Too many parts of the world testify to the difficulties religions have in tolerating each other. It is often concluded that the only way tolerance and plurality can be protected is to keep religion out of the public square. Ian Markham challenges this secularist argument. In the first half of the book, he advances a careful critique of European culture which exposes the problem of plurality. His analysis of the Christendom Group is contrasted with the outlook found in the USA, where a religiously informed culture may be seen to be tolerant. In the second half of the book, the author argues that plurality is better safeguarded by a theistic, rather than a secularist, foundation. He submits that too often secularists use relativist arguments, while theists want to appeal to the complexity of God's world. He concludes that in our post-modern world the religious affirmation of diversity offers genuine political possibilities for cultural enrichment.

PLURALITY AND CHRISTIAN ETHICS

NEW STUDIES IN CHRISTIAN ETHICS

General editor: Robin Gill

Editorial Board: Stephen R. L. Clark, Anthony O. Dyson,
Stanley Hauerwas and Robin W. Lovin

In recent years the study of Christian ethics has become an integral part of mainstream theological studies. The reasons for this are not hard to detect. It has become a more widely held view that Christian ethics is actually central to Christian theology as a whole. Theologians increasingly have had to ask what contemporary relevance their discipline has in a context where religious belief is on the wane, and whether Christian ethics (that is, an ethics based on the Gospel of Jesus Christ) has anything to say in a multi-faceted and complex secular society. There is now no shortage of books on most substantive moral issues, written from a wide variety of theological positions. However, what is lacking are books within Christian ethics which are taken at all seriously by those engaged in the wider secular debate. Too few are methodologically substantial; too few have an informed knowledge of parallel discussions in philosophy or the social sciences. This series attempts to remedy the situation. The aims of New Studies in Christian Ethics will therefore be twofold. First, to engage centrally with the secular moral debate at the highest possible intellectual level; second, to demonstrate that Christian ethics can make a distinctive contribution to this debate – either in moral substance, or in terms of underlying moral justifications. It is hoped that the series as a whole will make a substantial contribution to the discipline.

BOOKS IN THE SERIES

Rights and Christian ethics by Kieran Cronin

Power and Christian ethics by James Mackey

Biblical interpretation and Christian ethics by Ian McDonald

Plurality and Christian ethics by Ian S. Markham

Sex, gender and Christian ethics by Lisa Sowle Cahill

The moral act and Christian ethics by Jean Porter

The environment and Christian ethics by Michael S. Northcott

PLURALITY AND CHRISTIAN ETHICS

BY

IAN S. MARKHAM

Lecturer in Theology,
University of Exeter

CAMBRIDGE
UNIVERSITY PRESS

Published by the Press Syndicate of the University of Cambridge
The Pitt Building, Trumpington Street, Cambridge, CB2 1RP
40 West 20th Street, New York, NY 10011-4211, USA
10 Stamford Road, Oakleigh, Melbourne 3166, Australia

First published 1994

Printed in Great Britain at the University Press, Cambridge

A catalogue record for this book is available from the British Library

Library of Congress cataloguing in publication data

Markham, Ian S.
Plurality and Christian ethics/by Ian S. Markham.
p.   cm.   (New studies in Christian ethics)
Includes bibliographical references and index.
ISBN 0 521 45328 3.
1. Christian ethics.   2. Pluralism (Social sciences)
3. Secularism.   4. Political ethics.   I. Title.   II. Series.
BJ1275.M365   1994
241'.62—dc20   93-22811 CIP

New studies in Christian ethics 4

ISBN 0 521 45328 3 hardback

TAG

*To Lesley
with love*

Contents

General editor's preface

This is the fourth book in the *New Studies in Christian Ethics* series. It tackles one of the most troublesome issues within both Christian and secular ethics today and does so with considerable panache.

The issue is pluralism – or rather 'plurality'. Ian Markham wishes to avoid the term 'pluralism' as he believes it to be too identified with John Hick and with the specific problem of Christianity's relationship to other religions. In contrast, the central problem that concerns this study is how Christianity relates distinctively (but without being exclusive) to a pluralistic political and economic order. In what appears to be an increasingly fragmented world – intellectually, culturally, and morally – how is Christian (or any other kind of) ethics to be done? This is an important issue which has obvious relevance to many intellectuals struggling with values in an ever more complex world.

In the first part of this book Ian Markham faces some of the key issues raised by plurality and secularism in complex modern societies. In the second he considers some of the British attempts to come to terms with plurality – particularly the so-called Christendom Group – of which he is fairly critical. In the third section he turns to North American attempts to cope with plurality. The summer of 1991 that he spent with the Institute on Religion and Public Life in New York provided the background for his research in this area. He makes out a good case to the effect that American Christian ethics has been rather better at coming to terms with the fact of plurality than British versions of Christian ethics. In the final section he puts forward a very interesting thesis to the effect that Christian ethics and theological vision have something distinctive and rational to say which goes beyond the contentions of secular plurality.

As with Kieran Cronin's *Rights and Christian Ethics* which started the series, this is Ian Markham's first book. It is good to welcome both authors as distinctive younger voices bringing well-honed philosophical skills to Christian ethics. If once it might have been feared that philosophers were too clever for theologians, these two both show that today such fears are not well founded. A new era of rigour in Christian ethics seems to be dawning.

ROBIN GILL

Acknowledgments

Since 1986 I have been living with the issues that are explored in this book. During that time many a discussion and disagreement have contributed to the ideas within this study. In one sense it is both impossible and inappropriate to attempt to select those who deserve a mention. Yet not to mention anyone is equally misleading. So with grateful thanks to all who shared this project, special mention must be made of the following.

My theological outlook has been moulded by three institutions: Bodmin Comprehensive School where the RE teacher John Keast sensitively opened up the delights of academic theology; the Theology department at King's College, London provided my undergraduate training; and the Divinity School at the University of Cambridge, especially Canon Brian Hebblethwaite who supervised my research in philosophy of religion and ethics.

This particular study emerged from a three-month stay in 1991 at the Institute on Religion and Public Life in New York. The Institute did everything they could to ensure a successful summer. They provided delightful hospitality, from funding and office space to outstanding dinner conversations. Special mention must be made of the help and assistance of Richard John Neuhaus, Matthew Berke, and Jim Nuechterlein. During this time I stayed at the General Theological Seminary. For the kindness of Dean Fenhagen and his staff I am especially grateful. Mark and Dawn Goodman and Shannon Ledbetter also provided much needed distractions from the days spent in the Library.

The following either read parts of the manuscript or

stimulated a particular line of thinking: Ron Atkinson, Paul Avis, Sue Burns, Shaun Coates, Leslie Houlden, Vicky La'Porte, Giles Legood, Daniel Rossing, Chris Southgate, and Non Vaughan-Thomas.

My colleagues in Exeter have tolerated every step of the process: David Catchpole, Gordon Dunstan, Richard Burridge, Alastair Logan, Don Murray and Sally O'Shea have all, in different ways, made a significant contribution.

I am grateful to the editors of *The Heythrop Journal* for permission to reproduce sections of my article 'World Perspectives and Arguments: Disagreements about Disagreements', 30 (1989) 1 – 12. Thanks are also due to Alex Wright and Robin Gill for all the help and support they have given. Finally, my brothers Anthony and Michael provided the computer on which the book was written, and my wife Lesley has tolerated, reassured, and loved me during the entire process. To her, I dedicate this book.

Introduction: the secularist challenge

Many secularists view religion with suspicion, if not open hostility. Religious people, they claim, make dogmatic judgments about unresolvable issues. For Jews, it seems God presented the fullness of his truth in the Torah and, though interpretation is endless, further revelations are not needed; for Christians, Jesus is the only way to salvation, and those who do not accept this are doomed to an eternity in hell; for Muslims, there is one God, Allah, and Muhammad is his prophet. Each claim is asserted as the truth, thereby implying that everyone else is in error. These different truth-claims come packaged with different ethical codes. For some monogamy is required, for others polygamy is permitted. For some homosexuality can be tolerated, for others it is to be condemned. This diversity, explains the secularist, suggests that religious outlooks are difficult to accommodate in public affairs. Everything in the religious disposition seems to justify intolerance.

Much of religious history illustrates the point. The world of medieval Christendom conjures up images of the Inquisition and religious wars. For a society to succeed, argues the secularist, we need to reduce religion to the sphere of the personal and private. Religious people can demand of themselves a high personal morality, but should not impose it on anyone else. They should be allowed to believe whatever they like in the privacy of their own home, and to propagate their views, but they should not seek to impose their beliefs on those who do not share them: their ideas have no special privilege.

This secularist outlook has exercised a considerable hold over public polity in western Europe and North America. In Britain, for example, church attendance has fallen dramatically, and so has religious passion.[1] For the secularist, this is to be welcomed. Modern Britain compares very favourably with other countries in the world, such as Iran, which, the secularists argue, is still trapped in the old world of religious fanaticism and intolerance. From this perspective, a range of positions within the public square requires a secular society. The choice for the secularist is simple: either an intolerant society with religion in the saddle or a tolerant secular society with religion taking its place alongside other opinions and life styles.

The traditional Christian response to this argument has often been to refuse to make concessions. Christians have complained that the religious vacuum suggested by the secularist is nothing more than a quasi-religious or ideological claim which is imposed on everyone else – a religion of 'humanism' which denies any transcendent truth-claims. In the name of tolerance, it is claimed, secularists impose their atheism. Further, secular culture is deeply destructive. It is a culture in rebellion against God, and therefore subject to all the frustrations of sin.

Now there is some sense in this response, and in the second part we shall examine it in detail. But it ignores the force of the secularist challenge in one very important respect. It seems to imply a power struggle. The Christian complains of the secularist's intolerance of religion while, it often appears, wanting religion to be returned to power so religion itself can once again be intolerant. Every society must have some sort of 'idea', the argument goes; better that it be Christian than secular. It is a power struggle with an intolerant Christianity wanting to displace the intolerant secularism. Any real engagement with plurality has been side-stepped. Both sides seem to find it difficult to accept legitimate difference.

One of the greatest problems facing western culture in the late twentieth century is the problem of truth and tolerance in the public square. Religious traditions are right to complain that a secular society creates a dangerous vacuum of value at the heart of any culture. Secularists can legitimately expect certain standards of civility to be observed by contributors to the public discussion, which must include a willingness to tolerate certain fundamental disagreements.

This book is an attempt to consider the theological and philosophical problems posed by the secularist challenge. We shall start with the traditional Christian response to the secularist, taking the Christendom Group in Britain as a fairly recent representative. I shall show that, although there is much of value in their analysis, the problem of tolerance and plurality remains. Furthermore the failure even to concede tolerance as an achievement of modernity is an important aspect of their total rejection of the culture of modernity. This total opposition partly explains why their proposals were so unrealistic.

The spirit of the Christendom group continues to imbue the British approach to plurality. The crisis over immigration provoked by the speeches of Enoch Powell and, more recently, the Salman Rushdie affair presupposed the ideal of a unitary culture – a culture where one religious option dominates.

The approach of the Christendom group is contrasted with the outlook found in the United States. Here we find a culture preoccupied with the problem of religion and tolerance. A sustained discussion of the history and civil religion of America reveals a different cultural option emerging. The apparent impasse between the secularist and theist is being broken. It is possible for a religiously informed culture to be tolerant.

Building on this discovery, the theologian can go on the attack. The secularist argument is bankrupt at every level. Its strongest element was the need for tolerance as an important ingredient in civility.[2] But now the tables can be turned. A case can be made that the best way to protect the standards of civility in the public square is not to marginalize religion, but to bring it firmly into the square. It will be shown that the greater threat to tolerance and plurality comes not from the competing religious outlooks, but from secularism. However, this argument comes at a certain price. I shall show that tolerance and plurality do depend on a certain theological shift from a traditional to a more liberal stance – at least in certain respects. This is, of course, widely assumed. The extent of the required shifts has often been overstated, and throughout arguments are offered which show how as-conservative-as-possible forms of belief can nevertheless be tolerant.

The basic argument is an exercise in Christian ethics. However, it is a 'Christian ethics' of a certain type. The main issue here is the relation between culture and religion. It requires discussion of matters historical, philosophical, sociological, and theological. It explores the ethical questions from a cultural perspective. In this respect the *approach* of the book is heavily influenced by the work of Reinhold and Richard Niebuhr. The Niebuhrs discerned the appropriate ground on which ethical questions must be tackled. Most Christian ethics tends to work far too crudely. Church reports on social questions tend to start from certain theological principles and then leap to certain social implications, creating the absurd impression that the policy prescriptions arrived at are God's timeless requirements for all humanity. So, for example, from the theologico-ethical principles of 'freedom and learning' we get a commitment to vouchers for American schools. Clearly, this cannot be a timeless requirement for all people everywhere. Although others have already made this point, it is worthy of repetition. So in Part I I have described the appropriate method for such questions as theology and plurality, which I believe is making explicit the method found in the Niebuhrs.

The book divides into four Parts. In Part I (chs. 1 and 2), I shall locate both the problem and the method. The problem of tolerance is described in terms of plurality and secularism; I locate the foundations that underpin the secularist approach to plurality. In regard to the method, I suggest that Christian ethicists need to work with three modes of enquiry – the theological, the cultural, and the practical. In Part II (chs. 3, 4, and 5), I examine the 'traditional European' response. For many Christians, this is the rejection of modernity, and the call for the establishment of a Christian society. Others are happy to accommodate modernity, but still feel that too much religious and cultural diversity is threatening. And those who want to resist these calls for a unitary culture and endorse plurality often feel forced to give uncritical support to secularism. The idea of a religious commitment to diversity has not been discovered.

In Part III (chs. 6 and 7), I examine the background to the American experience and discovery. I discuss the insights emerging from the Civil Religion debate and the attempt, in the work of Richard John Neuhaus, to form a public philosophy. The final part is the longest and most innovative. In this I try to construct the theoretical argument against secularism, and show that rational discourse, genuine tolerance, and public polity need the presence of religious outlooks. This is an attempt to show, with the help of philosophical argument, the inadequacy of secularism.

Two qualifiers need to be added. The first is that many ethicists shy away from questions of such complexity. It is difficult to master all the relevant historical, philosophical, and theological material. Yet this practical difficulty can all too easily become the excuse for refusing to tackle these large interdisciplinary questions. I ask my readers to tolerate the brevity of much of my discussion, and trust the discussion is sufficient to establish my overall thesis. Secondly, many theologians and ethicists object to the term tolerance. They do so for good reasons. 'Tolerance' seems to suggest isolated individuals keeping their distance from each other. As will emerge in Part IV, tolerance is only the bare minimum in our relations with others, and for religious reasons it needs to develop into a richer exchange and mutual dialogue. However, I have retained the term because it is the starting-point. Historically, so many religious dispositions seem to compel the church toward intolerance. Even tolerant co-existence is preferable to intolerance.

It will be shown that the American discovery is that religious dispositions need not imply intolerance. The theologian must try to explicate the theological implications of this. In doing so I shall show that certain forms of secularism are built on the shaky foundations of relativism and subjectivism, which can and must be opposed by the religious commitment to truth. Secularism is no longer a secure foundation for plurality. Religious traditions need to welcome plurality as a part of God's world. This implies that disagreement, argument, and difference are all to be seen as within the providence of God. Seen in this light, religious institutions can offer the public square a moral perspective grounded in a commitment to plurality.

PART I

Plurality and secularism

For secularists, despite their lack of religious commitment, religious plurality creates social and political difficulties. It also raises theoretical problems relating to tolerance and its practical outworking in society. In this chapter I shall explore the narrative underpinning this view of plurality. First, however, I need to clarify the meanings of 'plurality' and 'tolerance'.

PLURALITY

Throughout this discussion I shall use the word 'plurality' rather than 'pluralism'. Plurality signifies the simple phenomenological reality of differing and conflicting traditions (or world views) arising in different communities with different histories. For my purposes it is important to stress that these differing traditions are not simply differing propositional beliefs about the world. A small vulnerable Asian Muslim community in the UK does not simply disagree with Christians over the status of Jesus. This belief fits into a total outlook and culture, with a distinctive language and history different from those of the majority Christian population (even though its Christian belief is now nominal). The problem of plurality involves the problem of different communities, with different identities, coexisting, and so raises questions of tolerance.

The term 'plurality' simply describes a state of affairs that is seen increasingly in our cities; it implies no judgment on its desirability or otherwise. The term 'pluralism', on the other hand, has come to describe a theological position. For John Hick, 'pluralism' points to a transformed outlook to different religions: no longer are we able to speak of one tradition as being true and those that disagree as false, instead we must talk of different and equally valid ways to the Real.[1] For Hick, pluralism is set against exclusivism or inclusivism.[2] This is a separate debate. Although the theme of this book will lead me to comment on that debate in chapter ten, I have tried to distance my argument as far as possible from the Christian theology of other religions.

Plurality is no great challenge to Hick-type pluralists. They have a theoretical structure in which religious disagreements are only apparent. Hick no longer believes that the beliefs of the religions 'really' conflict with each other. For Hick, Christians and Muslims only appear to disagree. This apparent disagreement is due to different cultural responses to the one true reality underpinning all major religious traditions. Coexistence is therefore easy because all disagreements become irrelevant. However, for those who believe that their religion is true, this is not an option. It is important to remember that most orthodox adherents in most religious traditions believe that their tradition is the truth, or at least more true than the alternatives. Plurality is therefore a challenge.

So from the fact of plurality we derive the need for 'tolerance'. Tolerance among committed believers of different traditions is an obvious need if social harmony is to prevail. It is precisely because of this that the secularist, with a position of neutrality, appears to be on such strong ground. Religious people are often tempted to express their commitment by excluding those who disagree; it is for this reason that the secularist suggests that religion must be kept out of the public square.

TOLERANCE

Tolerance is itself contentious. Tolerance has personal, group, and political dimensions. On the personal level, a landlady might exercise tolerance when renting her flat to a gay couple or an unmarried couple living together. On the group level, a predominantly Christian community in a city would exercise tolerance toward the Muslim minority, if they permitted a disused Methodist Church to be converted into a Mosque. And on the political level, a state exercises a policy of toleration when it makes legal provision requiring all to respect the festivals of minority religions. All three dimensions are linked. All require the willingness to accept differences (whether religious, moral, ethnic, or economic), of which, at whatever level, one might disapprove.[3]

For a person or group to be tolerant, two conditions must be met. First, that person or group must be in a position of power to allow or forbid the action or situation in question. Dilemmas involving the exercise of tolerance arise when the party in question has some degree of power. The landlady is in that position in respect to the couple seeking to rent from her. If the landlady decides to exercise her power by refusing to rent (or forcing them to move out), then she would be intolerant (i.e. because she disapproved of homosexuality or unmarried co-habitation she found it impossible to tolerate such situations in her flat). This power can be either explicit or implicit. In our example the landlady has explicit power (i.e. she is in a position to decide who may be her tenants). When the white majority in the community make life unpleasant for their recently arrived black neighbour, they are exercising implicit power (i.e. diffused power located in a community outlook). Many of the worst examples of intolerance are the result of implicit rather than explicit power.

The second condition is that one must disapprove, even if only minimally or potentially. The sense of disapproval or even antagonism is important. One does not tolerate that which is accepted or an object of love. If one is an ardent supporter of homosexual rights, then one is not being tolerant in letting one's flat to a gay couple. I do not tolerate my wife; I love her. No disapproval is involved; I am proud and fond of her. Nor does one tolerate that towards which one is indifferent. If you do not care about homosexuality, then you are not tolerating it. You are simply indifferent; it stands alongside other equally irrelevant issues such as the existence of the Loch Ness monster.

The equation between indifference and tolerance is the mistake made by Wolff, Marcuse, and Moore in *A Critique of*

Pure Tolerance. Their common complaint is that tolerance is a policy used in American society to allow all manner of injustice. So Marcuse writes, 'Tolerance is an end in itself. Tolerance is extended to policies, conditions and modes of behaviour which should not be tolerated because they are impeding, if not destroying the chances of creating an existence without fear or misery.'[4] The assumption here is that tolerance is equivalent to indifference. Marcuse would only be right if most Americans strongly disapproved of all this injustice, but reluctantly permitted it. But when it is put like this, Marcuse is clearly wrong to blame tolerance. He is really attacking indifference, which is a completely different problem.

Generally, tolerance can be seen as a half-way house between hostility and hatred on the one hand, and love and acceptance on the other. Hostility and hatred will result in an intolerant attitude and intolerant actions; love and acceptance will not need tolerance at all. Voltaire captures the sentiment lying behind tolerance in his famous quotation, 'I disagree with what you say, but I defend to the death your right to say it.'

THE SECULARIST NARRATIVE

To understand a position, it is important to engage with the historical narrative that justifies the position. The modern concept of tolerance is rooted in the secularist's narrative. This is part of the reason why many Christians are so unhappy with the concept. I shall now outline briefly the history of tolerance as found within the secularist narrative. The purpose is to discover the assumptions that underpin the secularist account of tolerance.

All societies must be tolerant to some degree. People are not identical, and differences are bound to provoke some disapproval and bring power into play. However, there is a marked difference between general toleration in everyday life, and tolerance as a slogan and state policy. Although both forms of tolerance exhibit the features I have just identified, and the boundary between the two may move and vary from one society to another, there is a difference of status. All cultures have had to reflect on the politically pragmatic question as to the limits of this general toleration. However, toleration as a state policy has been given a higher status. It is not simply pragmatic coexistence, but a principled linkage between toleration and the freedom of an individual to follow their conscience.

This move from pragmatic justification of tolerance to principled philosophical advocacy is seen most clearly with John Locke and Spinoza.[5] Signs of the shift are seen earlier. In the sixteenth century, and the first half of the seventeenth, the Socinians, Unitarians, and Anabaptists all made sophisticated cases for toleration.[6] But the difference in Locke was the different role suggested for the nation state. No longer was religious uniformity to be strictly required of all the people. So toleration in this sense starts with John Locke.

For many centuries, the church had taken the right to suppress those who were teaching error. From St Augustine to the Inquisition the same intolerant tendency was at work. Augustine, for example, felt that punishment for the Donatists was justified as it might save them from eternal damnation.[7] Of course there were certain exceptions to this intolerance even in the Middle Ages. Charlesworth considers that the Roman Catholic emphasis upon the value of the individual's informed conscience as the supreme arbiter must imply tolerance.[8] The Reformation, too, made tolerance an issue, simply because there was visible religious diversity.[9]

Yet overall these are exceptions in the sea of intolerant assumptions. It is difficult to disagree with A. J. Ayer that: 'Of all the forms of intolerance, religious intolerance has probably caused the greatest harm.'[10] It was as religious beliefs lost their power and were held less strongly that tolerance became possible and so came into consciousness. This is crucial to the secularist's narrative. It was with the rise of secularization (i.e., the decline of the political power of religious institutions and beliefs) that tolerance became a political option, and in due course even a necessity, for the state.

John Locke, writing in his first *Letter on Toleration*, published in 1689, argued that limited religious tolerance should be extended to 'dissenters' who did not follow the practices and beliefs of the established Anglican Church. The limit of this tolerance was drawn up to protect the internal cohesion of the society. So Roman Catholics were excluded because they owed their allegiance to the Bishop of Rome and not to the king; and atheists were excluded because their oaths could not be trusted.[11] Tolerance always comes within certain limits. Although we today are not impressed with such a limited tolerance, we can still recognize in it a remarkable historical achievement. Locke takes a strong social conflict of his time, that concerning Anglican monopoly of legitimate religious allegiance and official authorization, and argues for a policy of official state tolerance.

Locke makes a very significant assumption. Religious difference can be tolerated provided it does not undermine social cohesion. Locke is building on an important distinction used elsewhere in his work, that between the public and the private spheres: the state can permit much variety on the private level providing it preserves harmony and order on the public level. The public level is concerned with the minimum agreement required for social cohesion. One can see this distinction in the *Two Treatises of Government*.

It is generally agreed that Locke's main purpose in writing the *Two Treatises* was to develop a view of political obligation which did not depend on the Bible.[12] Locke's alternative ran as follows: humans are by nature free and independent. They can, however, acquire obligations to obey political authorities that restrict their freedom, by consenting to them. The founding of political society is an agreement of all the members to accept restrictions on their freedom. From then on those members are required to comply with the rules of their society because they have consented to do so in the original contract. The original members give their explicit consent and all subsequent generations give their tacit consent.[13] It is in this context that the liberal elevation of the individual is developed.[14] Each person opts into society, relinquishing certain individual rights for the benefit of living in community. The implications are clear (although Locke did not entirely see them): you only relinquish the minimum required for social living and security of your property. On this account, one concedes that murder and theft would be anti-social, but (in a modern, rather than a Lockian, example) homosexual relations in the privacy of one's own home are the concern solely of the individual, not of society.[15] In private, individuals are free to behave as they wish provided it does not infringe the rights of other individuals in society.

From Locke two assumptions lying behind the secularist challenge can now be identified. The first is the distinction between public and private. You tolerate anything that does not make claims in the public square. On this assumption, Locke's exclusion of Roman Catholics makes perfect sense, for Roman Catholics were making (and some continue to make) demands that all society ought to accept. The second is the strict distinction between the individual and the community. Society makes the minimum demands for harmonious behaviour between individual citizens. However, a third assumption behind the modern secularist narrative is not found in Locke. This is relativism, which may be approached by way of developments in the century following Locke.

The epistemological problem created by the Enlightenment comes out most starkly in the work of David Hume.[16] Hume was preoccupied with the question: how do we discover the truth? How do we know whether the ultimate reality is a Trinity or Allah or Brahma? Relativism starts with the observation that traditions are relative to specific cultural situations, and therefore it is impossible (or at least difficult) to discover which tradition is correctly describing reality. It is on this relativist foundation that John Stuart Mill formulated his arguments for tolerance. C. L. Ten has restated Mill's arguments in a sympathetic form and identifies three basic arguments in Mill's essay *On Liberty*.

The first is 'the Avoidance of Mistake Argument'.[17] As each opinion is contestable, we should not oppress an opinion because we might discover that we are oppressing a true opinion. This argument has limited value because one could still feel (a) one is unlikely to be wrong, and it is a risk worth running, or (b) even if the opinion is true it still ought to be censored (for example, as tending to immorality or disorder).

Mill attempts to overcome these objections with his second argument, the 'Assumption of Infallibility Argument'. Mill writes, 'Complete liberty of contradicting and disproving our opinion is the very condition that justifies us in assuming its truth for purposes of action; and on no other terms can a being with human faculties have any rational assurance of being right.'[18] Mill believes that discussion and the facing of objections are the only ways of establishing the truth of one's own views. So unless those views have faced objections, one can have no confidence that it is justifiable to oppress those who are objecting.

This flows into the third argument, which Ten calls the 'Necessity of Error Argument'. Ten summarizes this argument, 'It maintains that in the absence of freedom of discussion one will not appreciate the full meaning of opinion ... He [*i.e. the person holding an opinion*] will not appreciate to any considerable degree what he is committed to when he accepts the opinion. At the same time his acceptance of this belief will prevent him from accepting other beliefs that appear to oppose it, but may in fact be no more than complementary to it, or perhaps a refinement of it, or even completely unrelated to it.'[19]

These three arguments have a relativist tendency, in the sense that they question our capacity to achieve total and final truth. It is not relativism in the modern anti-realist sense (i.e. denying any possible way of ascertaining the truth in a correspondence sense), but Mill is taking seriously the lack of certainty surrounding our truth-claims. From Mill one can move in two directions. For many contemporary secularists Mill's mild and implicit relativism becomes more overt and anti-realist: truth is inaccessible; quest for truth (with a capital T) is doomed to failure; there are only different perspectives on the world; each is as valid as the other. Michael Creuzet in *Toleration and Liberalism* takes this route. He argues explicitly that toleration is possible only when one accepts that there are no absolute truth-claims.[20] Most secularists tend to go in this direction. The other direction continues to stress tolerance as a means to the truth: one tolerates difference because the world is complicated; it is in dialogue with different positions that the truth might emerge.

In chapter nine I shall make some use of these arguments. On this view tolerance is a means to an end, not an end in itself.

So far I have argued that the idea of tolerance within the secularist narrative is largely built on certain assumptions formulated in the last three centuries. The first is the distinction between private and public aspects of religions. The second is the assumption that society is made up of individuals to whose existence it is secondary. The third is the epistemological tendencies towards relativism. It is partly due to this history that some theists do not want to talk of tolerance at all. Theists do not want to affirm an idea which rests on relativist and individualist assumptions. It is not that they are intolerant, but they want a richer, more affirmative model for the relations between differing traditions.[21] Tolerance, with all its connotations of disapproval and coexistence, does not sit easily with the theistic commitment to love between communities. One must concede that mere tolerance is not the ideal. Tolerant coexistence is not a solution, but only, given the terrible history of religious intolerance, a good start. It is not realistic in certain parts of the world to expect religions to arrive at an 'affirming plurality'. In Northern Ireland and Israel toleration would be a dramatic leap forward. Tolerance must be viewed as the first stage that in time can be superseded by more positive relations. And it is a first stage that many strands of our religious traditions are finding it extremely difficult to attain.

CHAPTER 2

Plurality, culture, and method

Everything connects with everything else; or at least so it frequently appears. One starts by exploring the issue of plurality; and then one discovers that culture, politics, religion, history, and philosophy are involved. Boundaries are extremely difficult to draw.

It is therefore of the first importance to clarify our method of enquiry, which will be applied to the work of Demant, Bellah, and Neuhaus. In this section I attempt to make explicit the method that I consider Reinhold Niebuhr to have used. I shall show that the greatness of Niebuhr was partly due to an exceptional competence across three modes of enquiry – theological, cultural, and practical. For Christian ethics to be effective all three modes must be in operation.

The best ethicists manage to work effectively in all three; weaker ones are only effective in one or perhaps two of them. The first and major mode for Christian ethics, the *theological*, can be defined as ethical analysis, within the Christian tradition, that includes both ecclesiological and biblical reflections. Yet the extent to which this dimension dominates is more contentious. For Karl Barth, ethical reflection starts with the revelation of God in Christ and ends with the church.[1] The entire ethical enterprise stands alongside doctrine, midway between the church and the Bible. In so far as it speaks to the world, it does so by speaking to the church. Thus Barth's method is dominated by this mode of enquiry. In this respect, as in so many, he represents the extreme.

For the Niebuhrs and Demant (the leading thinker of the Christendom tradition) the theological inevitably necessitated movement into the cultural mode. This places them into a minority among ethicists. Many Christian ethicists move directly from theological principle to application, or, to use my terminology, from the first mode to the third.[2] Most church documents on ethical questions proceed in this way. So I shall discuss the third mode next.

The third mode is *the practical or applied mode*. This is the area of policy recommendations for individuals, communities, and nations. A primary concern here is the application of theological insights: what is the relevance of the Bible to questions about medical practice or political and social institutions? The practical Christian ethicist must engage medical, social, and economic expertise in a quest for relevance. Denys Munby and Ronald Preston have made this the theme of their work.[3] Christian ethical pronouncement on a subject without adequate grounding in that subject is as good as useless. Preston's resounding criticism of many ethicists, for example, is their lack of training in economics. If Barth is primarily theological, then Preston is primarily practical. One searches in vain for the theological system of Preston. In so far as there is one, it is his presupposing of the theology of William Temple and Reinhold Niebuhr. The thrust of his work is to ascertain the policy recommendations that flow from their theology.

For many Christian ethicists their subject consists of these two modes of working. The theological provides the context, the practical provides the application. However, writers in the Christendom tradition, and many contemporary ethicists in the United States, have insisted on a third mode. This is the *cultural mode*. To understand or remedy social problems, one must consider the particular cultural setting. Now the definition of the term 'culture' is notoriously difficult. Richard Niebuhr suggests that culture 'is that total process of human activity and total result of such activity to which now the name culture, now the name civilization, is applied in common speech. Culture is the "artificial, secondary environment" which man super-imposes on the natural. It comprises language, habits, ideas, beliefs, customs, social organization, inherited artefacts, technical processes, and values.'[4] Niebuhr then goes on to identify culture with human achievement and a world of value. Niebuhr is right to capture the all-embracing aspect of culture, and the only expression I would add to his list is 'world view' or the term I prefer 'world perspective'.

A world perspective is rarely consciously stated; most of us feel that most of our presuppositions are quite simply just self-evident. A world perspective is not a result of conscious decision, but a multitude of factors combining to develop a world perspective within us. These factors include: such specific factors as religion, and education; and such general factors as one's gender and economic position. One's world perspective will only be discovered by considerable reflection. Decisions in terms of life style will reveal much about one's world perspective. The term world perspective is free from any crude empiricist observational assumptions, and is not intended to be purely theoretical, but rooted in human practice and decision.

The relation between theology and culture is partly determined by the culture in question. Richard Niebuhr posits five models: (1) Christ against culture, (2) Christ of culture, (3) Christ above culture, (4) Christ and culture in paradox, (5) Christ the transformer of culture. I would argue that different models are appropriate at different times. Where a culture is in total opposition to the Christian narrative (for example, in Nazi Germany) then the 'Christ against Culture' would clearly be an appropriate model. Where a culture is religiously informed, then a different model might be appropriate. So Richard John Neuhaus argues very effectively that the 'Christ and culture in paradox' model is ideal for the contemporary western situation.[5] The point is that this mode of inquiry wants to take the world perspective seriously; and the Christian narrative must at different times engage with, reject, or affirm different elements, depending on the cultural situation.

For Demant, this mode of thinking is essential because he considers the Christian tradition to be addressing a culture in revolt and therefore in crisis. For more contemporary ethicists, there are many reasons why they might be forced into this mode. For some, for example Stanley Hauerwas, it is a result of their wish to articulate the ethical story of the Christian tradition.[6] For others, for example Neuhaus, it reflects the fact that ethical reflection must take seriously the religious and cultural dispositions of North Americans.[7] And there are others, for example Alasdair MacIntyre, who are forced to use this mode because it provides the only perspective from which one can judge the thought-forms of our post-Enlightenment, scientific, liberal, secular culture.[8] For whatever reason ethicists find themselves in the third mode, they have been given considerable assistance by the civil religion debate. This debate, initiated by the sociologist Robert Bellah, offers a new slant on questions which American historians had raised when they considered the influence of religion on politics. However, as we will see, Bellah provoked philosophers, political theorists, and religious ethicists to join the debate at the level of cultural reflection.

As I have said, the greatest of Christian ethicists have tended to work with all three modes. Reinhold Niebuhr, for example, showed exceptional theological competence in his Gifford Lectures, put into book form as *The Nature and Destiny of Man* (two volumes: 1941 and 1943). He formulated a theological system that showed how biblical symbols can offer insights into the deepest human problems. His writings achieved political influence not only within the church, but also in the largely secular spheres of government, business, and academia.[9] He also worked within our second mode of inquiry, the cultural. It was from this perspective that Niebuhr offered an analysis of the scale of the difficulties facing our contemporary culture. He believed that factors deriving from the Renaissance and Reformation have created a tension in our modern culture that requires a new synthesis.[10] Part of his greatness is seen in the successful engagement of all three modes, although there is a certain awkwardness in his movement from one mode to another. Conversely the failure to work with all three modes exposes the weakness in the work of other Christian ethicists. Joseph Fletcher's 'situation ethics' is a good example.[11] In Fletcher the simple requirement of all ethical decisions is to decide what is the 'most loving action' in any given situation, i.e. to reject all forms of legalism and opt for the flexibility of situation ethics. For Fletcher, there is no cultural mode. The

poverty of this system is exposed when one looks at situation
ethics as a cultural phenomenon. In essence it is a variation on
the 'act-utilitarianism' invented in the nineteenth century by
Jeremy Bentham. Situation ethics operates on the same method
(although for the utilitarians the criterion was goodness rather
than love). Utilitarianism was the main ethical legacy of the
nineteenth century, so it was hardly surprising that it found
theological expression. Further its popularity in the 1960s
reflects a cultural reaction against all forms of authority, in to
which Fletcher's opposition to legalism fitted nicely. This shows
that to accept situation ethics one needs to accept the utili-
tarian culture of the 1960s. Put like this, it is not surprising
that its popularity started to decline. I suggest that the main
reason why Reinhold Niebuhr is still considered to be important, and Joseph Fletcher has almost been forgotten, is this
need for effective Christian ethics to use all three modes of
enquiry

When one uses three modes the following procedure emerges:
the theological reflection works within a certain cultural
narrative; and then the emerging insights must again work
within the cultural setting to generate certain suggestions about
possible courses of actions. Or, to use my terminology, both
modes one and three need to work within the second, cultural,
mode.

These reflections on method will serve two purposes in this
study. First, these three modes will be used to compare quite
disparate thinkers. Any judgments made on the contribution of
these scholars will be offered on the basis of their effectiveness
within each mode. The second purpose is to clarify and limit my
task. The bulk of my contribution on plurality and religion
needs to be located in the second mode, although certain
theological and practical implications of my argument will be
suggested.

I have made much of my debt to Reinhold Niebuhr. This is
true not only in respect to method, but also in respect to
theological reflection on plurality. Having posed the secularist's
challenge and set out the appropriate method for exploring
these cultural issues, it is helpful to turn to Reinhold Niebuhr's

discussion. He will provide the framework for the substance of my argument.

In *The Children of Light and the Children of Darkness*, Niebuhr explicitly discusses the issue of plurality. He identifies three primary approaches to the problem of religious and cultural diversity in the western world. 'The first is a religious approach (typified particularly by Catholicism) in which an effort is made to overcome diversity and restore the original unity of culture. The second is the approach of secularism, which attempts to achieve cultural unity through the disavowal of traditional historical religions. The third is again a religious approach which seeks to maintain religious vitality within the conditions of religious diversity.'[12] Niebuhr dismisses the first, arguing that the Catholic position is in conflict with the presuppositions of a free society (i.e., it is intolerant). He rejects the second on the following grounds. Although tolerance probably would not have arisen without the spirit of indifference to religion that arose through secularization, it is a shallow unity that will break down because religion is not dying out.

My argument should be seen within this Niebuhrian framework. My 'secularist challenge' corresponds to his second, secularist approach. I have already explained in the last chapter how – what Niebuhr calls a 'spirit of indifference' – is built upon important philosophical arguments. So in Part IV I shall explore the philosophical assumptions. Further I shall show that Niebuhr's first approach, the Catholic response, is characteristic of much European Christianity. I shall concentrate on a group of Anglo-Catholics within the Church of England as representative of this attitude. Christendom as a culture is still visible in Europe. Splendid cathedrals witness to an age when an entire culture was dominated by Christian presuppositions. Nostalgia for Christendom is understandable, but deeply damaging. For it is at this point in my argument that I show how toleration is a *hinge issue*. Those unable to concede toleration as an achievement of modernity are often equally unable to

concede any other achievements to modernity. So for the –
appropriately named – Christendom Group the rejection of
tolerance ran parallel with a rejection of capitalism and
socialism. Frequently a judgment about tolerance will expose a
whole set of attitudes to modernity.

The positive argument of this book is also anticipated by
Niebuhr. Niebuhr commends his third approach – the religious
solution:

This solution makes religious and cultural diversity possible within the
presuppositions of a free society, without destroying the religious
depth of culture. The solution requires a very high form of religious
commitment. It demands that each religion, or each version of a single
faith, seeks to proclaim its highest insights while yet preserving an
humble and contrite recognition of the fact that all actual expressions
of religious faith are subject to historical contingency and relativity.
Such a recognition creates a spirit of tolerance, and makes any
religious or cultural movement hesitant to claim official validity for its
form of religion, or to demand an official monopoly for its cult.
Religious humility is in perfect accord with the presuppositions of a
free society.[13]

For Niebuhr, this 'religious humility' has radical implications
for systematic theology. On God Niebuhr writes, 'Profound
religion must recognize the difference between divine majesty
and human creatureliness; between the unconditioned character of the divine and the conditioned character of all human
enterprise.'[14] On sin Niebuhr writes, 'According to the Christian faith, the pride which seeks to hide the conditioned and
finite character of all human endeavour is the very quintessence
of sin.'[15] And this transformed theology leads to a very different
view of the world based on humility and love. 'Religious
toleration through religiously inspired humility and charity is
always a difficult achievement. It requires that religious
convictions be sincerely and devoutly held, while yet the sinful
and finite corruptions of these convictions be humbly acknowledged and the actual fruits of other faiths be generously
estimated.'[16]

My argument can be seen as exploring in more detail
Niebuhr's religious solution and the theological implications of

that solution. Also I shall show that this Niebuhrian argument was made possible precisely because Niebuhr was working in North America. He articulates what I call the American discovery, namely that tolerance not only can be accommodated with religious commitment, but needs religious commitment.

Before we start with an exploration of the traditional and largely European response, I must comment on the level of generalization that I am required to make. Working in parallel with the Christendom Group in Continental Europe were several advocates of tolerance; Jacques Maritain is probably the best example. And in the States, the evangelical equivalent of the Christendom Group has attracted a very sympathetic hearing in certain circles. The so-called Theonomy movement, founded by Rousas J. Rushdoony,[17] attempts to create a 'biblical politics' for committed Christians. Certain parts of the British and American experience overlap so much that the generalizations break down. Yet they remain defensible; the spirit of most ethical reflection in Britain and America corresponds to the positions outlined. In Britain there has been a much greater concerted attempt to oppose plurality and insist on a unitary outlook; in the States ethicists have tended to be much more sympathetic to plurality. That said, we can now start with the traditional, and largely European, response to the secularist challenge.

PART II

CHAPTER 3

Plurality and the Christendom Group

To understand why plurality was such a problem for the Christendom Group, we need to understand the theological system that is operating. Christianity is not one valid system among many valid options. It is the truth, which offers a powerful analysis of the contemporary world. People who disagree with Christianity are not only wrong, but will misunderstand the social, economic, and political problems. The secularist is a heretic, whose views must be challenged and corrected.

Compromise is not an option. Accommodation between truth and falsehood will only lead to confusion. The Christian narrative must be articulated by the church, and the secular culture called to repentance.

Most people today are puzzled by such sentiments. How can anyone be so certain that their religious narrative is true? In what sense can a religious narrative provide a critique of social and economic problems? It is because of this widespread bewilderment that we shall spend the next two chapters getting inside this approach. We need a sense of the all-embracing nature of the analysis. These chapters will show how the Christendom Group's affirmation of Christianity seems to exclude plurality.

Most of the present chapter will concern the Group's reflections on the cultural crisis pervading Europe during the 1930s and 40s. In the next chapter we shall examine their reflections on capitalism and ecology. I shall affirm their commitment to the explanatory power of Christianity, but criticize their failure to see that their understanding of Christianity, including their analysis of modernity, was defective precisely because they excluded plurality.

The origin of the Christendom Group is hard to date, as no formal membership list ever existed, but the Group formed a distinct identity in 1922 when *The Return of Christendom* was published.[1] The book was introduced by Bishop Gore and rounded off with an epilogue by G. K. Chesterton. Its thesis was that our age (i.e. western culture) had come adrift from its religious moorings. Modern ills such as the unleashing of uncontrollable economic forces, the disintegration of community, and the corruption of culture were blamed on the Enlightenment. Moreover, contributors to the volume argued, modern European culture had lost the harmony and balance possessed by medieval Christendom. After the publication of this volume Maurice Reckitt financed and organized the journal *Christendom*, which became the focus for those who identified with these sentiments.

Reckitt's inner circle formed the habit of meeting once a fortnight at a London restaurant. They became known as the Chandos Group, and their meetings became the hub around which much was planned and organized. It provided the inspiration for several publications, namely, *Coal: A Challenge to the Nation's Conscience*; *The Miners' Distress and the Coal Problem*; and, finally, *Politics: A Discussion of Realities*.[2] It was active in organizing publications and conferences up to the late 1950s. The membership of the Group included V. A. Demant, A. J. Penty, and P. Mairet. The most celebrated person to join was T. S. Eliot, who was also a member of the Moot Group, a conclave similar to the Chandos Group. This time the organizer was J. L. Oldham who persuaded J. Baillie, Reinhold Niebuhr, R. H. Tawney, A. Vidler, and K. Mannheim to meet regularly to discuss social and political questions from a theological perspective. On one occasion, just after Britain had declared war on Germany in 1939, the Group met to discuss the crisis. The minutes of the meeting recorded a remark by T. S. Eliot:

It is strange that in 1914 we did not expect war and were not confused when it came. Now we have been expecting it for some time but are confused when it comes. We are involved in an enormous catastrophe which includes a war. (He mentioned Demant's *Religious Prospect* as a book which had enormously helped him in clarification of issues but was terrifying in the magnitude of the task of Christianization which it implied.) Where will people be found even to understand the basis of the task? A programme of publicity must recognize many levels, being addressed both to the many and the few.[3]

It was reflection like this that provoked Oldham's letter to *The Times* arguing that our salvation may lie 'in an attempt to recover our Christian heritage, not in the sense of going back to the past but of discovering in the central affirmations and insights of the Christian faith new spiritual energies to re-generate and vitalize our sick society'.[4]

Out of the reflections of these three groups – Christendom, Chandos, and Moot – a distinct cultural analysis emerged. They were forced into the second cultural mode by the scale of the crisis facing European culture. Five main themes of these groups will now be teased out. Their most articulate spokesman was V. A. Demant. He came to prominence when in 1929 he was appointed Director of Research to the Christian Social Council. In 1933 Demant became vicar of St John the Divine, Richmond, Surrey; and, in 1942, he was appointed a canon at St Pauls Cathedral, London. This was the period during which he was most productive; and he was rewarded with the post of canon of Christ Church and Regius Professor of Moral and Pastoral Theology in the University of Oxford in 1949. This discussion will concentrate on Demant, but identify larger themes that he shares with his contemporaries. The five themes are:

1. The theological presuppositions and the natural order of society
2. Cultural analysis and the penumbra
3. The incoherence of liberalism
4. Capitalism and ecological concern
5. Recovery of Christian social conventions and assumptions.

In the remainder of this chapter we shall look at the first three of the themes articulated by Demant and his contemporaries.

THEOLOGICAL PRESUPPOSITIONS

In the United Kingdom the bulk of Christian social reflection was firmly based in the Anglo-Catholic tradition. It is perhaps ironic that the early Tractarians, who were so opposed to the Christian socialists of the 1840s and 50s, were soon succeeded by generations of priests who found the two traditions completely compatible.[5] It was partly the popularity of Anglo-Catholic ritual in the inner cities which forced many priests to bring these two traditions together. By the turn of the century most of those working on social and political questions were firmly rooted in the Anglo-Catholic community.

It followed that most of their theological presuppositions were Catholic. First, they tended to presuppose a realist epistemology, asserting a real correspondence between language and reality. They saw Christian theism as the most appropriate way to describe the complexity of human life and reality. By the 1950s Eric Mascall was giving new currency to Thomist theology.[6] For this circle of Anglo-Catholics, natural theology and, as we shall see, natural law, were valuable resources against modernity.

The second theological presupposition was a commitment to an underlying dualism between God and the world. For Demant this was reflected in the title of his unpublished collection of sermons, *Not One World: But Two*.[7] God cannot be reduced to an aspect of this world. God's eternity must be set against the temporal processes of human life. This, Demant argued, was crucial; it ensured that the world would always be judged by a standard from beyond itself. As we see later, Demant argued that, once the temporal process is taken to be all that there is, then totalitarianism becomes both intelligible and logical. The Christian claim is precisely that this world order is not everything.

The third theological presupposition is that Christian theology, through the natural-law tradition, provides a description of the way the world is. Demant, using the arguments of Christopher Dawson and Jacques Maritain, developed an interesting account of this tradition.[8] The claim that there is a natural order, partially discernible without revelation, lay behind the claims of what became known as 'Christian Sociology'. According to Demant, 'The Christian religion provides such a criterion for placing the different activities of man in their instrumental order, for it has a doctrine of the essential nature of man.'[9] Sociology is an attempt to examine and describe society. Christians with their natural-law insights can offer certain facts about human life which will assist any description of society. Therefore a Christian sociology will apply Christian natural-law insights together with the sociological methodology. No longer, argued Demant, should we attempt to recommend what 'ought to be', but rather we should be describing 'what is'. The church can provide an accurate analysis of the human predicament, not simple platitudes or exhortations for moral improvement.

Demant's natural-law system starts with the claim that there is a natural order for each individual life. For a balanced and whole human life, the spirit must be firmly grounded in the divine. So there needs to be a recognition of creaturely dependence on the divine. With this in place the rest of human life then takes on an appropriate character around this centre. So our main priority as humans is to pray. The next most important sphere of natural activity for humanity is that of the cultural and rational, which means that, after prayer, the second priority in the human life is to compose and create in art, music, and literature; the next is the generation of economic wealth; and the least (but still good and wholesome) is the sexual.[10] On this account of natural law, sin becomes the giving of priority to any of these secondary activities. Some will make economics and money the most important; others will let sexual activity take priority. Whenever such disordering occurs, a person is leading an unnatural life. It is unbalanced and bound to all the frustrations of sin. Redemption, for Demant, becomes restoration. We need to recover the initial, God-intended, balanced life, by acknowledging in prayer our creaturely dependence, and allowing God's redemptive activity in Christ to restore us.

Demant then offers an analogy between the balanced individual and a balanced society. Ultimately a balanced society should acknowledge the priority of the spiritual, with God at the centre, then the rest of a society's activities would fall into place. Next would come the cultural, then the economic, and, finally, the sexual. In his unpublished Gifford lectures, he argued that the truth of this analysis is illustrated by the common-sense priorities found in Plato's Republic, the Indian Caste system, and medieval Christendom. In all three the representative of the spiritual (philosopher, Brahmin, and priest) is the most important figure. Then comes the political/military ruler of social structures; and third come those involved in economic activity. This argument sounds very dated now, and the drawbacks are obvious. Yet the main point Demant made using this model continues to have some relevance. The problem with our post-Enlightenment capitalist societies is the priority given to economic activity. Although, cultural activity is physically dependent upon economic activity, economics is always a means to an end, never an end in itself. It is completely unnatural to make economic activity an end in itself. So the theological presuppositions in Demant's work all focus on his natural-law analysis. This is a cognitive claim. It is firmly theistic, presupposing the orthodox Christian division between God and the world, and enabling one to describe the world in a way which is deemed more accurate than naturalistic or non-theistic alternatives.

THE CULTURAL ANALYSIS

We have seen how Demant's natural-law system applied to both individuals and to society. It meant that the Christian tradition provided the resources to describe the natural order of humanity; and Christian sociology was simply the application of these natural-law insights to society.

It is not surprising that this method leads us in to our second mode of enquiry, the cultural. The Christendom Group claimed that our modern post-Enlightenment secular culture is less balanced than medieval Christendom. (In fact, chronologically, the Christendom Group started with this claim, and then Demant offered the natural-law analysis to make sense of it.)

The contributors to *The Return of Christendom*, and later the *Christendom* journal, all agreed that modernity is in trouble, that our culture has constructed an urban, technological edifice which destroys the communal roots of society itself. Our culture is so preoccupied with economic activity that it has lost sight of any *telos* for such activity. It creates so many options requiring human decision that living by moral values is no longer habitual, but requires the moral strength of a saint. On each of these three points at least, argued the Christendom Group, we have much to learn from medieval Christendom. There, the organic roots of community were protected, economic activity had an appropriately subordinate place, and moral conventions ensured that the 'good life' for most people did not in most situations require a deliberate moral decision.

Demant's natural-law analysis was taken up with enthusiasm by Christendom adherents. He explained the difference between modernity and Christendom using the Christian ethical tradition. Christendom is a balanced and natural culture, whilst modernity is unbalanced and unnatural. The Group believed that this cultural analysis provided a much-needed depth for ethical reflection. The world of the thirties – with the Wall Street crash, the Great Depression, and the rise of totalitarianism – prompted and seemed to justify a radical cultural analysis. It is from this perspective that T. S. Eliot's *The Idea of a Christian Society* needs to be read. Early on, he explains, 'My point of departure has been the suspicion that the current terms in which we discuss international affairs and political theory may only tend to conceal from us the real issues of contemporary civilization.'[11] Later, Eliot explicitly uses Demantian language, as when he pleads for a recovery of the 'natural life and the supernatural life'.[12] This is Demant's natural order for society.

Both Christopher Dawson and Jacques Maritain are important in developing the narrative which explained the shift from a balanced Christendom to an unbalanced modernity. Demant's own attempt is found in his unpublished Gifford lectures, *The Penumbra of Ethics*.[13]

The image of the penumbra was an attempt to offer an analysis which went beyond the conscious outlooks and doctrines of a society, to its cultural assumptions, world views, and conventions. In an intriguing analysis, Demant argues that modern culture continues to articulate Christian aims consciously, but has unconsciously undermined the Christian axioms on which the aims depend. The penumbra is the world of overlap between the light (i.e. conscious aims) and darkness (i.e. unconscious assumptions).

Demant's narrative points to the way in which many modern ideas are a result of the Christian heritage. The 'secular' arose precisely because Christianity permits the created order to have a degree of given autonomy under God. Modern science presupposes an intelligibility which makes sense if the world is created as a result of design. Liberal democracy and human rights require objective moral values which are intelligible only if there is a personal God. The very Christian heritage which made our modern world possible was undercut by developments within that modern world. This was an act of rebellion, of sin, of hubris which generated the subsequent dissatisfaction. For Demant our culture, although ostensibly still articulating a vision of the world which is Christian, has destroyed all the assumptions which made sense of that vision.

THE INCOHERENCE OF LIBERALISM

Demant's argument starts with a distinction between the inner and outer life of a culture. There is a conflict between the assumptions and aims of western culture. The inner life is linked with the assumptions and the outer life with the aims. In *The Religious Prospect* where this argument in respect to liberalism is most thoroughly developed, he uses the terms 'dogma' and 'doctrine'. The doctrines of an age are the conscious, articulated aims or objectives (the light beyond the penumbra), whilst the dogmas of an age are the habits or assumptions which provide the framework through which reality is interpreted (the darkness behind the penumbra).[14]

Working with this distinction, this theme is best explained in five stages:

(a) The first is that liberalism is the ideology of our age. The purpose of liberal doctrine is to protect the individual against the state.

Demant writes,

The liberal doctrine may be described as the body of beliefs that proceed from the conviction that, while the human being has his existence in social and temporal relationships, his being or essence as a person is not a function of those relationships in time and space. Man has his inner meaning as truly human by his link with something eternal. He sees the ultimate truth about himself, not in his actual historical situation, but in his relationship to a truth that transcends that situation and in the light of which he can view and judge it.[15]

Demant admits that most liberal theorists have not used this sort of metaphysical language. Nevertheless he insists that this understanding has been assumed in all the historic formulations of liberalism.

Demant brings forward three witnesses: first is Jose Ortega y Gassett, who was Professor of Metaphysics at Madrid University. His book *The Revolt of the Masses* written in 1932 was an attack on the utter lack of morality that led to the totalitarian movements of Europe. Demant quotes Ortega's definition of liberalism, which emphasizes the self-limitation of the state out of respect for minorities within the state. In other words, the state is tolerant of those who disagree with its own aims. Demant's second witness is John Stuart Mill. Demant mentions Mill in passing, insisting that the whole of *On Liberty* is an attempt to protect the individual against the power of the state. Demant's third witness is Professor H. J. Laski, then Professor of Politics and Political Theory at the London School of Economics. Again, Demant correctly finds Laski identifying liberty with the rights of the individual over against the state.

His three witnesses have established the important negative conclusion that liberal doctrine is concerned to protect the individual against the state, and this implies that the purposes of the state are to serve the individuals within it. Demant now develops this and draws out four positive aspects of the liberal doctrine.

First, there is an objective truth which can be reached by eliminating bias and cultivating disinterestedness. In liberal theory the means to this truth is the exercise of reason. This belief in an objective truth does not imply a dogmatism, because the world is complicated and therefore assertions have to be tentative and held with a certain humility. Although truth is complicated it is still accessible. (The opposite view – that the complexity of the world makes an objective truth inaccessible – can itself be dogmatic because it makes the struggle to understand the world redundant, and genuine discussion between people unnecessary.) It is a belief in an objective truth which explains the necessity of providing a climate where the freedom of speech, of opinion, and of the press are vital.

Secondly, there is an objective morality. Unless there is an objective morality it is difficult to see how one justifies the rights of the individual against the claims of the state. All talk of 'human rights' implies a standard, beyond the subjective will of the people, which all people should recognize. The liberal belief that there are obligations and rights binding on nations everywhere is intelligible only with reference to an objective morality.

Thirdly (and this is the legal extension of the second aspect), there is the liberal belief in 'Natural Law' and 'Natural Rights' in the constitution of existence which can be apprehended by all humans and appealed to against the laws of any particular state legislature. The importance of this aspect is that the state is subject to natural law, and is an embodiment, not the source, of true law.

The fourth aspect is the recognition of a universal character in all human beings. Beyond all the differences of race, sex, status in society, and behaviour, is a common essence which is part of human nature. This is the assumption behind democracy, which holds that every person may play a part in framing the laws under which she will live. These, Demant says, are the four conscious doctrines of liberalism.

(b) The liberal dogma denies the transcendent and has a tendency towards humanism and subjectivism. 'The dogma of liberalism', writes Demant, 'has been precisely that there is no dimension other than the temporal. Reality is the flux of becoming. There is nothing in the absolute which is not in the moving process of history.'[16] The dogma of liberalism is the dogma of our modern age which has its roots in the Enlightenment. Demant clearly links the modern tendency towards humanism and subjectivism with liberalism. In *God, Man, and Society* Demant charts the philosophical roots of the liberal dogma. Descartes is considered to be the origin. His philosophy separated the human from 'both his physical or spiritual environment, and also from his cultural and historical setting'.[17] Kant carried the Cartesian system to its logical conclusion, 'in whose system the human being is practically the artificer of reality, and only by an act of will or faith can believe that the world is what the mind has prefigured it to be'.[18] In Kant there is no way of knowing the objective truth about reality.[19] The mind becomes absolute and self-contained. Demant is deeply critical of Kant, believing that many damaging changes in religion, morality, and human self-perception can be traced back to his philosophy. He concludes: 'the change we are here describing tended to make this total universe a function of man's autonomous mind and will, instead of something given to him and of which he had to discover the truth by effort of a conforming mind and a submissive will'.[20] The only counter-tendency was the rise of science, which left the impression that the only aspect of the external world humans had to accept was the material world.

Significantly Demant does not then explain why these developments were so attractive to liberals. Why did liberals take to a world view which was subjective and humanistic? This is especially strange when so much of the conscious doctrines of liberalism would seem to be at odds with this dogma. Demant might have suggested the following: that liberals welcomed these philosophical claims partly because they appeared to resolve the conflicts between different moral claims by implying that all moral claims were relative. There are no absolutes.

Humanity is the sum of all there is; therefore moral arguments disappear because the only disagreement is over individual's preferences. This implied complete tolerance; for if there are no absolutes, the individual has no right to impose her moral beliefs on other people. Therefore there is never any justification for society taking action against minorities.

Thus far I have simply reported Demant's argument. However, this gap in Demant's argument is so crucial that it warrants a brief comment which anticipates my conclusions for this Part. Demant makes a strong case that liberalism slid from a conviction of absolute truth to a relativizing dogma. Yet his failure to understand the reason for this illustrates his failure to appreciate the significance toleration had in the development of liberalism. In other words, Demant has identified the philosophical basis of the secularist challenge, but failed to discern the primary reason why this philosophical basis was needed.

The result was liberal dogma. Human-rights language was linked with secular humanistic language. The dogma denied the transcendent, denied absolutes, and, in Demant's language, was a dogma of becoming.

(c) The liberal dogma contradicts liberal doctrines. The doctrine of liberalism, according to Demant, was the claim that the individual has certain rights over and against the collective. The liberal dogma was a denial of the transcendent and an insistence that all that exists is the temporal order.

The best way to show the contradiction is to use the attitude of the cynic. The cynic wants to know why the individual has rights over against the collective. If both are merely parts of a temporal order, then it is impossible to give a reason. (Demant believed that the collective could, because of its larger size, claim the loyalty of the individual. That, however, is the next stage of the argument.)

Then there is the liberal claim that there are absolute human rights which apply to all states everywhere. This is really another way of saying that there is an objective morality beyond the temporal order. I have noted that the secular liberal believes that a relativist view of morality provides a justification for state tolerance. However, the cynic can reverse this judgment and demand an explanation as to why he should not impose his moral preferences on others if he has the power and inclination. Once again the secular liberal has no response, because the cynic's morality is his own preference, and, as morality is relative, the liberal's dislike is not a rational objection. This is a strong argument which recurs throughout Demant's work (although he does not use the 'cynic' as it has been applied here). It was clear to Demant that the language of morality made objective assumptions. The logical conclusion of the liberal dogma, Demant believed, was a totalitarian state.

(d) The totalitarian doctrine fulfils the logic of the liberal dogma. The logical implications of the liberal dogma can be stated as follows:

1. There is nothing in humanity not derived from the temporal order.
2. The collective life on earth is of the temporal order.
3. The individual life is likewise of the temporal order, but it is a fragmentary part of the collective whole. It is something less than the life of the community.
4. Therefore 'in the contest between individual and society the less inclusive has no rights against but only duties towards the more inclusive'.[21]
5. Therefore the only end of the human life is in the enhancement of the collective.

So, then, in the totalitarian countries this liberal contradiction has been resolved. The liberal doctrines have been abolished and replaced with new totalitarian doctrines which concur with the dogma of the age. They demand that all individuals live for the nation state. This follows logically from the liberal dogma. The state decides the morality for its people. After all, in the temporal order the state is the highest authority. Everything must be done for the state. Demant gives three examples to prove this point. First, a former Commissar of Justice in Russia declared that 'every judge must remember that his judicial decisions in particular cases are intended to promote first the prevailing policy of the ruling class and nothing else'. The second example is Mussolini in *Il Fascismo :* 'The State becomes the conscience and will of the people. The State spreads the triumph of intellect throughout the domain of science, of art, of law and of humanity.' The third example is a Dr H. Nicola in Germany, who declares,

> it will be the task of the constitution to set forth as the central law of the National Socialist philosophy of life the racial ideal, the Nordic spirit of law ... these must be the guiding principles of the entire life of the people, in politics, in education, and in culture ... It is this which, according to German and Nordic conceptions of life, is considered as the Eternal Law, as unchangeable as the stars, as the Moral Law which lives in every true German.[22]

Therefore, Demant believed that the totalitarian states were popular because they were providing new doctrines for the modern dogma. The solution did not lie with a reaffirmation of the liberal dogma, but a reassertion of the traditional Christian one.

(e) The solution is the Catholic dogma. Demant was convinced that the traditional Catholic faith was the only dogma which could sustain the liberal doctrines. 'Catholicism' is meant in a broad sense. The primary meaning is that humanity belongs to two worlds – the temporal and the eternal. In this sense, it contrasts favourably with secular liberal humanism and continental Protestantism.

Religious liberalism had – as the name implied – allied itself with the liberal dogma and replaced the Catholic doctrine with a moral gospel. It suffered from all the defects that secular liberal humanism was facing. Continental Protestantism, whilst it is a clear assertion of faith, has also encouraged this sacred–secular divide. God is no longer active in the historic order because it has fallen, and therefore there is nothing to guide human beings. Demant then writes,

> In contrast to these two attitudes stands the view that reality is Being, the ground-pattern of Becoming, and not Becoming itself. On this view we can discern reality at any moment of becoming and do not have to wait for the consummation of all things to discover it ... Only an attitude which accords reality to both being and becoming, and the

interaction of them in the actual world, can give us insight and power to interpret and direct history. In this book I shall make that claim for Catholicism.[23]

For Demant, the only antidote to the rise of totalitarianism on the continent of Europe was Christianity. Secularism built upon the foundation of relativism was in trouble. It could not provide the necessary foundation for human rights. The only alternative to secularism was Catholicism, which provided a total metanarrative. It is a complete analysis of the human situation. With this outlook, it is not surprising that different world perspectives were ignored by Demant. Plurality was excluded by the totality of the Christian narrative.

Despite the changing world of the 1940s and 50s, Demant persisted in his analysis of liberalism, and extended it towards socialism. He saw the growth in the Welfare State (the state principle – as he called it) as involving the same unresolved contradiction as the totalitarian regimes of the 30s. For Demant, socialism denied individual human values and was a natural outcome of liberal failure.

In the next chapter we examine this extension of the Christian analysis towards socialism, capitalism, and economics.

CHAPTER 4

The totality of the Christian narrative: capitalism and ecology

In the last chapter the explanatory power of the Christian perspective was illustrated by the crisis within liberalism. In this chapter a distinctively Christian analysis is extended to economics. For Demant, the economic and political analysis is part of the truth of Christianity. It is all part of the totality of the Christian perspective.

CAPITALISM AND ECOLOGICAL CONCERN

The bulk of the argument is taken from Demant's Scott Holland Lectures of 1949, published in 1952, *Religion and the Decline of Capitalism*. It sounds a little strange in the 1990s to talk about the 'decline' of capitalism, a point which will be taken up later. In this account of his views, the 'current position' refers to 1949. The lectures are envisaged as a sequel to Tawney's *Religion and the Rise of Capitalism*. There are six stages to Demant's argument.

(a) *The current position.*
Demant retains the basic thesis that various Protestant forces were responsible for the development of capitalism. He describes the current position as 'the end of a short-lived experiment'.[1] The length of this experiment, he concedes, is difficult to measure, mainly because a free market never operates irrespective of other factors. He also concedes that the principles of sale and exchange have a history going back centuries. Nevertheless, says Demant, 'never before our own times did sale and exchange in the commercial sense constitute more than the fringes of economic life'.[2] In the end, he identifies 'the period of

capitalism, as ... the latter half of the eighteenth century and most of the nineteenth century'.[3]

The decline is apparent by the turn of the century, when the *laissez-faire* doctrines were found wanting. Socialism became attractive, ostensibly because of the unfairness of the market as an allocator of both resources and rewards. Since then there has been a dramatic shift away from capitalism towards socialism. Demant sees parallels with the rise of the totalitarian regimes on the continent. It is in this respect that the story links with the rise and fall of liberalism. Liberalism and capitalism went hand in hand; and totalitarianism is a more extreme version of the socialist declaration that the state has the central role to play in society.

(b) The nature of capitalism.

Capitalism, argues Demant, is distinctive in two different but related ways. First, it concedes a dramatic autonomy to economic life. It answers only to itself rather than to any higher authority. It is no longer a means to an end, but an end in itself. Capitalism involves the 'relative freedom of economic activity from social controls and its theoretical bulwark in the idea of economic life as the operation of natural law rather than a system developed by men'.[4] Capitalism, argues Demant, has run parallel with various other secularizing ideas, in particular the innovation that economics should be regarded as an autonomous science, free from any religious restraints.

The problem, which this account of Demant's views exemplifies, is that this description of capitalism is muddled. Some sort of competitive economic life is an essential part of any society where there are unlimited wants but limited resources. Economic life is, by definition, a question of the allocation of those resources for the purposes of production. This is the assumption behind the important idea of 'opportunity cost'. The resources used to produce x could have been used to produce a, or b, or c. These other uses are the opportunity cost. So, for example, for every production decision to make guns, there is the additional cost of every other possible production use for those materials. It is not economic life as such which is the distinctive feature of capitalism, but the development of the market economy. Adam Smith, partly in the light of his deistic presuppositions, argued that the free market is the best allocator of resources, and it is this ideology of *laissez-faire*, with all its implications of competitive individualism, which Demant feels lacks grounding in moral and spiritual values. It must be conceded that whenever Demant writes of economic matters, there is a distinct lack of precision.[5] The second distinctive feature of capitalism (his description of which Demant concedes to be contentious) is that the 'nerve of capitalism is the predominance of market relationships over the greater part of the social field'.[6] Demant gives several examples of this. The simplest is the way in which labour is treated as a commodity the price of which is regulated by its sale in the market. The value of any job, Demant says, should not simply be determined by the price it can fetch in the market-place. There is a strong moral case here: consider the relative rewards enjoyed by accountants and those of nurses in our own society. The accountant, it could be argued, should not earn much more than a nurse simply because he has a certain rarity value. This does not mean that he works harder or does a more worthwhile job.

Demant believed that the natural associations between people – for example, neighbourhoods, families, labour unions, professional associations – were being undermined by the constant expectation that nothing should happen without a contract. Instead of working with a sense of vocation, people work merely for a reward. Instead of showing pride in community and having the pleasure of contributing to local events, an individual stands back, refusing to participate for fear that others might get something for nothing and one will not have suitable financial recompense. A person's home is subject to rent which makes the owner a profit. For Demant this is unnatural. It has enthroned the contract and market principle at the centre of human life.

(c) The reasons for the decline of capitalism.

Demant lists four reasons for the decline of capitalism: the hostility it has elicited against itself; the break-up of its own institutional framework; its parasitism on the non-economic foundations of society; and the dissipation of the ethical dispositions which reared and sustained it.[7] Each of these related reasons will now be discussed in turn.

In speaking of the hostility that capitalism has brought upon itself, Demant does not simply mean the standard objection that capitalism, as a system, makes the rich richer and the poor poorer. There is also the elevation of a certain aspect of human society to the status of the key by which everything is understood. Capitalism makes 'the wage' the determining factor of all human activity. This means that it has disturbed the organic foundations of human life, leaving the human person dislocated and alone. The worker has nothing on which to depend, save what she can buy.

One additional element lies behind the hostility which capitalism has generated. Demant questions the quality of the goods which capitalism produces. Even the much heralded rewards of our society in terms of housing and clothes are, he claims, often shoddy and undesirable. He says, 'And if good food, good houses, good clothes and good furniture are objects of the right kind of materialist desire, then our technical society is making a bad job of its materialism. Many a simpler community does these things better.'[8] Here Demant is showing his training in anthropology. He always felt that many so-called primitive or less advanced societies were more successful – in terms of quality – than those in the West were willing to concede. They produce better food, better designed homes, and more interesting designs of furniture than the West.

The second reason he gives for the decline of capitalism is the break-up of its own institutional framework. He means that capitalism requires a framework of stability or (to use his term) establishment in which the market can operate. Historically, capitalism presupposed certain feudal structures, which it then proceeded to undermine. Demant is, at this point, heavily dependent upon the work of Joseph Schumpeter in *Capitalism,*

Socialism and Democracy. As the market principle developed, it was in a context where 'underneath ... and keeping society together, were ties and responsibilities surviving from the feudal and local social structures'.[9]

Demant's third reason for capitalism's decline was that it was parasitic on non-economic factors. (Clearly this is related to the second reason. Demant has an organic conception of society. People are born into families; families are part of communities; and all communities identify with a country. Industrialization and specialization are deeply damaging to this organic foundation of society. People no longer live and work in the same community. Their colleagues are strangers: they do not visit each other's homes, because they all live too far apart from each other. This geographical effect is a result of increasing specialization and dramatic improvements in transport. The triumph of capitalism undermines the very institutions that make humanity feel at home within a culture.

The final reason for the decline of capitalism is that it is undermining the ethical dispositions that engendered it. Capitalism depends upon a high code of ethics. Promises need to be kept. Certain conventions need to be observed. However, the impersonal nature of industrial, technological culture erodes these conventions.

Capitalism, then, is in decline, according to Demant, because the economic sphere is given too much significance; it takes precedence over every other factor. Work is judged by the amount of economic activity it generates, not by the quality of the product. Governments operate a policy of employing people simply for the sake of employing them, not because the product is satisfying human needs. Furthermore, there is no control of the economic area. Anything which satisfies a need, or, alternatively, anything for which a need can be generated by advertizing and then sold for a profit, satisfies the criterion by which all is judged. The 'progress' it produces takes place regardless of the social costs. To take one example, improved communication and travel represent genuine progress, providing the benefits outweigh the costs. Therefore, writes Demant, the railway and the steamship have been net gain to human communities. But with the motor car and the aeroplane, along with the satisfactions they give, numerous disadvantages arose which have to be offset against the satisfactions. I refer to traffic problems, knocking about of villages and towns, noise, the taking of good land badly needed for food and houses, material wanted for good furniture, increase of restless mobility, less care for the place we live in, encouragement to divide sharply places where men live and where they work. Instead of linking communities those developments tend to disintegrate them.[10]

(d) The rise of socialism.

When a society is in rebellion against God the natural balance and order of that society are lost and the result is frustration and pain. In an attempt to alleviate this pain a society will swing from one layer to another, searching for the key. The rise of socialism is part of the problem, not the solution. Demant sees both capitalism and socialism as symptoms of the same crisis. It is 'a swing-over from the market principle to the state principle'.[11] Demant uses the term 'swing-over' to capture the idea of the dialectical swing from one layer of human existence, seen as the key to everything, to another, seen in turn in a similar light. Where the market has failed, human society hopes that the state will succeed.

The crisis which brought the downfall of the market principle was the erosion of community. It is hoped that the state will compensate for this. Demant, as we shall see, is convinced that in this quest it will fail. However, he recognises that there are certain attractions to the state principle. There does not appear to be anything else which can solve the problems confronting society. Socialism, for Demant, is not some distinctive economic structure of common ownership, but the increasing involvement of the state as the solution to the country's problems. The notion of state power makes explicit a parallel which Demant always felt was legitimate, that between social welfare politics and totalitarianism. Their difference was one of degree rather than kind.

To sum up: the rise of socialism is the hope that the state principle can bring healing to human society and overcome the

divisive effects of the market principle. Demant sees in this hope
a swing from one inappropriate layer of human existence to
another, as will be shown presently.

(e) *The inadequacy of socialism.*
To give to the state the status of the most important key to all
human life is, for Demant, as unnatural as to give it to the
market. There are two detailed reasons why this is so. The first
is that 'the state can never be an object of emotional attachment
which could replace a man's roots in home, property, neighbourhood and craft association'.[12]

The second reason, related to the first, is that the essential
features of socialism have the same parentage as those of
capitalism and, therefore, reflect many of the same features.
'Both the state principle', writes Demant, 'with man treated as
bare citizen, and market principle with man treated as bare
economic unit ... represent very advanced constructions of the
human spirit and intellect, built on to the substance of society
made up from clan, associative, geographical, and religious
Groupings'.[13] The basic problem with the state principle is that
it remains something imposed on top of humanity, instead of
something that revives the roots of human life. It is an unnatural
superstructure that stifles the natural organic growth of human
society. The implication is that the problem is not which one of
these alternatives we are to pick, but how can we recover the
roots which made both possible and then atrophied as a result
of them.

In the end Demant does not see much potential for the
Welfare State. In a very perceptive passage, he interprets the
shift from capitalism to socialism as meaning 'that the causes of
dissatisfaction are then projected upon governments instead of
upon the propertied and managerial classes. In fact, as society
becomes less pluralist and more unitary under state direction,
all social resentments become directed against the state, and the
state tends to redirect them against foreign powers.'[14]

So Demant is in a rather strange position. He was wrong to
believe that capitalism was in terminal decline; but he was right
to believe that socialism would not succeed. Demant has been

much criticized for implying the terminal decline of capitalism. And yet what frequently goes unnoticed is his equal conviction that the 'state principle' cannot succeed. In fact, Demant's model does not entail that capitalism is in terminal decline; when dissatisfaction with the Welfare State sets in, society will swing again, and there is no reason why it should not be a swing back to individualism. The implication of dissatisfaction with the state principle is precisely that in time that too will decline. It now appears that socialism was an even shorter experiment.

(*f*) *Neither capitalism nor socialism but ecology.*
If neither of these forces can provide the healing which our society so desperately needs, then what is the solution? The model that Demant uses demands that we rediscover our roots in the eternal. To adopt this will, he claims, restore the appropriate, natural balance to society. The economic element and the state can then resume their appropriate roles. There is a need to concentrate on the inner life, the penumbra, to sort out the problems which exist at the sub-economic and sub-political level. Demant believes that there are, at this level, three main elements: the vital, the cultural, and the religious. When describing the importance of the first element, his writing resembles the tract of some ecological Group:

The first is the life-giving power of the earth upon whose organic products the most theoretical technician or paper planner depends in order to live. Warnings about dangers here have been given loudly enough. The earth upon which we live is being drained of its power to support animal and human life. Its vital reproductive cycle is broken under the spur of technical urban and commercial aggression. An acre or two of forest is destroyed to make one New York newspaper per issue; in our small island cultivable land is covered with bricks and concrete, not even for houses or military defence – both of which are vital priorities after food – but for an alleged technical progress which exaggerates the misbalance between superstructure and foundations.[15]

The similarities between Demant's programme and the ecological one have not been stressed sufficiently. For Demant, the ecological theme was the main point of the Christendom Group. At the end of his life he was asked to sum up the work of the

Christendom Group; he wrote: 'One basic tenet of this movement is an economic one, namely that the pattern of industrial society is fraudulent and self-destructive. It holds that we cannot have too much production; people compete for jobs not for goods; useful food products are left to rot, in order to maintain earning opportunity.' And he concluded,

The earth's self-recovering rhythm is broken under the spur of technocratic, megalopolitan and commercial aggression. This betrays man's stewardship of the earth. More and more of the earth's surface becomes incapable of reproducing the sources of life. The land is over-driven by technical farming, reckless use of chemical fertilizers and pesticides, and loss of agronomic land for urban development, airports and roads. Cities become less desirable for human habitation. The costs of economic growth rise rapidly.[16]

T. S. Eliot makes exactly the same point in *The Idea of a Christian Society*.[17]

The second element, which requires attention, is the cultural, which Demant links with community. Culture implies the priority of a community over the raw economic drive. It is exemplified in a political decision to renovate existing Victorian terrace houses, where there is a genuine sense of community, rather than knocking them down and housing everyone in high-rise flats where no sense of the corporate seems possible. The third element is the deepest of all. A civilization which has lost a sense of the transcendent has lost the necessary foundation for a balanced life. It is only when this dimension is at the centre of life, that society can place everything else in perspective.

As for political prescriptions, Demant devoted his entire life to the quest for something which was neither capitalist nor socialist, but different from both. In the late 1920s he followed Reckitt in his support for 'Guild Socialism', a version of socialism which wanted a new partnership in industry, between managers and the unions, modelled on the medieval guilds.[18] In the thirties Demant was sympathetic to Major Douglas' social credit proposals. An eccentric economic theory committed to overcoming the apparent deficiency of purchasing power in the economy with a simple 'social credit' – a dividend. The problem with both of these proposals is that they are hopelessly impractical, and, perhaps more fundamentally, incompatible. Guild socialism wanted to undermine the capitalist edifice; whilst social credit wanted to free the system to work more efficiently. A. J. Penty spotted this incompatibility, but this simply stimulated the Christendom Group into trying to modify social credit to make it 'workable'.[19] It was, it must be admitted, a blind alley.

Since the emergence of the Green movement, it has become clearer what the Christendom Group were seeking: a weaker and looser state structure; controls on economic growth (on the grounds that there is an ecologically desirable limit for such growth); greater controls on planning and road development to protect the environment. It was a sustained attempt to recover the quality of life which had been undermined by urbanization. They wanted to recreate the space for small communities to flourish. But primarily they wanted a recovery of certain basic Christian dispositions and conventions which they believed to be necessary to ensure the vibrancy of a culture.

THE RECOVERY OF CHRISTIAN SOCIAL CONVENTIONS AND ASSUMPTIONS

T. S. Eliot's definition of a Christian society met with broad approval from the Christendom Group: 'It would be a society in which the natural end of man – virtue and well-being in community – is acknowledged for all, and the supernatural end – beatitude – for those who have eyes to see it.'[20] Eliot described this as his minimum for a society to be called Christian. Of course, ultimately, Christians want everyone to be Christian within a society, but this is unlikely to be attained in our modern pluralistic culture. So what this definition suggests is plurality within strict limits. Public policy – even when power is exercised by those who are not Christian – should protect a broadly Christian ethos. Eliot made much of the established church. Britain both past and present is, by establishment, opposed to a neutral society. The state then has an obligation to build up the family and expect chastity prior to marriage and fidelity within it. Further the state should encourage all that generates respect for persons and property. For Demant, this meant that attention must be paid to the penumbra; legislation should be framed with a view to protect the world views, conventions, and habits of the cultural subconscious.

Demant's main anxiety is the sheer size of the technological, urban edifice. The organic foundations (or establishment – as he calls it in the Giffords) are being eroded. He writes in his *Christian Sex Ethics* that the current preoccupation with sex is a result of modernity's crushing depersonalization, and that it is this which gives the rediscovery of intimacy and affection disproportionate importance. He writes, 'this is just a resort to sexual activity as a kind of narcotic … Economic anxieties, worries about esteem and status, intolerable personal relations, hating one's work or despising it, general feelings of failure or cowardice – all this sort of anxiety can be momentarily shed in the sexual embrace.'[21] Because we are unnatural in our social relations, we have become unnatural in our sexual relations. If communities were smaller, more intimate, more natural, then much would be put right. So it is an appeal for the rediscovery of community.

Demant did not explicate further policy recommendations. He sat on the Wolfenden committee, and supported its recommendations to legalize homosexuality, when one might have expected him to oppose it. Certainly, his reasoning has been used in support of a conservative moral agenda. It can be argued that, to protect marriage, one should make divorce so difficult that people do not lightly embark on extra-marital relations. It is certainly true that it is easier to remain faithful if one is never given the opportunity to be unfaithful. Another area of concern is the effect of television, newspapers, and, above all, pornography. It is presupposed here that options are created for people by these media which otherwise would not be there. So violence in a street brawl on the screen might well create an actual street brawl off the screen. Our media provide people with ideas for immoral behaviour. As Demant put it there is something inadequate about a culture which only enables those who are saints to be moral.

However, his major area of concern was education. The

educators have the power to create the framework in which people experience the world. T. S. Eliot returned to this theme time and time again. No educational system is value-free; therefore it is preferable that the system is Christian, reflecting what, for a Christian, are the true values.[22] In a society committed to pluralism, it is difficult to see how this suggestion can be implemented. This is the problem that the Christendom Group failed to face. It is to this problem that we now turn.

CHRISTENDOM AND PLURALITY

For the Christendom Group the choice was simple: sinful secularism or Christianity. And in deciding between these options our culture must opt for the truth. The destructive tendency of modernity exposes the poverty and falsehood of the secular world view. The strength of medieval Christendom illustrates the truth of the theistic world view. For the Christendom Group, the argument was reducible to three points:

1. Secularism excludes Christianity, and Christianity excludes secularism. Only one of these world views can be true.
2. Modernity is in trouble precisely because of its secularist tendencies.
3. Therefore we must recover and realize the truth of the Christian world view.

This traditional Christian response is mistaken on three counts. First, the Christendom Group analysis ignored the single greatest factor behind secularism, namely, the religious wars of western Europe during the seventeenth century. Religious traditions have found it difficult to live together. Religious adherents have found it difficult to tolerate fundamental religious differences. Whenever one sect or denomination has had sufficient power it sought to exclude other sects and denominations with less power. Medieval Christendom is not attractive to a modern secularist. For all the drawbacks of modernity it is at least free of medieval intolerance.

Secondly, the traditional response could not adjust to a

changing pluralistic society. In Britain during the 1920s, it was still possible to point to Christianity as the main religious option. All the trappings of establishment – the monarchy, bishops in the House of Lords, and academic chairs confined to Anglicans – conspired to create the impression that Christianity was the only major religious option. However, even as the Christendom Group was writing, the world was changing. Communication, travel, and immigration were creating a pluralistic culture. The choice was no longer Christianity or secularism, but Christianity or secularism or Judaism or Islam or Sikhism or Hinduism, and so on.

The secularist can legitimately use the fact of plurality as a decisive objection to this traditional Christian response. A vacant public square at least protects the minority religious viewpoint from persecution by an alternative religious viewpoint. Christianity needed secularism to learn the lesson of tolerance.

The third mistake is the most important because it is theological. Demant's view of Christianity was incomplete, because it ignored the fact of plurality. I have attempted to present his views sympathetically, because he tried to illustrate the total nature of the Christian world perspective. Christianity, for Demant, explains contemporary cultural problems, such as the rise of totalitarianism and the crisis of capitalism. And yet his cosmic Christianity could not accommodate the numerous traditions that differ from Christianity. Plurality is a fact that requires Christian analysis. Demant could not see this.

Demant wanted a unitary culture that offered small concessions to different world perspectives; his social agenda was intolerant. In the end, Demant's understanding of Christianity was not total enough because he ignored plurality.

CONCLUSION

The Christendom Group did try to work in all three modes, though the bulk of their work was in the second, i.e., the cultural, mode; for their primary concern was to offer a cultural analysis that offered depth to ethical reflection. They worked in the first mode (theology) because they were Anglo-Catholics using the natural-law tradition underpinned by a broadly Thomist framework.

The Christendom Group's activity in the second cultural mode was a result of two factors. The first was the Catholic natural-law tradition which, Demant claimed, provided a distinctly Christian resource to explain our current cultural malaise. The second factor was a sense that modernity compared unfavourably with medieval Christendom. Working within these parameters the Group saw a culture in crisis. The dominant liberal ideology was fundamentally incoherent; the major political options were evading the true extent of the crisis and ignoring the real options; and cultural assumptions were constantly being eroded by the extent of our technological, urban edifice.

This generally gloomy appraisal was provoked by the tyranny of Stalin (representing the evil of the left) and the Great Depression and Hitler (representing the failure of capitalism and the right). The fairly dramatic decline in church attendance in the United Kingdom made creeping secularization the obvious culprit. Demant managed to retain this general analysis even in the self-confident sixties. He still saw disaster lying just around the corner.

The Christendom Group's major problems were found in the third mode (application). Their support for certain 'cranky' options, such as Guild socialism and social credit, was clearly unfortunate. Their ecological concern is more important. But the problem remains: what are the policy recommendations that will recreate our community roots?

I have argued that this mixed assessment of the Christendom contribution is partly due to the failure of the Group to grapple with the fact of plurality. They failed to discern any achievements in the post-Enlightenment world view. Modernity is entitled to take some credit for attempting to find ways to accommodate diversity; its wholesale rejection is not appropriate. Furthermore rejection of modernity almost inevitably made the Group's policy prescriptions either irrelevant or hopelessly impractical.

A more discerning evaluation of modernity is needed. Demant *et al.* can offer a significant contribution to the debate, once a central weakness in their position has been confronted. The development of secularism was partly a result of religious intolerance. Religious traditions need to discover tolerance. Demant's call for a recovery of medieval Christendom is not an option, because plurality is with us and will not go away. Christians must find a way to embrace alternative religious traditions within the public square.

Unfortunately, British culture does not seem able to affirm plurality. In the next chapter, we find the spirit of Christendom living on in contemporary Britain. This spirit cannot affirm diversity; diversity is to be feared.

CHAPTER 5

Plurality and contemporary British Christian ethics

Although the Christendom Group identified legitimate areas of concern, it is not surprising that their approach went out of fashion. The Group's main critics were Denys Munby and Ronald Preston. Both were very critical of the Group's tendency to make economic pronouncements without economic expertise. However, for my purposes, Munby is the more significant. He attacks explicitly the failure of the Group to grapple with plurality. With the exception of Munby, one finds a surprising paucity of ethical reflection on the problems of plurality and tolerance. The little offered has arisen in response to the crises provoked by the speeches of Enoch Powell and, more recently, the *fatwa* against Salman Rushdie.

So in this chapter, I shall start by reporting Preston's criticisms of the Christendom Group, and noting his lack of interest in questions about plurality. Then I shall discuss at greater length the contribution of Munby, concentrating on his book, *The Idea of a Secular Society*. Munby represents the strand of British Christian ethics that affirms secularism as the only way to affirm plurality. Finally, I shall show that the Christendom spirit with regard to plurality can be clearly seen in the debates surrounding Enoch Powell and Salman Rushdie. Four different approaches to plurality are represented in this chapter: Preston's neglect; Munby's capitulation; Powell's affirmation of a Christian unitary culture; and British Muslims' affirmation of an Islamic unitary culture. The last two show that the spirit of the Christendom Group lives on.

Ronald Preston was trained in economics, which helps to explain why many of his frequent references to the Christendom Group, and to Demant in particular, complain about the lack of economic expertise.[1] It is true that Demant was not trained in economics and, at certain points, he is most unsatisfactorily imprecise. Nevertheless Preston is not entirely fair to him. Behind the sometimes confused rhetoric of Demant, certain legitimate economic claims are being made. For instance, he believed that the relentless push for economic growth was deeply damaging to the environment, and that there must be an ecological limit to such growth. Although many economists would take issue with such judgments, Preston is wrong to imply that all would. In the last chapter we looked at Demant's article prepared for the *Dictionary of Business Ethics* called 'The Work of the Christendom Group in the Field of Business and Economic Thought'. This proved to be his final writing before he died; and in it one can sense the old man reflecting upon his career. Therefore the bibliography for this short article is very significant. He does not refer his readers to anything by the Christendom Group; instead he lists *The Diseconomics of Growth* by H. V. Hodson, and *The Costs of Economic Growth* by E. J. Mishan. Both books go some way towards endorsing Demant's economic judgments. He believed that the Green movement basically encapsulated the Christendom Group's main themes. The difference between Demant and Preston is not just a matter of economic expertise versus economic ignorance, but of conventional, pro-growth economics against ecological, no-growth economics. Whoever is correct on this issue, ultimately the main difficulty with Demant is not his ignorance of economics.

Preston makes three further criticisms of Demant. First, he blames Demant's alleged disregard of the experts on certain theological mistakes. Preston, in his discussion of the Malvern Conference, comments on the legitimate Thomist assumption that the doctrine of the Fall of humanity should not be pushed so far as to imply that human reason cannot apprehend any divine truth. He writes, 'It is the next stage in the argument that causes difficulty. It is assumed that because human reason is not fallen so far that it cannot apprehend divine truth, it can therefore arrive at the truths of a divinely given natural order for the social and political world without being trained, or using the work of those trained, in the different sciences which study that world. This appears a complete *non-sequitur*.'[2] In the same review, Preston criticizes W. G. Peck (and clearly feels that the criticism could apply to the rest of the Christendom Group) when he writes, 'Mr. Peck's economic errors have a theological origin in a theology which forbids him to take economics seriously, because he has an unsatisfactory view of natural law, which in turn goes back to the inadequacies of the Thomist synthesis which he takes as a norm.'[3]

Preston is, again, not entirely fair to the Christendom Group. It is not that divine truth is so blindingly obvious that experts are not needed (this would be a theological error), but that the economic experts are held to be operating with inappropriate assumptions. This is a dispute about the nature of economics. Preston is correct to say that economic experts, within the value-free models they develop, make very few assumptions, and it would take exceptional economic expertise to show that the assumptions are inappropriate.[4] But the model of natural law used by Demant is intended to be flexible and to provide the basis for general criticisms. The claim that Demant makes a theological error is not justified; the claim that he evinced a lack of precision about economics is.

Secondly, Preston is also rightly critical of the norm used by the Group – the civic and agrarian society of the ancient and medieval worlds. As a result, writes Preston, 'he [Demant] hardly ever does justice to the problem of production which capitalism has tackled pretty successfully'.[5] This is a fair criticism that applies not only to the problem of production, but also to the growth in plurality. Here, too, his medieval-style norms prevent an adequate grasp of modern social reality.

Preston's third criticism is that Demant has too weak a doctrine of the state. Preston believes that Demant has forced himself into a highly simplistic polarization. He writes,

Demant's fear of the omnicompetent state, valid enough against totalitarianism, seems misplaced when the problem now is whether in a self-conscious participatory 'Western' type of political democracy the electorate will be sufficiently far-sighted not to want incompatible things, and to allow the state enough power to guide the complex interlocked economies of advanced industrial societies in a way which avoids economic and social disasters. Demant is a high churchman with a low doctrine of the state.[6]

Once again, Preston is right. He identifies correctly Demant's opposition to modernity. For Demant the Christian narrative is set against modernity in every respect. What Preston misses is that this failure is best seen in Demant's inability to engage with plurality. One could conceivably make a case for the view that a decentralized, agrarian, Christendom culture is preferable to our modern capitalist society. Some in the Green movement would want to say exactly that.[7] However, it is impossible to argue that a return to religious wars or the suppression of religious diversity is preferable to peaceful coexistence between religious Groups. It is for this reason that plurality and tolerance can be seen as hinge issues; and Demant's failure here is more important than his failure to affirm capitalism. If Demant could not even concede tolerance as an achievement of modernity, it is not surprising that he could not make any other concession. Preston helpfully identifies the extent of this opposition to modernity, and in so doing explains why Demant's political prescriptions proved so irrelevant.

The actual problem of plurality is strangely neglected throughout Preston's work. Naturally, one should not expect everyone in Christian ethics to reflect on every ethical issue, but it remains surprising that the tolerance and plurality questions do not even get a mention. It is for this reason that Munby is particularly important to us.

DENYS MUNBY

In 1962 Munby used the Riddell Memorial Lectures to provide a reply to T. S. Eliot's *The Idea of a Christian Society*. Munby's reply is excellent, and clearly operates in all three modes.

Within the second mode (cultural), Munby celebrates the achievement of a 'neutral' society as one of the benefits brought about the increasing secularization of British society.

He identifies and affirms six marks of a secular society. First, 'a secular society is one which explicitly refuses to commit itself as a whole to any particular view of the nature of the universe and the place of man in it.'[8] In other words it does not have any particular metaphysic that requires people to live in a certain way. Secondly, it is pluralistic. Munby writes, 'A secular society is in practice a pluralistic society, in so far as it is truly secular.'[9] Thirdly, it is tolerant. In response to Patrick Devlin's view that the limits of toleration are indicated by the presence of 'disgust' at some action (for example homosexuality), Munby retorts, 'It is precisely the glory of a secular society that it does not allow our "disgust" with the behaviour of others to lead to action against them. A secular society is one which tries to set bounds to the natural persecuting tendencies of human nature.'[10]

The fourth mark of a secular society is a minimum structure to resolve disagreements and a common framework of law. Munby is very careful to distinguish these structures from an 'overall aim'. He writes, 'The liberal secular society, by contrast with most previous societies, does not set itself any overall aim, other than that of assisting as fully as possible the actual aims of its members, and making these as concordant with each other as possible.'[11]

Fifth, a secular society solves problems by examination of the empirical facts. In a delightfully quaint affirmation of the self-confident sixties, Munby believes that specialists in economics and sociology can provide the necessary data to ensure that society operates efficiently. Instead of government based on superstition or tradition, he seems to envisage government in the hands of academic specialists who rationally evaluate all the appropriate options and select the best course of action.

Finally, it is a society without official images, precisely because it is pluralistic. 'If there are no common aims', Munby explains, 'there cannot be a common set of images reflecting the common ideals and emotions of everyone.'[12]

Due credit must be given to Munby for his attempt to reflect ethically on the problem of plurality. However, his opposition to Eliot is so total that it is a complete capitulation to the secularist challenge. This description of a secular society is built on the assumptions already outlined in chapter one. It presupposes Groups of individuals who construct society for mutual convenience. Munby affirms the arguments of the secularist because he believes that a secularist framework is the only way to accommodate plurality. He is completely persuaded that religion must be kept out of the public square, otherwise plurality will be threatened. He is a Christian who has just capitulated to the secularist challenge.

This must be contested. First, he fails to see the intolerant possibilities lurking within a neutral society. For example, let us imagine a predominantly religious but officially neutral society with a very small minority of humanists. The different religious Groupings are tolerant of each other and, apart from thrusting the occasional tract into a passing hand, do not put much pressure on the humanist. Now imagine that this neutral society decides to implement Munby's suggestions. We must have no controls on activities during sensitive religious festivals; no legal entitlement to holidays in order to observe these festivals; Muslims would be forbidden to try to persuade the society that greater controls on alcohol are needed; and pro-lifers would be unable to oppose unlimited access to abortion. Such a society would have in effect legally imposed humanist values upon all its members. It would have made humanism the easy tradition to observe and created legal obstacles for any other tradition. Religious tyranny of former times has been replaced by secular tyranny.

The second difficulty with Munby's position is that the neutral society has a tendency to restrict legislation to the absolute minimum required for coexistence.[13] This would provide a constant block on any ethical movement. At one time it was only a small minority of people who believed that slavery should be illegal. It required this minority to persuade the majority that they were right. To exclude a priori such a possibility would be tragic. We ought to welcome those who are trying to suggest legal changes to create a more just society: in this sense those campaigning for better treatment of animals are in a comparable position to those who are campaigning against abortion. Whether or not these movements are right, their case rests on an appeal for greater justice. Both want to see ethical progress against the wishes of many in society. A society must engage with such arguments and attempt to evaluate their validity.

A further difficulty is Munby's commitment to a value-free expertise, rationally applied that can solve all problems. I have already described his fifth mark of a secular society – this confidence in a detached liberal rationality that can solve all contemporary problems – as quaint.[14] Take two examples of contemporary problems which, Munby claims, a secular society is well equipped to tackle. Both are relatively specialized. First, he takes the economic problem of wage-cost inflation and the call for a national-incomes policy. Here Munby proposes that technical questions require expert analysis. Then he tackles the issue of promotion on the basis of merit rather than class. But these are hardly major social issues. Whether or not there is a national-incomes policy will not determine the survival of a society. Issues such as abortion or the freedom to publish contentious books perceived as an attack upon Islam are less easily resolved on Munby's criteria.

The final difficulty is that tolerance and plurality are not best safeguarded by relativist and individualist assumptions. Parts III and IV will show how religious traditions are discovering a religious commitment to plurality, and an alternative foundation for tolerance is emerging.

Within the first mode (theological) Munby argues that a secular society creates the possibility of a much broader sense of God's action. God as creator is active throughout the world. Therefore a society embracing plurality enables the Christian to discover God in different traditions. He links the theological possibilities of plurality with other movements that want to locate God beyond traditional confines. God is not simply active in religion, but within 'secular' movements. God is not just in theology, but in all branches of human inquiry. God is not just represented by the clergy, but is to be found in all people.

This view of Munby's is attractive. He grounds a commitment to plurality in the doctrine of God as creator. As God is active in all traditions and communities, so we ought to welcome this diversity. However, his uncritical support for the secular society sits uneasily with a theological affirmation of God's activity in the whole world. It seems strange to insist that religion which affirms God's total and global activity must be marginalized. Also he ignores the persistence of the particular truth-claims of each tradition that pose the central problem for plurality.

Thus far we have had Preston's neglect of the issues and Munby's largely uncritical acceptance of the secular society. These two responses are fairly typical among British ethicists. We find them compounded by the responses to two debates in British society about plurality: these were occasioned by the Enoch Powell speech of 1968 and the publication of *The Satanic Verses* by Salman Rushdie in 1988.

ENOCH POWELL AND IMMIGRATION

Enoch Powell is a contemporary contributor to political debate who has represented Wolverhampton and then South Down in Ulster in the House of Commons.[15] He was Professor of Greek in the University of New South Wales at the age of twenty-five. As an Anglican, he is committed to Christian reflection on ethical questions. For my purpose, Powell was the popularizer who articulated concern with the growing racial plurality of our British cities.

Powell's views came to prominence when, in a speech to the West Midlands Area Conservative Political Centre in Birmingham on the 20th April 1968, he argued against free immigration from the former colonies and complained about the changing character of British cities.[16] He claimed that the 5 to 10 per cent of the British population who were from the Commonwealth represented an unacceptable threat to the stability of British cities.

To understand Enoch Powell one must first locate him on the map of political philosophy. He has very clear views on the nature of the nation state. He rejects the liberal individualist tradition of Locke, preferring to see the nation as inseparable from culture.[17] This organic view of the nation, sometimes known as communitarian, stresses the common history, religion, and symbols that unite a nation.[18] People do not opt into a nation, but are born into it. Nationhood is linked with a certain language, a certain religion, and a certain history. Now Powell admits that the combination of language, religion, and history that produces a particular sovereign nation state is a mystery.[19] Nevertheless, an entity emerges that identifies with a set of shared symbols and demands self-rule. Powell writes, 'Nationhood is an absolute. There is no such thing as semi-nationhood, or semi-nationalism ... Nationalism, if it is real, cannot be brought off with less than the complete article. This is not because the nationalist is less reasonable or more greedy than his fellow men; it is because nationhood is the complete article.'[20] National cultural identity is the basis of a stable society. For Powell, to tamper with or destroy that cultural identity is treasonable. These sentiments are to be located in the Conservative political tradition that can be traced back to Hooker, and of which Edmund Burke was the prime exponent.[21] For Hooker, to be English is to be an Anglican. Culture and national identity are not to be separated. Powell should be located in a tradition that started with Hooker and has recently been reaffirmed by T. S. Eliot. For Powell, unlike the Christendom Group, this affirmation of a unitary culture is not the discovery of a theological truth, but, like them, he does want to limit the extent of the diversity that is tolerable within the state. As we shall now discover, in many respects he illustrates all the problems that the Christendom Group had with plurality.

For Powell, anything that undermines the culture of a nation will destabilise that nation. With the growth of immigration during the fifties and sixties, different cultural outlooks were introduced into Britain. For Powell these people are alien:

Of the great multitude, numbering already two million, of West Indians and Asians in England, it is no more true to say that England is their country than it would be to say that the West Indies, or Pakistan, or India are our country. In these great numbers they are, and remain, as alien here as we would be in Kingston or in Delhi; indeed, with the growth of concentrated numbers, the alienness grows, not by choice but by necessity.[22]

He describes in graphic terms the fear indigenous English people allegedly feel as they watch their cities being 'taken over'.

For Powell, it is comparable to treason for a government to permit so much immigration. He denounces successive British governments when he writes, 'It was not for them to heed the cries of anguish from those of their own people who already saw their towns being changed, their native places turned into foreign lands, and themselves displaced as if by a systematic colonization.'[23] For Powell, the government are guilty: 'for no government has the moral right to alter, or permit to be altered, the character and the identity of a nation without that nation's knowledge and without the nation's will. It is a moral issue, and it is a supreme issue.'[24]

Such a striking challenge to plurality by a Christian politician would be expected to provoke considerable response by the church. It did in certain places: the media explored the issues from a moral and religious angle in a popular way; and the Church of England Synod placed immigration firmly on their agenda.[25] But the quality of the debate was poor. Powell had foreseen the response: the call from the church was for integration.

Trevor Huddleston is representative. He described the speech as evil; it was evil because it ignored the destructive impact such sentiments have upon the immigrant community who are trying to settle within Britain; it was evil because it ignored the global impact – a colonial power that had occupied other countries apparently could not accommodate a small influx of immigrants. In the last analysis, why could British people not welcome their Commonwealth friends into their homes and lives? These people have so much to give; they could enhance social life considerably. Huddleston explains, 'I would be perfectly happy if there might be ten million coloured people in this country at the end of the century, and I would thank God for it, because it would at least bring some fresh blood into a very tired old country.'[26] For Huddleston, it is a Christian's responsibility to persuade people to be much more positive towards immigration and the assimilation of fresh elements into society. Powell simply dismisses this view as unrealistic and wrong. He explains to Huddleston, 'A politician would wish that human nature, and that the nature of his own people, was perhaps better than he supposed it to be; but unless he acts upon his judgment of what is … it seems to me that he is guilty of betrayal.'[27] People are suspicious of different cultures; and this is a datum that a politician must accept.

For Powell, even if integration were desirable, neither the immigrants nor the indigenous inhabitants are interested in bringing it about.

> The other dangerous delusion from which those who are willfully or otherwise blind to realities suffer, is summed up in the word 'integration'. To be integrated into a population means to become for all practical purposes indistinguishable from its other members. Now, at all times, where there are marked physical differences, especially of colour, integration is difficult though, over a period, not impossible. There are among the Commonwealth immigrants who have come to live here in the last fifteen years or so, many thousands whose wish and purpose is to be integrated and whose every thought and endeavour is bent in that direction. But to imagine such a thing enters the heads of a great and growing majority of immigrants and their descendants is a ludicrous misconception, and a dangerous one to boot.[28]

The mistake that Huddleston has made is to ignore the toleration option. This does not require complete integration and acceptance, which is why many Christians are unhappy with it. But toleration accommodates Powell's realism. Powell is right to draw attention to the fears of the indigenous population. Tolerance is a call for different communities to live together in peaceful coexistence. It is true that these communities will disagree about religion; and there are numerous differences in terms of history and custom; but these different communities need to discover tolerance as the half-way house between whole-hearted acceptance and outright hostility. This suggestion did not even emerge in the debate.

It is worth noting that part of the reason for the neglect of

Powell is that some of his more horrifying prophecies did not come true. A level of coexistence in practice did emerge, even if no one articulated the theory.

One final point is worth making. Powell viewed with horror the American experience of plurality. Powell did not visit the States until October 1967 (which was very surprising for the Secretary of State for Defence), and was appalled: 'What really frightened Powell and his wife was the reality of the colour clash in the cities they visited in the States'.[29] Roth goes on to report that 'Powell expressed his fears to an American visitor shortly after he had returned to London: "Integration of races of totally disparate origins and culture is one of the great myths of our time. It has never worked throughout history".'[30] Powell frequently used the United States as an illustration of the horrifying danger that would face British society unless we corrected our course. This perception of the States explains much. What Powell did not see is that American cities were discovering a different way for the varied inhabitants to live together. In among the serious problems within New York, there were signs of hope.

So Powell illustrates the major problem raised by the Eliot approach to plurality. For Powell, plurality has no virtues and must be resisted. For those opposed to him, the limited objective of tolerance was bypassed. The church ignored the option and wanted an whole-hearted endorsement of immigrant communities. A similar polarization can be found with completely different players in the recent tragedy of Salman Rushdie.

SALMAN RUSHDIE AND TOLERANCE

As one looks back on the Rushdie affair, much of it seems strangely unreal. A novelist writes a global, mystical, novel packed full of sophisticated allusions to Islam. Thousands of Muslims in Bradford take to the streets to demonstrate. They ceremonially burn the book. Some time later, a religious leader in another country issues a legal judgment requiring death, supplemented with a bounty for the person who carries it out. The author goes into hiding. The matter remains unresolved.

The purpose here is to show the failure of British society to understand the significance of the episode. However, many of the themes of this book will emerge in my discussion. For the tragedy of Salman Rushdie is a tragedy of British secular society.

The Satanic Verses was published on 26th September 1988. Penguin's own editorial consultant had advised against publication because the book would cause offence to Muslims.[31] Sure enough, thousands of letters and phone calls were sent to the publisher asking for the novel to be withdrawn. On 5th October, the Indian Government decided to ban the book; Bangladesh, Sudan, Sri Lanka, and South Africa all rapidly followed suit. Early January 1989 saw Muslims in Bradford, Yorkshire, symbolically burn a copy of the book.

It was on St Valentine's day that the most dramatic episode in the story occurred. The Ayatollah Khomeini, probably in response to demonstrations and deaths in Pakistan, issued his *fatwa* against Rushdie.[32] This sent the author into hiding and added impetus to the demonstrations. Rushdie's responses varied considerably: at first he issued an apology for the hurt he had inadvertently caused to Muslims. Later he complained about the intolerance of the mullahs, and even said, 'Frankly I wish I had written a more critical book.'[33] On the 4th February 1990, in his most sustained explanation of his position called 'In Good Faith' and published in *The Independent*, he claimed that he had never been a Muslim.[34] But by the end of that year, he announced to the world that he had embraced Islam, a conversion that was viewed with some suspicion because, although he conceded that he would not publish a paperback edition, he still refused to withdraw the hardback.[35]

This leads on to a survey of the responses stimulated by the episode. However, to understand the passions involved, we need to understand why so many Muslims found the book offensive.

Pipes is correct to remark: 'To understand its impact fully, *The Satanic Verses* ideally should be read excerpted, out of context, and preferably in translation – for that is how most of his critics became acquainted with it.'[36] Much of their passionate reaction derives from misunderstanding due to translation. Nevertheless there are legitimate grounds for offence. Much of the novel is about Islamic images.[37] The most contentious passages occur when the character Gibreel has a dream, and his identity becomes interwoven with the Angel Gabriel who is responsible for imparting the words of the Qur'an to Muhammad.

Mahound (an ancient Christian name for Muhammad) is depicted as a pragmatic businessman who receives convenient revelations from God. Rushdie uses the 'Satanic verses' episode in the novel to illustrate Mahound's pragmatism. These verses refer to an alleged revelation Muhammad was given that suggested the three main goddesses in Mecca should become intermediaries between humanity and God. Almost without exception, Muslim scholars consider this entire story to be extremely unlikely.[38] In Rushdie's treatment the overwhelming impression is that the Satanic verses show that the Qur'an is not a revelation from God, but a result of human invention.[39] This, coupled with the depiction of Muhammad, left Muslims understandably aggrieved.

One of our problems as a culture is that we have lost a sense of reverence for the sacred. For Christians, a number of helpful analogies have been suggested. The best comes from Ali A. Maxrui who suggests that the Mahound tale would be equivalent to the Virgin Mary being depicted as a prostitute, Jesus as the son of one of her sexual clients, the twelve apostles as Jesus' homosexual lovers, and the Last Supper as an orgy.[40] It would be very disturbing for Christians to have the central symbols of their lives parodied in such a way. For religious beliefs are not just incidental propositional claims about reality; they are life-dominating. Religious convictions are linked inseparably with one's identity. Perhaps the only secular equivalent would be insult against one's parent or partner. For instance, a mother for most children commands respect and reverence. To hear others insulting one's mother is the ultimate abuse. 'Attack me if you must, but do not bring my mother into it', is the attitude of most people when someone offers such abuse.

But even if we grant the offensive nature of the novel, would that in any sense justify the killing of the author, or even a banning of the novel? This has become the central question of the debate.

Responses to the question formed around two different poles. On the one hand, there were those who felt that offence to a large section of society was sufficient for action of some sort; on the other hand, many saw the 'liberty to publish' as a central tenet of our civilization, which must be protected at all costs.

The bulk of the British media was much more sympathetic to the latter pole. The modern secular spirit, appalled by the passion that 'a work of fiction' had generated, seized the moment to proclaim its credo. This credo had three components. First of all, and most importantly, it affirmed the importance of free speech. Numerous examples abound (from Anthony Burgess to Norman Stone), all expressing the same sentiment: however much we might disagree with a book, that is no reason to ban it. *The Daily Telegraph*, no friend of Salman Rushdie's left-wing politics, used an editorial to write:

Mr. Rushdie himself, with his huge conceit, fastidious distaste for Thatcherite Britain and impenetrable literary style, is an implausible hero for any save the likes of Mr. Harold and Lady Antonia Pinter. Yet to almost all of us, Mr. Rushdie's right to publish his book was, and remains, beyond dispute ... British publishers should encourage Penguin to proceed with the paperback edition. To flinch from publication now would be a surrender to those forces of fanaticism with which we cannot compromise, if we are to sustain the traditional values and licence of our own society.[41]

Perhaps it is not surprising that the media, with its obvious vested interest in avoiding censorship, should take this position. However, as critics were quick to point out, free speech has always been confined to certain limits. Lesslie Newbigin writes, 'Freedom to do and say what one likes is not a human right. We prohibit the sale of harmful drugs to those who want to use them, and we punish harmful speech when it injures a particular individual.'[42] Richard Webster documents both the explicit and the implicit protection that Christians are given in Britain. So the Monty Python film *Life of Brian* was not only actually banned from certain areas of Britain, but was shunned by the

BBC and ITV for fear of upsetting Christians.[43] Clearly, the secular credo needed a further reason to justify the insistence on free speech even when it clearly causes so much distress.

This further reason, which provides the second component, is the widespread fear, suspicion, and horror of Islam. The Salman Rushdie affair provided an excuse for ferocious attacks on Islam. Fay Weldon described the Qur'an as 'this violent frightening poem'.[44] And in slightly less restrained prose, a popular tabloid, the *Star*, writes:

Isn't the world getting sick of the ranting that pours non-stop from the disgusting foam-flecked lips of the Ayatollah Khomeini? Clearly this Muslim cleric is stark raving mad. And more dangerous than a rabid dog. Surely the tragedy is that millions of his misguided and equally potty followers believe every word of hatred he hisses through those yellow stained teeth. The terrifying thing is not that a lot of these crackpots actually live here among us in Britain, but that we are actually becoming frightened of them. The whole thing is crazy. And it has to stop.[45]

These sentiments are very ugly and, needless to say, quite inappropriate.

Sadly, the *Star* is fairly typical. The best study of the Rushdie affair was written by Sardar and Davies in *Distorted Imagination*. They rightly link the vitriol written about Islam during the Rushdie affair with the general impression of Islam within western culture.

Whether the standard treatment is meted out in academic and professional works, literature and fiction, or newspapers and television, there can be little doubt that the total picture that emerges from the perpetual onslaught suggests Islam to be a mediaeval monolith – a monolith with fanatical, inarticulate and incoherent followers; prone to degenerate into violence at the slightest excuse; zealously against reason, thought and literature; for book burning; intolerant of free thought and free expression; and ready to suppress critical material even to the extent of assassination. It will come as a surprise to many that the reality is somewhat different. Islam does not sanction suppression of thought or banish freedom of expression.[46]

It is as unreasonable to judge Christianity by the Inquisition as it is to judge Islam by Shiite extremism in Iran. This affirmation of mainstream Islam is an important corrective to much of the hysterical media polemics.

The third component is that secularization will slowly eliminate this passion about the irrational. As one writer put it in a brief letter to *The Independent on Sunday*:

The events following the publication of Salman Rushdie's *The Satanic Verses* highlight the fundamental obstruction to the further development of society. Belief, that is the dogmatic rejection of reason and the acceptance of ideas on the basis of 'faith' alone, provides man with a box to hide from the realities of life. Belief, be it religious or political, has been the major cause of war, conflict and disunity ... To build a better society and a better world we must be prepared to question and to reason; belief obstructs the path towards achievement of this ultimate aim.[47]

A comparable line is taken in Daniel Pipes' study of the Rushdie affair.[48]

The arguments at the other pole were mainly concerned with trying to make an unsympathetic media and public understand Muslim feelings. With the widespread attacks on Islam, there was a tendency to create a united front that obscured certain very important differences. So, for example, even within fundamentalist Islam, very few were entirely happy with the *fatwa*.

The idea of capital punishment for insulting a religious figure sounds absurd to modern western ears. However, it is important to remember that that sense of absurdity is relatively recent. The Hebrew Bible provided a basis for a quite different attitude: 'When any man whatever blasphemes his God, he shall accept responsibility for his sin. Whoever utters the Name of the LORD shall be put to death: all the community shall stone him; alien, or native, if he utters the Name, he shall be put to death.' (Lev. 24:15–16, New English Bible) Though this is describing blasphemy against God not insult against a prophet, it still places a high premium on reverence. With this teaching absorbed into the Christian tradition, capital punishment in this sphere came to be extended to heresy. St Thomas, for example, argued that as the civil law punished relatively trivial offences with death, then surely heresy, which is much worse, must be punished with death. He wrote:

With regard to heretics there are two points to be observed, one on their side, the other on the side of the Church. As for heretics their sin deserves banishment, not only from the Church by excommunication, but also from this world by death. To corrupt the faith, whereby the soul lives, is much graver than to counterfeit money, which supports temporal life. Since forgers and other malefactors are summarily condemned to death by the civil authorities, with much more reason many heretics as soon as they are convicted of heresy be not only excommunicated, but also justly be put to death.[49]

All three traditions, Christians, Jews, and Muslims, have much in their tradition that justifies death as the punishment for blasphemy and heresy.

Ironically, perhaps, Islam of all the three faiths has historically had the most elaborate procedure to ensure justice. And this is where the trouble starts with the Ayatollah's *fatwa*. For most Islamic jurists, a *fatwa* can only be issued after the accused has been given a fair trial. The punishment should never be carried out by a bounty hunter, but only by the appropriate Islamic authorities.[50] So according to Islamic law, the Ayatollah Khomeini's ruling was suspect.

It is interesting that Khomeini did not ask for the book to be banned, but wanted the author dead, while most Muslims in Britain were campaigning for the book to be banned. In Britain much was made of the blasphemy laws which protect the Christian religion. Many Muslims and some Christians felt that these ought to be extended to cover other religions. This was the line taken by Archbishop Robert Runcie in February 1989.[51] The basic argument used was that free speech should not legitimate insult, and that it can survive without it. People are permitted to take issue with Islam, but not in an abusive and hurtful way.

These are the arguments clustered around the two poles. For my purposes, three conclusions emerge. First, the entire episode has illustrated the intolerance of secularism. In a careful critique of Rushdie's arguments, Gavin D'Costa identifies this intolerant secularism as typified by Rushdie:

My argument has been that Rushdie's world view should be acknowledged for what it is: inimical to any authority outside the self, hostile to any idea of beliefs which derive their authority or sanction from outside the self, and consequently fundamentally unable to understand or deal with alternative and contrary world views except in terms of pejorative encodings, e.g. blind faith, fundamentalism, and a form of zombiism (those who continue to live in a world that is godless as if it were not!). Cartesian doubt, a Kantian agnosticism, and the Romantic view of the artist are the European sacred cows of Rushdie's world. If they collapse, so does the universe of discourse that produces and legitimises such a world view. Only once these issues are made explicit, torn free from the dominant discourse which renders them as 'liberal tolerance', can the real questions raised by living within a religiously pluralist society be pursued'.[52]

D'Costa shows that Rushdie does have a creed; furthermore, it is an intolerant creed. *It is a creed where religious certainty is inappropriate; where the right to offend is an absolute; where secularism denies any validity to any other tradition.*

Coupled with this secularist creed is a deeply offensive racism. Many Rushdie supporters used his tragic plight as a weapon to inflict damage on Asian communities. While Rushdie himself was appalled, the people for whom he had spent much of his life speaking found themselves victims of much racial abuse from his own 'friends'. This racist abuse was not only found in the rantings of the *Star* newspaper, but in the baiting of children on the streets of our cities. *The Observer*'s Beirut correspondent, Julie Flint, was sent to Bradford: '"Rushdie" has joined the lexicon of classroom slang. White children shout it on the streets and scrawl it on the underpasses: "Salman Rushdie is our hero... Rushdie rules". Asian youngsters are stopped on the street and asked: "Have you seen Salman Rushdie? If you did, would you kill him?" "Rushdie, Rushdie" is a popular chant when Bradford city play away from home.'[53] It is not surprising that such cruel taunts often end in violent incidents. Clearly the Rushdie affair seems to sanction much of the abuse heaped on the Islamic community.

Secondly, the *fatwa* is clearly illegitimate. It is evident that most Islamic authorities have wanted to distance themselves from the Ayatollah Khomeini's judgment. The main reason why some supported the *fatwa* was that it took seriously their offence and pain. In this respect Sardar and Davies are right, extreme 'fundamentalists' are a reaction against secularist provocation. They write, 'In all its various manifestations, from born-again Christianity to Ayatollahism, fundamentalism is a direct creation of secularism. It is the last refuge from the abuse and ridicule of the secular mind, a declaration that man is much more than a manikin. Essentially, fundamentalism is a grotesque projection of the worst nightmares of secularism on the world stage, an acknowledgment of the war that the secular mind has declared on the sacred.'[54] The limited popular support the *fatwa* did receive can be blamed partly on the insensitivity of our pervading secular culture.

Nevertheless, it can never be right to kill a person simply for writing a book. Living, vibrant religious traditions must be open to thoughtful evaluation. Although it is true that Islam has a comparatively good historical record on tolerance, and much within the tradition to justify tolerance, it still has more to learn. A re-examination is desperately needed because Ayatollah Khomeini's *fatwa* is at odds with so much of the Qur'anic tradition.

Sardar and Davies illustrate the necessary theological manœuvres that need to be made:

Islam law, as it is derived from centuries-old *fiqh*, the juristic interpretive legislation, needs to be rethought. The tradition of thought upon which the Ayatollah Khomeini's *fatwa* relies, derives from *fiqh*, and not from the basic sources of Islam, the Qur'an and Sunnah. The development of the body of opinion on which the *fatwa* is based is a function of how jurists in history have reasoned according to their historical circumstances. Such human reasoning cannot be elevated to the same status as the eternally valid and superior sources of the Qur'an and Sunnah.... The legal tradition of the *fiqh* is something that has been made by Muslims in history and is the aspect of the received tradition that needs most urgent reassessment and critical endeavour by Muslims today. Hence, the *fatwa* is and must be open to debate, as well as to clear and unequivocal disavowal.[55]

Along with a reappraisal of the legal tradition, the temptation to campaign for an Islamic state-within-the-state must be resisted. An Islamic parliament has been founded. Kalim Siddiqui has expressed a hope that an Islamic society can be established in Europe. Such a position is the Muslim equivalent of the positions taken by the Christendom Group and Enoch Powell. All want a unitary state dominated by one single ideology. In Britain it seems that neither the Christian nor the Muslim tradition has discovered dynamics that would enable them to embrace a plural and tolerant society. Fortunately, many Muslims and Christians offer a pragmatic justification for coexistence, but very few ground it within their theology.

Thirdly, the responses of the churches were sensitive, although not very imaginative. One or two voices discerned the greater issues, but much of the church was bemused. Many ethicists simply followed Preston's neglect or Munby's capitulation. A few discerned the wider agenda, but most did not.[56] Much of the debate was preoccupied with the status of the blasphemy laws.[57] As we have blasphemy laws in Britain, then it is an option to extend them. However, this overshadows the deeper questions about religion, plurality, and tolerance.

In this chapter three main outlooks on plurality have emerged in British culture. The first is neglect; the second is capitulation; the third is the 'Christendom' spirit. The first (neglect) ignores the problem; the second (capitulation) surrenders to the secularist; and the third (the 'Christendom' spirit exemplified by Demant, Powell, and Siddiqui) cannot accommodate plurality.

We shall now turn to the American experience. I shall argue that the problem of plurality preoccupied the founders of the United States. Here was a country in the making with religious adherents from a wide spectrum.

PART III

CHAPTER 6

Plurality and the American experience

We have seen how the traditional Christian response to the secular challenge has failed to accommodate plurality. One of the facts (and achievements) of modernity has been the development of tolerance. This is not to imply that medieval Christendom was, in every respect, intolerant, but that in general the celebration of difference is a post-Enlightenment phenomenon. The failure by the Christendom Group to accommodate plurality was a symptom of a greater failure to concede anything to modernity. The Group's utter rejection of modernity can be explained, in part, by alarm at the decline in institutional Christianity since the early nineteenth century. The 1851 census brought home the message that church attendance was already a minority activity. Christian ethicists have naturally felt that cultural damage would result from this decline.

We find in the United States a completely different situation. Part of the data which Christian ethicists must explain is the powerful and persistent religious sensibility of Americans. All ethical reflection must start from the actual situation. Those working in America have the advantage of working within an intensely religious culture. Yet it is also a highly enigmatic and contradictory culture; it is constitutionally committed to a sharp distinction between church and state, yet the coinage carries the message 'In God we Trust'. Most Americans are Christians, yet their fundamental Christian intuitions are constitutionally forbidden from forming any part of their law-making. I shall argue that the best way to make sense of this tension is to suppose that the American experience is preoccupied with the very problem with which this book engages. How can a culture accommodate different religious perspectives?

We shall begin with a brief survey of some of the historical issues, exploring this tension between the religious dispositions of Americans and the legal restrictions on religion. The tension illustrates how important the issue of religion and plurality is. The issue of tolerance, initially confined to the differences between the non-conformist sects, was complicated by the arrival of immigrant communities of diverse religions. Although still predominantly Christian, America has successfully incorporated large numbers of Jews and Muslims into the body politic.

In 1967 Robert Bellah, the sociologist, claimed that America had developed a distinctive religious option which accommodated the American commitment to plurality. This claim stimulated an academic cottage industry examining a phenomenon which he dubbed 'civil religion'. Civil religion, Bellah claimed, is a distinctly American form of self-understanding using religious symbols. In the second section of this chapter we shall give careful scrutiny to the civil religion debate. Although the details of Bellah's position are difficult to sustain, I shall argue that he is right to discern a growing American religious commitment to plurality and tolerance. In this respect Bellah is affirming an aspect of modernity. With this crucial affirmation of modernity, I then describe Bellah's more general cultural reflections. Whereas the Christendom Group failed to accommodate plurality, Bellah's analysis provides a useful contrast.

Despite all the tensions and difficulties embedded in American cultural life, the chapter will conclude on a positive note. I shall show that Bellah's 'civil religion' is nothing more than religious traditions discovering tolerance. The American situation has demanded that religious traditions learn to respect and affirm differences. For the first time in the history of Christianity, the privilege of being the dominant religion in a culture has not led to intolerance. This discovery is so dramatic that it is not surprising that Bellah thought he had found a different religion. However, as we shall discover in the next chapter, American ethicists and theologians have started to show that this discovery is a legitimate development of the Christian tradition. The 'civil religion' mistake was to confuse the development of religious traditions with the creation of a new tradition.

HISTORY

The history of the United States is complicated. It does not start with the European settlers. When they arrived they found a country already inhabited – some one and half million indigenous Indians were already occupying the land. The temptation to idealize the early settlers can easily ignore the heinous crime which was perpetrated against the Indians. And yet it is precisely because the Indians were rendered powerless that the European settlers following in the wake of Christopher Columbus, brought with them the dominant religious sensibility which has proved so important in defining American self-identity.[1]

The basic story is well known. The first European settlers arrived in Virginia in 1607. Others came and developed communities in Maryland and New England. For the first 160 years these settlements, as part of the British Empire, acknowledged the authority of the English crown. The relationship was awkward: the American colonies were disparate, distant, and disorganized and the British government was too pre-occupied to impose the necessary structures. As a result of two political crises provoked by British taxation policy – the stamp act of 1765–1766 and the Townshend Acts of 1767–1770 – a movement for independence emerged. On 4 July 1776 the Second Continental Congress adopted the Declaration of Independence, which had been drafted by Thomas Jefferson. One purpose of the Declaration was to explain precisely why independence from Britain was necessary. The beginning part, however, offered a more generalized statement of political principle.

When in the Course of human events, it becomes necessary for one people to dissolve the political bonds which have connected them with another, and to assume among the powers of the earth, the separate and equal station to which the Laws of Nature and of Nature's God entitle them, a decent respect to the opinions of mankind requires that they should declare the causes which impel them to separation. – We hold these truths to be self-evident, that all men are created equal, that they are endowed by their Creator with certain unalienable Rights, that among these are Life, Liberty and the pursuit of Happiness.

This statement established the ideals that were later given institutional expression in the Constitution of the United States. At the Constitutional Convention in Philadelphia, held between 25 May and 17 September 1787, the basic structure of the United States Government was formulated. Slowly the discovery was made that it was a Constitution which could not accommodate the problem of slavery. Although, of course, every effort was made to mitigate the 'problem' of slavery by the North, it remained an unresolved sore. From 1861 to 1865 the Northern and Southern states fought a terrible civil war which was, directly or indirectly, related to the issue of slavery. With the victory of the North and the abolition of slavery, the United States started the process of recovery involving dramatic population growth and the expansion of industry. The United States entered the twentieth century in such a strong position that it was almost inevitable that it would rise to the status of a world power.

The very familiarity of the story creates a misleading impression. At every point there are considerable ambiguities and complexities. Three such areas are of particular importance for my purposes. The first is the language of the settlers. The picture of non-conformists fleeing English persecution and therefore determined to create a tolerant America is quite misleading. John Winthrop, first governor of the Massachusetts Bay Colony, made it clear that he wanted to create a model society based on Calvinist principles. He likened his journey to the movement of the people of Israel into the promised land and talked of a 'covenant'. In a sermon preached on board the '*Arbella*' as it approached the New World in 1630, Winthrop said:

Wee are entered into Covenant with him for this worke, wee have taken out a Commission...Nowe the onely way to avoyde this shipwracke and to provide for our posterity is to followe the Counsell of Micah, to doe Justly, to love mercy, to walke humbly with our God.[2]

This sort of language was by no means unique to the Massachusetts Bay Colony. For example, John Rolfe of Virginia described his community as 'a peculiar people, marked and chosen by the finger of God'.[3] However, Chidester is right to describe the Massachusetts Bay Colony as 'the most effective theocratic experiment in America'.[4] The Puritans rejected democracy as completely inappropriate; their task was the creation of the kingdom of God on earth. The Puritans believed that their experience ran parallel with the biblical experience of the people of Israel. As the Israelites were in slavery in Egypt, so the Puritans were denied the appropriate freedoms in England. As the Israelites had to endure many trials before entering the promised land, so the Puritans made a dangerous sea voyage. And as the Israelites had to fight to establish themselves in the promised land, so the Puritans had to work hard to make Virginia hospitable. Not only did the experience run in parallel, but the Puritans shared the Jewish sense of being chosen. The Puritans believed that they stood at the centre of a cosmic drama, chosen by God to create a beacon of hope in a dark world. It was this same sense of cosmic drama which pervaded the Salem witch trials of 1692, although by then the original theocratic government of Winthrop's time had already been eroded by the English crown, which, by the end of the seventeenth century, had brought New England entirely under the control of the British government. Nevertheless, the Puritan sense of covenant and divinely appointed mission in the world continued to be part of the American spirit.[5]

The second area of interest is the complex history surrounding the two most important documents defining the American identity: the Declaration of Independence and the Constitution of the United States. Here the overtly religious language of Puritanism was eclipsed by the language of rationalistic 'deism'.[6] In the Declaration the deity is invoked as creator; and it reads: 'We hold these truths to be self-evident, that all men are created equal, that they are endowed by their Creator with certain unalienable Rights'. The great designer, the source of a 'self-evident' morality, provides the justification for democracy. When we come to the Constitution, neither God nor religion figure very much at all. The one reference in the original Constitution is found in Article VI, which states that 'no religious Test shall ever be required as a Qualification to any Office or public Trust under the United States'. And then in 1791 the first ten amendments were approved, of which the first states: 'Congress shall make no law respecting an establishment of religion, or prohibiting the free exercise thereof; or abridging the freedom of speech, or of the press; or of the right of the people peaceably to assemble, or to petition the Government for a redress of grievance.' It might appear that this clear statement of non-establishment is a fundamental rejection of earlier Puritan impulses. Or as John Murrin puts it, 'The Federal Constitution was, in short, the eighteenth-century equivalent of a secular humanist text.'[7] However, the reality is more complex. All of the Founding Fathers claimed to be Christians, although only a few were orthodox. Most subscribed to a vaguely deist, rationalist faith which included belief in a designer, in a unitarian God, in a denial of original sin, in religion as justifying an unrevealed natural morality, and in the generally private nature of religion. Perhaps as a result of the Puritan spirit, the founders were a little inconsistent on providence.[8] George Washington, for example, certainly expected divine support for the American people.[9] Therefore an anti-religious spirit was not intended in the Constitution. Rather, as John F. Wilson explains, 'the overriding preoccupation of the founders [was] with designing and achieving an adequate national government. Their meaning derived from that context ... At root the outcome the founding generation intended, and sought, was neither pro- nor anti-religion in the abstract. "The Founding Fathers" overriding concern was to neutralize religion as a factor that might jeopardize the achievement of a federal government.'[10] In other words it was not that religion was unimportant, but that it was too important. If the States, already embracing much plurality in religion, were going to stay together, then religion had to be eliminated as a source of discord. Plurality of faiths had to be tolerated.

The effect of the first amendment can be seen in the subsequent rulings by the Supreme Court. The major case to produce a substantial development was *Everson vs. the Board of Education* (1947). The case involved a New Jersey law that provided public bus transportation for children going to Catholic parochial school as well as public school. In judgment, Justice Black, writing for the majority, argued:

Neither a state nor the Federal Government can set up a church. Neither can pass laws which aid one religion, aid all religions, or prefer one religion over another. Neither can force nor influence a person to go to or to remain away from church against his will or force him to profess a belief or disbelief in any religion. No person can be punished for entertaining or professing religious beliefs or disbeliefs, for church attendance or non-attendance. No tax in any amount, large or small, can be levied to support any religious activities or institutions, whatever they may be called, or whatever form they may adopt to teach or practice religion. Neither a state nor the Federal Government can, openly or secretly, participate in the affairs of any religious organizations or Groups or vice versa. In the words of Jefferson, the clause against establishment or religion by law was intended to erect 'a wall of separation between church and State'.[11]

This statement appears to enshrine a secular state in the Constitution. What emerges here is a basic tension at the heart of the American experience: from the Puritans a religious self-understanding which provides a framework for interpretation of American identity; from the founders a commitment to toleration and plurality which has been enshrined in law.[12]

The third historically complex area is the distinctive nature of 'the black experience'. The Constitutional commitment to human rights and freedom did not originally apply to black persons. It was believed that Africans brought over to the United States were then blessed with the opportunity to hear the Christian gospel.[13] To the crime against the indigenous Indians, there was now added the crime against the Africans. The scar of slavery continues to be visible within America. And the distinctive black perspective must be taken seriously. For the bulk of the two-and-a-half centuries when the vast majority of blacks were slaves, these slaves continued to affirm 'the open-ended syncretism of varied African traditions'.[14] However, there is not much documentation about the political implications of this religion. With the mass conversions to Christianity starting in the mid-eighteenth century there emerged a distinctive black Christianity, and a black Christian politics as well. James Reichley suggests that this new consciousness amounted to a 'politics of cultural resistance'[15] which he defines in the following way: 'The predominant pattern was one of accepting the power realities of the slavery system as a matter of fact but refusing to assent to them as a matter of right.'[16] In other words, the power realities were such that the Negroes could not revolt without getting themselves killed, but their theology did provide the means of affirming their dignity despite the dehumanizing institution of slavery.

So from the black slave perspective religion was not irrelevant to politics, but was not pro-active. With emancipation, religious–political activity was able to become more overt. However, Reichley suggests that, 'the story of the black church and clergy in black politics is a tale of continuity rather than change. From the earliest stages of black inclusion in the political process in the *antebellum* North down to the present, black religious institutions and their leaders have played a central but never dominant role in black electoral politics.'[17]

Herein lies an irony. For much the same could describe the tension between the Puritan and secular strands of the white European experience. For both black and white, it would appear that religion plays a central, yet never dominant, role in politics. The evil of the white experience partly lies in the way the racism was justified by the use of biblical images.[18] Yet it is wrong to see these different traditions as completely unrelated. Theodore Weld developed a constitutional argument against racial inequality in 1835, and he 'described the treatment in the North of free Negroes and abolitionists as "denials of rights to the equal protection of the laws, the safeguards of due process, and the privileges and immunities of citizens"', the very language that would become enshrined in the 14th Amendment of the Constitution'.[19] Abraham Lincoln, the president during the civil war, was responsible for incorporating the blacks into the tradition of the founders. Or as Pierard and Linder put it, 'the public faith was expanded to include blacks, who could partake in the blessings of the political system established by the founders and presumably enjoy a share in the destiny of the chosen nation. Consequently, most blacks find it easier to regard Lincoln as the "Father of the Country" than either the Pilgrims of 1620 or George Washington.'[20] In his second inaugural address, Lincoln used the language of covenant and revelation to articulate his response to the evils of slavery. The covenantal language implied repentance and judgment: the language of revelation captured the wholly appropriate extension of rights language to the black community. In the Civil Rights movement under Dr Martin Luther King the language of the Constitution was used to justify their campaign. In both the black and white experience, religion has had a similar role to play in the political sphere; and both traditions have been forced to develop as they interact.

This brief historical survey has set the scene. Both black and white America were, right from the outset, a religious nation. To accommodate diversity the founders opted for the separation of church from state, which has subsequently been interpreted by the Supreme Court in largely secular terms.[21] However, as Bellah discovered, American religious traditions took a different route. While the founders believed that plurality required the exclusion of religion, the religious adherents discovered that their religion can and should affirm plurality. It is to the civil religion debate that we now turn.

THE AMERICAN FAITH: CIVIL RELIGION

It was Jean-Jacques Rousseau who invented the term 'civil religion'. In *The Social Contract* (1762) Rousseau argued that a society needs some sort of shared values to keep everyone together. Christianity, he felt, was inappropriate; so he suggested a 'civil religion'. The contents would include a belief in

God, an after-life, as well as the value and importance of the nation. It seems likely that Rousseau was influenced by Locke. In much the same way, Rousseau influenced Durkheim, who developed this same theme. A stable society, Durkheim argued, will coalesce around a set of beliefs and symbols which express the shared values of a society, and these will be treated as sacred. These shared symbols enable a society to stay together during periods of conflict, for they serve as a framework for order, stability, and integration. Durkheim in turn has been a major influence on one of the major contemporary American sociologists, Robert Bellah.

In *Daedalus* (Winter 1967) Bellah began the civil religion debate by arguing that the speeches of John F. Kennedy represent an American form of civil religion. In Kennedy's Inaugural Address of the 20th of January 1961, there are three references to God which provide the frame for the rest of the speech. Kennedy, Bellah argued, stood in a tradition which can be traced back to the founders. It is a religious tradition which is *related to, yet distinct from*, the Judaeo-Christian tradition. It is a civil religion which Bellah later admitted had been analyzed under different names.[22] Some had described it as 'the American Way', or 'the religion of the republic', or 'the American Democratic Faith'. Bellah's use of the term 'civil religion' was deliberately intended to evoke associations with Rousseau and Durkheim. And he felt that one's first obligation is to understand this phenomenon.

The subsequent development of the debate is complicated. However, those believing that an American civil religion does exist have identified the following features.

Beliefs. 'The North American civil religion' has a basic creed. The main belief is in a unitarian God, whose main characteristic is to incline towards law, order, and judgment. Next comes a belief in providence. This God is responsible for protecting his people. The familiar historical story outlined at the start of this chapter is taken as evidence of God's providential activity. For how otherwise could this people have achieved independence against the major world power of the late eighteenth century? How else does one explain the spectacular national success? All this, it is argued, points to God's favour and providential activity. The third belief is a commitment to democracy and plurality. Will Herberg, amongst others, has pointed out that this is the point at which the civil religion conflicts with the particularist claims of Christianity and Judaism.[23] This is the point at which commentators discern a separate religious tradition. It is true that a commitment to plurality does distinguish civil religion from the New Right's vision of a 'Christian America', for example. However, I shall argue later that this need not be viewed as a separate religious tradition, but as a development of the particularist religious traditions.

Texts. All religions have certain sacred texts. The most important ones for American civil religion are the Declaration of Independence and the Constitution. Other documents which some would add to the canon are Lincoln's Gettysburg Address and his Second Inaugural.

Institutions. The most important institution is the Presidency. All the presidents of the United States have believed in God (at least in their public personae) and most have identified with a Christian tradition. They have all used the language of the civil religion in their speeches, and played down their denominational allegiances. Many have appeared to hold a faith which does not extend much beyond the three beliefs of civil religion already outlined.[24] Further, the office of the president has been given a sacred status by many Americans. The most striking examples of presidents regarded in this way are Washington and Lincoln. W. Lloyd Warner provides an excellent illustration of the religious esteem given these two, by quoting a Memorial Day oration extolling their supreme virtues:

No character except the Carpenter of Nazareth has ever been honored the way Washington and Lincoln have been in New England. Virtue, freedom from sin, and righteousness were qualities possessed by Washington and Lincoln, and in possessing these characteristics both were true Americans, and we would do well to emulate them. Let us first be true Americans. From these our friends beneath the sod we receive their message 'Carry on'.[25]

Sacred Calendar. As with all religion there is also a sacred calendar, marked by public holidays: Independence Day,

Thanksgiving Day, Washington's birthday, Lincoln's birthday. It bears a resemblance to a religious calendar. The current argument over the status of Martin Luther King in this calendar (which has been recently established as a national holiday) has the feel of a religious controversy.

A Living Tradition. Civil religion is a tradition, Bellah claims, that can be traced back to the founders. Like all religious traditions, it has been through difficult times. Bellah identifies two crucial and identity-forming experiences which it has endured. The first was the War of Independence (the Revolution), the second the Civil War. Bellah argues that it is now entering its third trial, and it is this contemporary analysis which makes Bellah so interesting. In effect he is participating in the tradition he has identified. He believes that in the American situation this civil religion can be a healthy phenomenon. It is healthy when the civil religion stands over and against the people demanding ever higher standards of civility. Jones and Richey, in their introduction to Bellah's essay, 'American civil religion in the 1970s', point out: 'Critical of the strain of civil religion ascendant in the Nixon administration, Bellah strikes a note of crisis. His essay belongs to what Robert Friedrichs has termed prophetic sociology. Or to put it differently, Robert Bellah is a prophet in his own religion.'[26]

This prophetic tone is also found in Bellah's book *The Broken Covenant.* Bellah, the theologian of civil religion who keeps the tradition alive, will be considered in more detail later in this chapter. But first we must look at some difficulties with the concept of civil religion.

Bellah's argument has not gone uncontested. Some of the objections are very technical and beyond the scope of this study,[27] but three main objections are germane to the discussion here. First, as George Kelly has argued, the concept of 'civil religion' is a symptom of secularization. It is a twentieth-century substitute for a robust religious faith; and Bellah's success is that he offered a concept which appealed to both secularists and modern theologians. Kelly concludes, 'The civil religion talked about for the past fifteen years in academic conventicles is a species of *docta ignorantia*, of disenchantment.'[28]

Prophets of secularization are constantly announcing the death of religion, and then events confound them. Kelly's analysis is flawed; it ignores the vibrant links civil religion has with established religion, and it ignores the discernible continuities which can be traced back to the founders. Kelly might insist that the 'deism' of the founders was the start of the secularizing impulse; however, as has been already noted, their brand of deism, committed as it was to a doctrine of providence, was often internally inconsistent. Civil religion is not best understood as a minimum creed in the same sense of pure eighteenth-century deism.

The second objection comes from those who do not want a civil religion. Germany, argues Moltmann, had a civil religion;[29] the Boers, points out Noll, had a civil religion.[30] America, argues Richard John Neuhaus, has never had a civil religion in the German or South African sense.[31] Against Moltmann, Bellah argued that although civil religion in America can be a good thing, this does not entail that civil religion everywhere is a good thing or exactly the same kind of thing. Against Neuhaus, Bellah can only repeat that there appear to be some data which the concept civil religion usefully explains.[32]

The third objection is a development of the Neuhaus criticism. It is the most fundamental of all. John F. Wilson believes that the very existence of 'civil religion' should be called into question. He suggests certain criteria that a civil religion needs to meet if it is to be called a religion. On these criteria, civil religion fails.[33] Neuhaus agrees with Wilson, 'Civil religion is not a religion. It does not look like a duck, walk like a duck, or quack like a duck, the burden of proof rests with those who say it is a duck. After nineteen years of trying they have not made their case.'[34]

However, all attempts to define the criteria for a religion are doomed to failure. It is very difficult to arrive at a definition which embraces the enormous diversity of religious forms in the world. There are no official creeds in Judaism; Hinduism prides itself on a plurality of beliefs and practices, and deliberately refuses to be exclusive. Yet both are clearly religions. It is better to follow Wittgenstein's advice when it comes to definitions. Search for the family resemblances; search for the characteristics which link some religions but not others; and the others will be linked by other characteristics. A concept like 'religion' resembles a rope – certain strands link to other strands and, in this sense, all the strands are part of the rope.

Yet Neuhaus and Wilson are right to point to a certain vagueness in the concept. Richey and Jones identify five different meanings of the concept of civil religion. First, it is simply a folk religion. Second, it is the transcendent universal religion of a nation. Here, civil religion may stand over against the various religions of the folk. Third, civil religion is a religious expression of nationalism; it is the religion of the American flag. Fourth, it is an affirmation of the American commitment to democracy. It is the democratic faith. Fifth, it is Protestant civic piety.[35]

Now this is crucial. These different meanings demonstrate that it is not obvious whether there is a civil religion which stands over against and distinct from Christianity, Judaism, and Islam. It is true that no American calls herself an adherent of the American civil religion. Many Americans consider themselves both religious and patriotic, but these loyalties are not felt to be in tension. *Part of the reason why civil religion can appear to have a separate identity is the commitment to plurality*. Sidney Mead suggests this when he points out that the civic religion (as he calls it) is completely opposed to the exclusive creeds of Christianity and Islam:

This theology [of civic religion] is not only not particularistic; it is designedly antiparticularistic, in this respect reflecting the predominant intellectual slant of the eighteenth century ... This is the theology behind the legal structures of America, the theology on which the practice of religious freedom is based and its meanings interpreted. Under it, one might say, it is religious particularity, Protestant or otherwise, that is heretical and schismatic – even un-American![36]

And Will Herberg makes the same point:

America's civil religion is not and cannot be seen as, authentic Christianity or Judaism, or even as a special cultural version of either or both. Because they serve a jealous God, these biblical faiths cannot allow any claim to ultimacy and absoluteness on the part of anything or any idea or any system short of God, even when what claims to be the ultimate locus of ideas, ideals, values, and allegiance is the very finest of human institutions; it is still human, man's own construction and not God himself.[37]

The assumption that Mead and Herberg are making is that Christianity and Islam cannot embrace plurality and tolerance, therefore civil religion must be viewed as a separate religion. For them, civil religion in its commitment to plurality and tolerance is by implication completely at odds with the intolerant exclusivity which is normally implied in both Christianity and Judaism. However, there is another way of looking at this. While it is true that throughout most if its history, the church has not embraced plurality, the Christian tradition is not static, it contains elements that are conducive to plurality. Instead of postulating the development of an altogether new religion more compatible with a commitment to plurality, the American experience may be more accurately understood as the Christian tradition discovering the virtue of tolerance.

This sheds some light on the Neuhaus position, in which exclusivist religion is able to embrace plurality: Neuhaus is able to reject the very existence of civil religion because he believes that one can be a Christian and an American (i.e. a believer in democracy and pluralism). So defined, all Christians throughout the world ought to be supporters of American values.

Bellah's construct indicates, at the very least, that Americans are a deeply religious people. One will only believe in the existence of a civil religion, related to, yet distinct from, the historic faiths, if one believes that the affirmation of plurality and tolerance is incompatible with the major historic religions. In the next chapter we shall look in some detail at the arguments of Neuhaus for the affirmation of plurality within the Christian tradition.

However, before concluding this chapter, there remains one further area which must be considered. Bellah's 'civil religion' is a religion which affirms elements of modernity. Bellah is affirming the greatest achievement of modernity, by his commitment to plurality and tolerance. Failure to make such a commitment was, I have argued, the single greatest failure of the Christendom Group. With this error corrected one can begin to see more clearly the contribution of a religious perspective to contemporary society. So it is interesting to see Bellah playing the role of the theologian for this civil religion. For it is here that Bellah clearly offers his cultural analysis. It is Bellah as the theologian of civil religion that I want to examine next.

BELLAH: THE THEOLOGIAN OF CIVIL RELIGION

It is important to make clear that Bellah does not give himself this title. He is, in fact, an Episcopalian who, as a sociologist, believes that civil religion in America can be a good thing. Yet, as I have already shown, in his writings on civil religion there is this theological-cum-prophetic element. From 1967 to 1975 his cultural reflections were always made within this context. However, from 1975 onwards a second distinct phase emerges: the civil religion context disappears and a pure cultural analysis develops, the prophetic tone continuing, now without any overt religious framework. It is this prophetic, almost apocalyptic, tone which justifies the label 'theologian'.

Bellah's work can be helpfully analyzed with the use of my three modes. Bellah works mainly with mode two (cultural) and mode three (practical application). There is a civil religion theology (first mode), but it is also a theology of culture. We can now concentrate on the other two modes.

Since Bellah's 1967 article one can trace changing attitudes to America in his work. Although Bellah does talk in this article about America entering a third trial for civil religion, he appears fairly sanguine that America will cope. The third trial 'is the problem of responsible action in a revolutionary world, a world seeking to attain many of the things, material and spiritual, that we have already attained'.[38] The problem for America is to use her global power with responsibility – to share her success with the rest of the world. Bellah's hope is that the United Nations can become a part of the American civil religion. He wants civil religion to become inclusive and universal.

He was much less sanguine when he returned to the issue of civil religion in the mid-seventies. He was writing in the context of Vietnam and Watergate.[39] The third trial, he explained, was upon us much quicker than expected. Nixon was a heretic who was betraying the civil religion; primarily, the tradition stressed the responsibilities of America, whilst Nixon used it to provide an uncomplicated affirmation of American goodness.

This theme is developed in *The Broken Covenant*, which is Bellah's major mid-seventies contribution to civil religion. He explicitly describes the book as 'an exercise in the analysis and interpretation of cultural meaning rather than in sociological explanation',[40] which clearly suggests that he is working in our second mode. The major problem explored here is the conflict between the American success ethic and the Puritan under- standing of the covenant. He explains that 'there is far more tension between basic American values and the capitalist economic system than is usually assumed. Much as the Puritans encouraged work as a calling, they were always aware of the dangers of making wealth and power into ends in themselves, dangers not only to one's eternal salvation but also to the coherence of the community.'[41] The point Bellah is making is that the central American tradition does not mean making millions with a complete disregard of the community. A tradition of social responsibility has to be nurtured. The obscene celebration of wealth on television and in magazines creates a source of frustration for those marginalized. Images portraying a need for a particular car or gadget creates a frustration and discontent. Americans are betraying their Puritan and biblical heritage. Bellah concludes with passion:

Today the American civil religion is an empty and broken shell ... The external covenant has been betrayed by its most responsible servants and, what is worse, some of them, including the highest of all, do not even seem to understand what they have betrayed. Nor can we discount the events that were disclosed in the second presidential term of Richard Nixon as the work of a small band of wicked men. The men in question, it seems, were not notably more wicked than other Americans. When the leaders of a republic no longer understand its principles it is because of a history of corruption and betrayal that has affected the entire society.[42]

He goes on to promise that the broken covenant would not go unpunished. The punishment lies in the success of American society. It is the economic technological success which has partly generated the blindness; 'Our economic and techno- logical advance has placed power in the hands of those who are not answerable to any democratic process: weakened our families and neighborhoods as it turned individuals into mobile, competitive achievers; undermined our morality and stripped us of traditions.'[43] For Bellah, the main drift of American society is towards the edge of the abyss. He expects that such a drift is likely to be 'a prelude to authoritarianism if not fascism'.[44]

What is Bellah's remedy in the face of such a gloomy prognosis? He suggests that the covenant needs to be reaffirmed. Presumably by this he is suggesting that the symbolic power of judgment and repentance be rediscovered. Politically, he suggests that a form of democratic socialism might deliver a healthier economic base.[45] And this combination he hopes might regenerate the social 'mores' which are now being undermined under capitalism.

Much of the *Broken Covenant* is the embryo for the substantial study in the mid-eighties called *Habits of the Heart*. This was a concerted attempt to provide sociological evidence for cultural analysis. *Habits* was a collaborative project which involved, along with Bellah, Richard Madsen, William Sullivan, Ann Swidler, and Steven Tipton. It was not intended to be about civil religion, which is not even mentioned. Yet it develops themes already identified in *The Broken Covenant* and is the best attempt so far at an 'empirical' cultural analysis, therefore it must be included in this survey. The methods used in the study involved interviews, discussions, and arguments with middle- class Americans scattered around the country.[46] The territory chosen for study is the 'habits of the heart'. This expression comes from de Tocqueville and describes the 'mores – consciousness, culture and the daily practices of life'.[47] This is the same territory covered by Demant's expression – penumbra. And we shall see that there are striking similarities between the judgments of the *Habits'* authors and Demant. Effectively, Bellah illustrates how aspects of Demant's analysis can be retained even with a more judicious evaluation of modernity. One similarity of approach is the reason given for studying these 'mores'. The authors argue that it is here that one has an insight into the state of society, its coherence and long-term viability; and it is here that dangers and problems will be anticipated.

The major finding of *Habits of the Heart* is that the celebration of individualism is undermining the commitment to community: individualism is thus eliminating any communal or Group identity. This highly damaging state of affairs has become accentuated during the last eighty years. Until the start of this century it was agreed even between opponents that government depended upon the existence of virtue among the people. It was this virtue which helped to resolve the conflict between private interest and public good. In other words there was an understanding that community obligations were part of one's private interest and responsibility, and both leaders and ordinary citizens needed to cultivate civic virtue.

Later visions of American society have undermined this assumption. The powerful images of individualism have set private interest in opposition to public good. With 'our concern for the economy being the only thing that holds us together, we have reached a kind of end of the line. The citizen has been swallowed up in "economic man".'[48]

The authors of *Habits of the Heart* label this state of affairs the 'culture of separation'. This has three features. First, there is intellectual fragmentation. Culturally, we have lost any unifying vision of life as a whole. Facts are set against values. Science and arts are set in opposition, causing a crisis in education. Scientific activity lacks the appropriate cultural context, thereby creating the impression that each area of life can be an end in itself.

Secondly, there is social disintegration. Families do not

identify with communities, and communities do not identify with each other. Special-interest Groups are formed which exclude the marginalized. To reverse this trend toward disintegration, a social ecology is required. In the same way that humans must learn to live in harmony with nature (ecology), so humans need to live in harmony with each other (social ecology – also called moral ecology). It is put like this:

Without derogating our modern technological achievements, we now see that they have had devastatingly destructive consequences for the natural ecology. We are engaged in an effort to mitigate and reverse the damage and regain an ecological balance whose complete loss could prove fatal. Modernity has had comparable destructive consequences for social ecology. Human beings have always exploited and oppressed one another, but modernity has given us a capacity for destructiveness on a scale incomparably greater than in previous ages. Today, social ecology is damaged not only by war, genocide, and political repression, but also by the destruction of the fragile ties that bind human beings to one another, leaving them frightened and alone. It has been evident for some time that unless we begin to repair the damage to our social ecology, we will destroy ourselves long before natural ecological disaster has time to be realized.[49]

The foregoing critique bears a striking resemblance to the analysis of Demant (outlined in my Part II) and there is a further parallel in respect to the third feature Bellah *et al.* describe. A constant conflict is found between human decency and brutal competition. In the media it is this conflict which produces the best drama and humour. One of the recurring themes of American television is the situation where a friend is caught between pursuing economic advantage and supporting a colleague at work. Often the colleague is given the support, but the fact that there is a dilemma at all is evidence of a cultural problem. More generally the world of television is one where divorce is common, society is frequently inhospitable, and intimate friendship can only be found in small Groups.

This culture of separation is one which cannot survive. With characteristic Bellah style, the authors point out, 'the culture of separation, if it ever became completely dominant, would collapse of its own incoherence. Or, even more likely, well before that happened, an authoritarian state would emerge to provide the coherence the culture no longer could.'[50] Fortunately, the situation has not yet gone this far. And it is part of the solution to develop those 'mores' which continue to thwart the likely looming fascism.

Habits of the Heart offers the following proposals to help foster 'culture of coherence'. The task is difficult; it needs a transformation at a variety of levels. The state cannot do everything; and individuals, by definition, cannot recreate a community by themselves. Instead, 'out of existing Groups and organizations, there would also have to develop a social movement dedicated to the idea of such a transformation'.[51] The Civil Rights movement provides the paradigm of a significant culture-transforming movement. Bellah's proposal is envisaged as a sequel to, and fulfilment of, the Civil Rights movement. (By way of comparison one might note Christopher Dawson's and V. A. Demant's equivalent proposal. In *Beyond Politics*, Dawson proposes a voluntary non-political organ for the preservation and enhancement of the cultural life of the community which Demant suggested could be called 'Friends of Civilization'.[52]) The *Habits* team also insists upon an effort 'to restore the dignity and legitimacy of democratic politics ... *Of course*, a political discourse that could discuss substantive justice and not only procedural rules would have to be embodied in effective political institutions, probably including a revitalized party system.'[53]

At this point, it is worth pausing and reflecting on not only the striking similarities with the Christendom Group in terms of analysis, but also in the sharing of the same impracticalities. That little 'of course' is really a prime example of wishful thinking. Existing institutions are not sufficient for the task; instead Bellah requires an almost utopian political system.

The substantive economic proposal made by the group is that there should be a minimum and maximum wage. This would change the character of work. The classic dilemma of university graduates between poorly paid yet fulfilling work on the one hand, and well paid yet soul-destroying work on the other, would disappear. One could become a high-school teacher and not be absurdly poor, or become a stockbroker and not be obscenely rich. Here the authors show a 'left of centre' political commitment, a thrust towards egalitarianism.

Three more contributions by Bellah need to be mentioned in this chapter. The first developed the cultural analysis and appeared in 1987 in a volume of essays edited by Bellah and Greenspahn called *Uncivil Religion*. In the concluding article Bellah reflects on the problem of truth commitment and intolerance. So often a religious commitment to the truth leads to intolerance. It is a symptom of our cultural malaise that often the only suggested solution is to relativize all moral judgments. Bellah writes,

To dissolve all boundaries, to relativize all moral judgments, would not only threaten the survival of the traditional religious communities, also it would lead to a society in which no one would really want to live. But on the other hand, we do not need to create iron curtains between communities either. That too leads to pathology. To wish to maintain the life of one's own community, to see it as a community of memory and hope, is not to deny that it overlaps with other communities, that individuals belong to more than one community, and that all communities are ultimately included in the human race. The dialectic of personal and Group identity is close to the heart of a healthy personal and Group life.[54]

We return to the central theme of the book. Bellah wants to affirm plurality without being a relativist. Culturally and politically, this combination of plurality and religious commitment is a particular American discovery.

The second contribution was written in the context of the demise of communism in eastern Europe. Has this altered Bellah's proposals for cultural regeneration? The answer, broadly, is No. Bellah believes that Americans are not entitled to indulge in triumphalism. He almost uses the mid-eighties language of equivalence – America and Russia represent extremes both of which are equally wrong:

[T]he greatest threat to our genuine human happiness, to real community, and to the creation of a good society comes not only from a state whose power becomes too coercive (we can never underestimate that danger), but from market forces that become too coercive, that invade our private and Group lives and tempt us to a shallow competitive individualism that undermines all our connections to other people.[55]

Russia had a coercive state which could not survive; America has a coercive market which could await the same fate. He goes on to claim that Europe has a much better balance.

This time Bellah's solution is that 'we need to use all the resources we have to confine the economy to its own proper sphere and keep it from drowning the whole of our lives'.[56] He suggests that the church is one such resource. Vibrant Christian communities can help resist market imperialism. In this article it looks as if Bellah has now completed a journey. Initially, cultural analysis was in the context of civil religion; then it was pure cultural analysis; now it is cultural analysis as an Episcopalian.

The third contribution develops this analysis. *The Good Society* is a rather disappointing sequel to *Habits*. Much of *The Good Society* is good sense. The study documents the deteriorating condition of children in American society, the insensitivity of American management, and the dangers of the market becoming the sole criterion for assessment of human activity. Andrew Greeley attacks the ambitious nature of the study and the complete disregard for specialists. He writes,

There may be nothing wrong with ignoring the work of fellow social scientists, but there is a suggestion of narcissism in writing as though no one else were concerned about the problems of American institutions and no one else had studied them carefully and thoroughly at that. The net result of this neglect is that institutional reform is made to appear a good deal more simple and easy than it really is.[57]

This is Greeley's most damning and important criticism. Ultimately, Bellah and his team fail in the third mode. Apart from setting up western European democracies as a possible model that manages to balance market and planning, his concrete proposals are highly generalized.[58] Greeley again: 'Bellah's institutional paradigm for reform is a mix of attention, communal concern, and generosity. If we give up our greed and our focus on our own individual welfare, the problems of our nation, it would seem, are well on their way to a solution. One

wishes that institutional reform was quite so easy.'[59] Bellah is
interesting when it comes to cultural analysis (the second
mode), but much weaker in respect to application (the third
mode).

In this chapter I have attempted to use Bellah's work to point to
a distinctive cultural development of the Christian tradition.
Bellah's analysis points to a culture committed to a religious
outlook yet, as a part of that outlook, affirming plurality and
difference. I have suggested that this is such a striking cultural
discovery that it is not surprising that many sociologists and
historians thought it should be treated apart from the traditional
faiths, and created this entity called civil religion.

Bellah has also used American religious dispositions to offer a
variety of cultural judgments. Some of these judgments have
clear links with the analysis of Demant discussed in the earlier
chapters. *Habits of the Heart* is impressive; and, in comparison
with the analysis of the Christendom Group, it is much more
thorough and less impressionistic. Yet, when it comes to policy
proposals, Bellah *et al.* are less convincing. Many of their
pronouncements are sentimental rhetoric to which any politician could assent. Bellah is strong in cultural analysis, but
much weaker in practical prescription. Clearly, some of the
Demant problems remain. However, Bellah's more constructive
attitude to modernity has made a significant contribution to the
public discussion.

The religious outlook of America is the first cultural attempt
to marry commitment and plurality. We now need to reflect
theologically on whether this is a legitimate development of the
main religious traditions. If it is not, then the idea of a separate
entity known as civil religion has much more validity. If it is
legitimate (which I am certain it is), then new and exciting
possibilities can and will emerge as the religious voice demands
to be heard in the public square. It is to the work of Richard
John Neuhaus that we now turn.

CHAPTER 7

Plurality and public philosophy

Part of the truth of Christianity, for the Christendom Group, was a clear vision of the appropriate structure of society. The main element of such a vision was the apprehension of the transcendent in and through the church. They did not discuss the problem of harmonizing this vision with the growing plurality of Britain. But even if they had been more sensitive to this reality, it is by no means certain that they would have known how to respond. They had no intention of surrendering the truth-claims of Christianity, and, in so far as Christianity makes truth-claims that contradict other philosophies and religions, there was an obvious problem accommodating plurality. Moreover, by rejecting tolerance, members of the Christendom Group found themselves rejecting all the achievements of modernity, thereby ensuring the marginalization of their geninue insights.

Yet, as we have seen, the American context is quite different. This problem of truth and plurality was a major cultural difficulty right from the start. The constitutional separation of church and state has existed side-by-side with a disposition to affirm plurality – for religious reasons. In the work of Robert Bellah this affirmation seeks to harness the religious disposition of American people in order to challenge reigning economic and liberal assumptions. Bellah was able to fuse a Demant-type analysis of modernity with a more plausible, albeit still unrealistic, political programme because he had a more balanced attitude to modernity.

However, Bellah is neither an ethicist nor a theologian; and the harmonizing of truth and plurality requires reasoning that is specifically theological, while taking the measure of modernity requires a philosopher and an ethicist. It is at this point I introduce the work of Richard John Neuhaus. Neuhaus wants to construct a 'public philosophy'. Every culture, Neuhaus argues, will have some sort of philosophy, whether secular humanist, Jewish, Christian, or militantly atheist. Neuhaus wants to persuade people that a 'religious' public philosophy is as legitimate as, indeed superior to, a secular humanist one.

RICHARD JOHN NEUHAUS: A JOURNEY THROUGH THE MODES

To the superficial observer, Neuhaus has changed his position dramatically. From 1961–78 he was the pastor of the Lutheran church of St John the Evangelist in Brooklyn. This was the setting for his angry attacks against wealth, power, and racism, and the base for his opposition to the Vietnam War that resulted in his arrest and imprisonment. For much of this period he was, in many respects, the archetypal angry, young radical contemplating revolution. Now in the 1990s, he is the co-ordinator of a think-tank which is identified with neo-conservatism. Some of his ideas have been embraced – at least rhetorically – by the Bush administration.[1] With his move from left to right, he appears to be yet another case of an angry young man growing old.

Yet in Neuhaus' own description of his journey, he insists that there is much more continuity than change. When he was recently invited by *The Christian Century* to reflect on 'How My Mind Has Changed', he starts, 'Thirty years ago, when I was 23 and trying to situate myself in a confusing world, I determined to be, in descending order of importance, religiously orthodox, culturally conservative, politically liberal and economically pragmatic. That quadrilateral still serves.'[2]

I shall argue that some of the changes in Neuhaus' thought are best understood as a changing emphasis on our different modes. From the start all three modes were present in his work, but at certain times one mode would be more significant than the other modes. His radicalism was born out of his pastoral involvement and it was always a campaign for change. He was living and working in the practical sphere – the third mode. As he became disillusioned with the selective priorities of the left, so he then moved away from one set of allies to form different allegiances. This seemed to free him to develop his theology (the first mode) and cultural analysis (the second mode).

Much of Neuhaus' work in the third mode is not documented. His considerable skills as an organizer in the Civil Rights movement and in the anti-Vietnam War organizations developed before his most prolific writing period. At the time of his first book, co-written with Peter Berger, *Movement and Revolution*, he still firmly identified with the left, but was already uncomfortable with its package of policies. In 1967 he complained that pro-choice on the abortion issue is not the obvious left line. All human life strives to fulfil its potential, and the right to life does not depend on what stage a human being is at. Therefore, Neuhaus argued, the fetus as a potential human life is entitled to the right to life.[3] This theme continues to be very important for him. He recalls: 'Breaking ranks with the left over abortion, I experienced the illiberality of certain liberalism. Its wrath was impressive.'[4]

His continuing commitment to the left was not to the package of policies, but to the scale of the vested power interests which must be overcome for the poor. This was almost the only disagreement between Neuhaus and Berger in *Movement and Revolution*. Berger described a conservatism which was committed to justice but also sensitive to the complexities of politics. He conceded that in principle Neuhaus' conditions for a 'just revolution' were legitimate: when all other avenues of change are exhausted, then it is legitimate to resort to revolution. But, insists Berger, America in the early seventies was not in such a state; Neuhaus was less sure.[5] The America of Neuhaus' experience was ugly and oppressive: 'American society countenances several forms of killing. Poor people are killed by hunger or by the absence of medical care. Thousands are slaughtered regularly in rituals connected with the American cult of the automobile. Loneliness and the inability to succeed in a competitive society drive other thousands to suicide each year'.[6]

It is this slaughter, resulting from various kinds of injustice, he argues, that has led some in the Movement to advocate violent revolution: 'This is the last, and perhaps the most rapidly accelerating, movement within the Movement. Truth spoke to power and power was deaf. Love appealed to power and power was heartless. Humility petitioned power and power was cruel. Reason argued with power and power was stupid. Now violent power must address violent power.'[7]

It is this same practical commitment to the poor which generated his opposition on another left issue – ecology. 'The whole notion of "issue-orientated politics"', explains Neuhaus, 'is alien to the poor. It assumes an ability to consider an issue on its merits, objectively, so to speak. It assumes a freedom from the tyranny of immediacy, a freedom to reflect on the common weal and not just on that slice of public policy that impinges directly on one's own survival and welfare.'[8] In other words, to take up issues is the luxury of the fortunate; to pick and choose the questions that matter suggests a list of priorities which can and do change. For a person at the bottom, struggling and hurting, then there is only one priority – that of justice.

Neuhaus believes that the ecological issue is not just a distraction, but is actually opposed to the interests of the poor. For Neuhaus, the problematic aspects of the ecological movement are the calls for population control and protection of wilderness, and the general elevation of nature over people. He has three objections. First, the involvement of the captains of industry and commerce in the campaign provokes Neuhaus' suspicion. Industry has spotted the marketing and manufacturing potential of ecology. Its leaders can see the money-making possibilities. Further, they like the idea of restricting development in their towns and villages to keep their locality 'nice' for them. They support the ecological movement because it supports their selfish desire to keep what they have and not share it with the poor. Secondly, the discerning observer will find the advocates of population control mainly wanting poor black families to have fewer children.[9] Some ecologists are now saying that world survival is contingent on America hoarding scarce global resources and not supporting aid programmes in the developing nations. After all, they argue, aid simply encourages Third-World people to have more children. Advocates of strict immigration controls often use carefully coded racist language. This is an ugly tribalism which ignores the contribution that immigrants can make, both culturally and in terms of economic growth.

This leads to the third response; an ecological problem is not necessarily a crisis. Neuhaus concedes that

there should be no dispute about the need for a new sensitivity to the fragility of the biosphere and for a political assault on the short-sighted economics that exploits natural resources and leaves out of its cost accounting the lethal effects upon the ecology and, consequently, upon the quality of life. In short, there must be a dramatic improvement in mankind's performance as caretaker of the creation of which he is part.[10]

Talk of a crisis ignores the achievements of the twentieth century; the cities have cleaner water, cleaner air, and better constructed homes and buildings. God-given human initiative and creativity are solving many of the ecological problems. Neuhaus hopes that economic growth, coupled with technological ingenuity, will solve the problem of resources. Despair, he argues, is not warranted.[11]

This attack against the 'no-growth' ecologists indicates that Neuhaus was never part of the socialist left. An immigrant coming to America is not a 'problem' to be fed, but a person who can use the opportunity of a free economy to create wealth, to support himself and others. If one defines socialism as a commitment to some sort of common ownership with the emphasis on the redistribution of wealth, then Neuhaus clearly is not a socialist. In America, socialism so defined was never really an option. It was not surprising that Neuhaus never really identified with it.

The bulk of the book has Neuhaus firmly in the practical-third mode. There are occasional hints of a wider canvas of concern. He criticizes the idiosyncratic nature of much contemporary theology; all these 'theologies of' are a distraction from substantial theological reflection.[12] And, towards the end, he suggests that a 'covenantal' model of American self-understanding might serve better than the current dominant liberal model. The Lockean–liberal model views America as a nation of individuals all sacrificing certain rights for the convenience of living in a Commonwealth. Instead of this, Neuhaus argues for a 'covenantal' model which explicitly acknowledges one's ultimate responsibility to God. The nation must repent if it fails to meet the transcendent obligations. It emphasizes the cultural and communitarian aspects of the American experience. This is Neuhaus discovering our second mode of enquiry.

In 1975 at the start of *Time Toward Home* he wrote, 'This is a book of theology, cultural criticism, politics, philosophy and ethics, among other things.'[13] Neuhaus has now discovered all three modes. The book takes off where *In Defense of People* finished. For his cultural analysis, Neuhaus uses the civil religion debate. Although he disagrees with Bellah's claim that there is a separate religion related to, yet distinct from, the traditional religions, he does accept that 'there is in American society a vague but real cluster of symbols, values, hopes and intimations of the transcendent which overarch our common life'.[14] Neuhaus believes that this public piety should be taken seriously as articulating a truth about the American situation. And, in the hands of theologians, it can be used to articulate an appropriate American self-understanding. Or as Neuhaus puts it:

Of the various themes in that public piety or 'civil religion' the single theme that seems to me most compelling in our time is that of covenant. It is firmly rooted in the most hallowed statements of American purpose and consciousness. It is emphatically historical in character, keeping present reality in tension with future contingency. It comprehends the experience of judgment, of betrayal and healing, of repentance and forgiveness. After the Indochina horror, the divisiveness of myriad racisms, the corporate death wish indulged by assassinations and the entire emetic of Watergate, the American people long for judgment.[15]

In other words, although Neuhaus does not use the term, this is an exercise in 'public philosophy'. He wants Americans to see themselves in a 'covenantal' relationship with God, partly because it is true and partly because it is helpful.

There are three strands to Neuhaus' covenantal understanding. First, it is objective, although it is not revealed. He
states that, 'To believe in the American covenant is either an act
of supreme arrogance or of supreme trust ... We have no explicit
word with regard to the American experience. The American
covenant is therefore more tenuous, more contingent, more
radically experimental.'[16] So for Neuhaus it must be distinguished from the revealed covenants God made with Israel
and the church; nevertheless it is still legitimate to speak of a
covenant.

There is something a little odd here. It is impossible to use the
term 'covenant' without the implication that in some sense God
is 'making a deal'. On the traditional account, God promises
his support if the nation behaves in a certain way. Therefore a
covenant without some sort of revelation sounds like a contradiction in terms. For how does one know that God has
agreed to the covenant without some sort of revelation?
Neuhaus responds to this criticism by arguing that the theistic
commitment to providence implies that all of human history is
under the control of God. Therefore all nations have an
obligation to discern the purposes of God for them. This
'discernment of God's providential activity' can legitimately be
called covenantal.[17] For Neuhaus, America has been called to
create an open community which should realize democracy and
justice for all. This is why many of the nation's founders and
citizens continue to think of America in this covenantal way.

The second strand is to emphasize that the 'covenant' should
not generate arrogance, but humility; it does not imply privilege
so much as responsibility. There are real dangers in any nation
thinking of itself as 'chosen'. As Mark Noll points out, failure to
recognize this distinction has been the problem of the South
African Boers.[18] Neuhaus attempts to avoid confusion on this
point by pointing to the notion of accountability: 'The logic in
the idea of America as a covenantal nation induces humility
rather than arrogance. Covenant is a relationship of mutual
accountability. A nation that is accountable is vulnerable to
history, it is always under judgment, it is held to account by the
Power of the Future.'[19] Neuhaus expects to be judged both as a

Christian and as an American. He will be judged for his part in the American covenant.

Neuhaus' third strand emphasizes the pluralistic character of the covenant, a crucial point, and welcomes the growing plurality of America. He does not want a 'Christian America' in any sense that involves Christian coercion; rather he welcomes the immigrant communities bringing their Judaism, Islam, etc. However, for Neuhaus, there is an awkwardness here. He starts by implying that at this point the 'covenantal' understanding needs to be complemented by the 'contractual' understanding. We need the liberal social contract to create the space for individual human rights. Neuhaus writes,

If the covenant is not to restore old oppressions or create new ones, it must be checked and undergirded by contract. One clause in the contract is that all covenants are open to communal deliberation and decision. A further clause is that community can never agree to any covenant that would foreclose challenge by even the most marginal member of the community. Within these provisions we can entertain rumors of a promising and judging future calling us to contract.[20]

Here he appears to be admitting that an alternative tradition, apart from covenant, is needed to protect pluralism. However, he later writes:

We noted earlier, for example, the utterly crucial character of the contractual agreement that freedom of thought and opinion be encouraged. Our insistence upon this point is not grounded in laws of nature nor in any of the other sources to which social contract theory might appeal. Our insistence upon such liberty is for the sake of the Kingdom. Because ours is such a provisional and partial moment of history, because we see through a glass darkly, because the Spirit blows where he wills, it is essential that we maintain maximal openness to the diverse sightings of the Kingdom's coming. Thus, as people of the covenant, we concur in some of the affirmations of classical liberalism, but such concurrence is always provisional and is reached through a quite different line of reasoning.[21]

This time pluralism is justified within the covenantal framework. Simple human limitations require diversity; for it is in diversity that we can all get much nearer to the truth.

Neuhaus joins Bellah in affirming the discovery of pluralism as an American achievement. The main difference is that Neuhaus believes that Christian theology should affirm such a discovery. The tension between the need for a contractual or a covenantal justification illustrates his sensitivity to the problem pluralism can be for certain forms of Christianity. Initially he suggested the contractual supplement because, at that stage, he was not certain whether the traditional Christian heritage could justify the pluralism. Later on, as overtly theological arguments receive fuller development and become dominant, they provide a sufficient defence of pluralism by themselves. One further difference between Neuhaus and Bellah needs to be noted. As we shall now discover, Neuhaus, unlike Bellah, has come to believe that many other elements of the American experience can and should be affirmed from a theological perspective.

By the mid-seventies, Neuhaus was trying to work effectively with all three modes. He wanted to use Bellah's civil religion to create an American self-understanding which was sound theology and had positive social implications. He had clearly broadened his interests. In 1976 he was a signatory to the Hartford Declaration, which called for a revitalized theology. The signatories included Peter Berger, Avery Dulles, Stanley Hauerwas, and George Lindbeck. And, as co-editor of the subsequent book, Neuhaus was turning his considerable organizing ability to 'sorting out' academic theology.[22]

His next contribution to Christian ethics lost sight of the second (cultural) mode and concentrated on the other two (theological and practical).[23] This was the clearest statement of his theological presuppositions. He emphasized the public nature of the Christian gospel and therefore its political and social implications. The main theme is that Christians are called by God to participate as God brings about his kingdom. In the sacramental life of the church, one has a symbol of the 'politics of God'.

In baptism, all that is deadly dies and a new creation is proclaimed. Baptism gives new life not only to the person baptized but also a promise in solidarity with all life that emerges from the primordial deeps represented by the water of creation and rebirth. The Eucharist signals the communal solidarity, now in the bond of need and grace, that will one day be realized in the *polis* of the New Jerusalem.'[24]

Neuhaus firmly roots the ethical enterprise in the eschatological. We are trying to realize the future now; we do so sensitive to the realities of sin and evil (and Neuhaus seems very comfortable with objective devil terminology); and we do so confident of the ultimate vindication by God. He interprets the Lutheran 'Two Kingdoms' language in this way, describing it as useful in that it 'highlights the tension between the "now" and the "not-yet" of Christian existence'.[25]

Having set out his theological framework, he then offers practical policy prescriptions.[26] The bridge from theology to policies consists of 'social ethical considerations' (others have called them 'middle axioms').[27] These considerations consist in fifty-seven statements which inform his policies.

The actual policy prescriptions emerging from the procedure give us a good insight into where America and Neuhaus had ended up in 1977. The following selective list illustrates the point:

1. Supports unilateral steps towards nuclear disarmament (p. 86).
2. Wants 1% of GNP to go to development (p. 96).
3. Supports an open immigration policy (p. 108).
4. Agricultural workers have a necessary right to operate a closed union shop (p. 108).
5. Single people have a right to adopt children (p. 113).
6. Supports the legal availability of contraceptive devices to both adults and minors (p. 113).
7. Supports a national health programme (p. 119).
8. Supports a minimum wage (p. 128).
9. Supports voucher payment redeemable at any state school (p. 132).
10. Supports the legalization of prostitution (p. 140).
11. Disapproves of state gambling (i.e. lotteries) (p. 141).
12. Supports the control of firearms (p. 144).

This list illustrate how localized and specific many of the policy recommendations are. However, such a selective list is unfair, as it appears rather arbitrary and inconsistent. In a review of this book, James Nuechterlein captured the general flavour of Neuhaus' policy recommendations when he wrote,

Neuhaus' general stance might best be described as post-liberal – a modish term, but difficult to avoid in this instance. More often than not, his political views fall on the left side of the spectrum (though they do so less consistently than expected or than one suspects would have been the case a few years ago), but he very seldom dispenses conventional liberal wisdom and is frequently skeptical of the standard secular pieties. In fact – and this is most surprising for one who not so long ago was seriously considering the need for revolution in America – Neuhaus at times sounds suspiciously like a neo-conservative.[28]

Nuechterlein is very helpful here. First, he correctly anticipates the political direction of Neuhaus' proposals. He then expresses legitimate concern about the theological basis of some of these political prescriptions. He takes as an example Neuhaus' view on migrant agricultural labour needing to operate closed union shops: 'Whatever one's views on the issue itself, it is difficult in the extreme to find a theological or moral imperative that would require arguing that "the churches should" support closed union shops for farm workers or anybody else.'[29] Nuechterlein has rightly indicated the difficulty of moving from, to use my terminology, the first-theological mode to the third-application mode. This I suggest would be mitigated if Neuhaus had developed the second-cultural mode. One of Nuechterlein's most forceful criticisms is that it does sound odd to move from a cosmic theological principle about, say, the Incarnation, to a particular policy position only applicable to America in the 1970s. Cultural analysis can both help to justify such a move and provide the appropriate context for understanding the policy. For the cultural perspective makes clear that a particular policy prescription is only one of many social expressions of a certain theological principle.

Thus the rediscovery of the cultural mode in *The Naked Public Square* in 1984 takes on special significance. This is Neuhaus' best-known book. The context of this study was the increasing political strength of the new religious right in general (though with particular attention to the 'Moral Majority'). It is an attempt to understand some of the issues which have provoked this movement. Although Neuhaus is critical of the religious right, he expresses sympathy with one of its main themes. The secularists claim that the 'public square' must be protected from religious warfare, yet this has become a rubric by which they impose their own anti-religious philosophy. For the public square to be dominated by secular humanist assumptions is clearly undemocratic; secular humanism is just as much a comprehensive world view or world perspective as Christianity. To impose its orthodoxy is not only undemocratic, argues Neuhaus, it is also dangerous.

The danger lies in the relativist implications of a form of liberal pluralism. Neuhaus explains: 'Pluralism is a jealous god. When pluralism is established as dogma, there is no room for other dogmas. The assertion of other points of reference in moral discourse becomes, by definition, a violation of pluralism. Pluralism, relativity, secularization – all come to be much of a piece.'[30] Neuhaus goes on to document the clear danger of a state of affairs where there is no moral regulation at all. He lists the following policy shifts as examples of the unthinkable becoming thinkable in American society:

Today perfectly respectable, indeed distinguished, persons propose in public the doing of what earlier was thought unthinkable. That nuclear strategy should be based upon the indiscriminate mass destruction of civilian populations; that babies should be examined until five days after birth and be eliminated if found defective; that 'triage' solutions should be implemented, checking population growth by the starvation of millions who have the least chance of survival in any case; that children of aged parents should be authorized, with medical agreement, to administer a lethal pill to their parents, thus allowing them to 'die with dignity' ... This, then, is the burden of our historical moment – to be facing moral dilemmas of unprecedented complexity at a time when we are inclined to throw away the compass and map and to scuttle the ship.'[31]

Neuhaus is claiming that if one leaves the public square completely naked, then Nietzsche's vision of the world belonging to the most powerful will be realized. Indeed, 'the truly naked public square is at best a transitional phenomenon. It is a vacuum begging to be filled ... The totalitarian alternative edges in from the wings, waiting impatiently for the stage to be cleared of competing actors.'[32]

Neuhaus emphasizes that this outcome represents an extreme scenario which is by no means inevitable. The need is for Americans to allow space to the religious outlook alongside other world views within the public square. The problem is that the religious outlook is not very tolerant. When people think they have the absolute truth about God and the world, they tend to find it difficult to cope with disagreement.

At this point Neuhaus takes issue with the intolerant religious person. Democracy is not a compromise following from the demise of medieval Christendom; it is part of God's plan for the world until the eschaton. 'Democracy is the appropriate form of governance in a fallen creation in which no person or institution, including the church, can infallibly speak for God. Democracy is the necessary expression of humility in which all persons and institutions are held accountable to transcendent purpose imperfectly discerned.'[33] With this attitude to the world, the church needs to be in conversation with those who disagree, and the church can be welcomed into the public square by the secularists. Neuhaus explains:

One enters the public square, then, not as an anonymous citizen but as a person shaped by 'other sources' that are neither defined by nor subservient to the public square. The public square is not a secular and morally sterilized space but a space for conversation, contention, and compromise among moral actors. Compromise is not mere fudging, then. It is not morally compromising. Within a universe compromised by fallen humanity, compromise is an exercise of moral responsibility by persons who accept responsibility for sustaining the exercise that is called democracy.[34]

All this might seem quite attractive; and we might want the positive outlook of Neuhaus on our public square, but surely these sentiments would not be shared by the Moral Majority. Yet, in fact, all the evidence is that most fundamentalists share Neuhaus' opposition to intolerance. For example, the most recent survey of American attitudes was made in Muncie, Indiana. Known as Middletown III, and directed by Theodore

Caplow of the University of Virginia, it shows that compared to the 1920s the people of Muncie are now both more religious and more tolerant. Caplow thought that this was a new phenomenon in the history of Christianity. Neuhaus, in an article on fundamentalism, suggests the following explanation for this phenomenon:

the people of Middletown believe it is wrong, morally wrong, for anybody, and most especially for the state, to mess around with other people's souls. In other words, it is the will of God that we be tolerant of those who disagree with us about the will of God. Respect for those who believe differently or do not believe at all stems not from religious indifference but from religious commitment.[35]

Although this might seem surprising, I suggest that such an outlook is to be expected given the distinctive American culture. Indeed, as I have argued throughout, the harmony of religious commitment and tolerance should be seen as an American discovery.

Neuhaus – pastor to a black community for many years – is now offering his pastoral services to the fundamentalists. He is on the side of the misunderstood and denigrated. He disliked the middle-class liberal attitude when it patronized blacks, and now he discerns the same attitude patronizing the fundamentalists. Thus he concludes:

The activist Fundamentalists want us to know that they are not going to go back to the wilderness. Many of them, being typical Americans, also want to be loved. They explain, almost apologetically, that they did not really want to bash in the door to the public square, but it was locked, and nobody had answered their knocking. Anyway, the hinges were rusty and it gave way under pressure that was only a little more than polite. And so the country cousins have shown up in force at the family picnic. They want a few rules changed right away. Other than that they promise to behave, provided we do not again try to exclude them from family deliberations. Surely it is incumbent on the rest of us, especially those who claim to understand our society, to do more in response to this ascendance of Fundamentalism – and indeed of religion in general – than to sound an increasingly hysterical and increasingly hollow alarm.[36]

So where is Neuhaus today? *The Naked Public Square* provides the most sustained statement of his current cultural analysis. He joins V. A. Demant and Robert Bellah in believing that there are totalitarian dangers facing our liberal secular society. But unlike Demant, and even Bellah, he wants to theologically affirm much more of the American experience. His most distinctive contribution lies in his strong affirmation of religious commitment to plurality and dialogue.

On the theological front, Neuhaus has made an ecclesial transition from the Lutheran church to Roman Catholicism. Some of the reasons for the shift can be seen in his study of Catholicism, *The Catholic Moment*. He believes that the reasons for the Reformation no longer apply to the post-Vatican II Roman church. The authentic gospel is being preached. However, his theology of public life appears to be unchanged. Of the five different models of church and culture in Richard Niebuhr's classic *Christ and Culture*, he prefers to see the church and the world in paradox. He explains, 'church and world in paradox, then, is not a model chosen by us but an acknowledgment of a situation forced upon us. It is not a matter of our preference but of our provisional moment so far short of the consummation.'[37] This retains the eschatological emphasis we have already found in *Christian Faith and Public Policy*. We live in the 'now' conscious of the 'not yet'.

However, on the applied front, Neuhaus has, compared to the 1970s, a slightly different list of policy prescriptions. First of all, his cultural analysis seeks to make the religious perspective available to the public square. To this end, he is the co-ordinator of a think-tank called 'The Institute on Religion and Public Life' and produces a journal called *First Things*. Secondly, the revolution in Eastern Europe and the demise of the Soviet Union have confirmed his judgment that socialism is no longer an option. Capitalism is the only way forward. It is in this respect that he is much more sympathetic to modern capitalist America than Bellah. His major concern is, however, that the poor be given the opportunity to join the wealth creators. He believes that this critical support for capitalism is the basic message of the pope's latest encyclical *Centesimus Annus*.[38]

The third strand of policy prescriptions calls for a government policy that defends, but does not interfere with, what he calls 'mediating structures'. Here continuity can be seen with the Neuhaus of the mid-seventies. In 1977 Neuhaus and Peter Berger published a short booklet entitled *To Empower People: The Role of Mediating Structures in Public Policy* whose basic argument was that government policy ought to build up the organic structures of a society. Mediating structures are defined as 'those institutions standing between the individual in his private life and the large institutions of public life'.[39] The authors concentrate on four such structures of family, neighbourhood, church, and voluntary association. They offer three propositions which sum up the argument of the essay: 'The first proposition is analytical: *Mediating structures are essential for a vital democratic society*. The other two are broad programmatic recommendations: *Public policy should protect and foster mediating structures*, and *Whenever possible, public policy should utilize mediating structures for the realization of social purposes*.'[40] The basic idea is that these mediating structures can be used to empower people, enabling them to take greater control of their own lives. The essay sketches out some of the implications: a voucher system in education would give families greater choice and power; child-care provision should be provided in the neighbourhoods; families with handicapped children need funding to prevent institutionalization; and the legal confusion over the churches needs to be clarified so they can be supported in their welfare activities. These are themes that remain central to the Neuhaus agenda.

NEUHAUS AND PLURALITY

Neuhaus is the most effective operator in our three modes of enquiry currently working in America. He moves with delightful clarity from an orthodox theology, to cultural analysis, to a realistic political agenda. Unlike the Christendom Group, Neuhaus does not want a unitary culture: he writes 'publicly assertive religious forces must be mindful that the remedy for

the naked public square is not naked religion in public'.[41]
Instead he commends the civil public square, built upon civil
society.

This civil society, argues Neuhaus, is made up of a multitude
of different communities. He writes,

American society is best conceived as a community of communities.
Citizens move in and out of communities, crossing lines and languages
in often confusing ways – confusing to themselves and to others ...
Americans who live ... in diverse communities with diverse languages
and diverse ways of dreaming their dreams engage one another in the
civil public square. The public philosophy that is needed is precisely a
philosophy that sustains that diversity.[42]

This vision is not a tyranny of one vision over others – least of
all the imposition of secularism – but the engagement, argument, and disagreement of different accounts of the good in
the civil public square. Each account of the good is attempting
to persuade others of its insights. This vision is not a convenient
pragmatism, but a Christian imperative grounded within the
Christian world perspective.

Diversity is not a threat, whereas T. S. Eliot's call for a
Christian idea to society, Enoch Powell's fears of an 'alien
wedge' or Kalim Siddiqui's hope for an Islamic state are all
calls for a unitary culture unable to cope with diversity.
Neuhaus wants to embrace difference; plurality should be
welcomed.

CONCLUSION

Neuhaus provides interesting theological arguments for affirming both plurality and capitalism within a traditionalist
Catholic framework. We have travelled a long way from the
European traditional response to the secularist challenge.
Neuhaus believes that the church can accommodate plurality,
and if he succeeds in demonstrating this he undermines the
main secularist argument against religion. In taking this
position on pluralism, Neuhaus has been freed to affirm many
other elements of American society, and to decry the unjustified
exclusion of religious values from the public square.

The chart, using the three modes, illustrates the differences

CHRISTENDOM GROUP V. A. Demant	CIVIL RELIGION R. Bellah	PUBLIC PHILOSOPHY R. J. Neuhaus
FIRST MODE *Theology*	**FIRST MODE** *Theology*	**FIRST MODE** *Theology*
– Anglo-Catholic, Thomist. – Natural Law Model. A natural and balanced society has God at the centre, and then the cultural, political, economic, and sexual activities take their appropriate place around the centre.	– 1967–1980 Civil religion can be healthy. It affirms a transcendent reality by which America must be judged. – 1980 Episcopalian. Hoping the churches will provide the community links America needs so much.	– Lutheran: Augustinian. – 1990 Catholic. Christians live in the world yet are conscious of the world to come. Christians must try to realize God's rule on earth now.
SECOND MODE *Cultural analysis*	**SECOND MODE** *Cultural analysis*	**SECOND MODE** *Cultural analysis*
– Liberal secular modernity is a culture made possible by the Christian religion and yet in rebellion against it. – The liberal ideology is incoherent. It both affirms human rights yet undermines any reason for such language.	– There is a conflict in our culture between individualism and community. – Our culture is a culture of separation. – The market is becoming too dominant. – There are certain totalitarian dangers facing our culture.	– America should use 'covenantal' language to understand her role in the world. – Certain legal decisions excluding religion from the Public square are undemocratic. – Religion offers the necessary values

– which are needed for the difficult decisions.
– A secular state has certain totalitarian dangers.

Tolerance: Important insight which can be protected by religion.

THIRD MODE
Practical

– Articulation of the religious outlook in the public square.
– Neo–Conservatism affirmation of capitalism as the best economic system available.
– Policies support not undermine the mediating structures.

– Capitalism and socialism are both symptoms of a frustrated unnatural society
– There are dangers of totalitarianism.

Tolerance: A symptom of the problem with liberalism

THIRD MODE
Practical

– Guild Socialism and Social Credit.
– Rediscovery of Christian social conventions.
– Ecological concern.

Tolerance: Important element for a society.

THIRD MODE
Practical

– Welfare/democratic socialism.
– Supporting the community ties which identify people together.

between Demant, Bellah, and Neuhaus. The divide between Bellah, Neuhaus, and Demant is partly the divide between America and Britain. The Americans have discovered how one can, and should, be committed yet tolerant. The rest of the book will explore the claim that plurality and tolerance can be better defended with a religious world perspective than a secularist one.

PART IV

CHAPTER 8

God and truth

It is given to certain cultures at certain times to discover a different way of understanding their religious tradition. Often the discovery is embedded in existing beliefs; sometimes it is a distinctive innovation. More often than not, it is a combination of the two. The discovery, if it survives, becomes so 'obvious' that people wonder why it was not discovered before. It was given to the eighth century BCE prophets of Israel to discover the high moral standards God expects of his people. It was given to medieval Europe to experience the all-pervasive influence of the Christian narrative, thereby showing the way in which everything we value can be understood. It was given to the Reformers to discover the democratic implications of the gospel.[1] And now I have shown it has been given to the Americans the discovery of a religious affirmation of plurality.

The West is still in the process of crystallizing this truth, and even America continues to exhibit certain intolerant tendencies, by Christians and secularists. Therefore what is needed now is a theoretical argument, in explicitly Christians terms, for tolerance and plurality.

In this chapter a cluster of claims will come together. The main claim is that theism provides the only secure basis for the affirmation of diversity within a mutual quest for truth. I shall attempt to show that the anti-realist foundation of secular tolerance can only be refuted by an affirmation of theism. For, ultimately, theism is the only sure safeguard of a realist epistemology.

We start with the MacIntyre and Stout debate. Here we find tolerance is the hinge issue that determines the more general attitude to modernity. I shall then use MacIntyre's line of argument (against that of Winch) to examine the anti-realist/realist debate. This leads into a discussion of God.

Both Bellah and Neuhaus give MacIntyre much credit for discerning the problems with contemporary liberal culture. MacIntyre, in his classic *After Virtue*, argued that modernity is in trouble, and as a consequence there is a moral crisis at the heart of our culture. The argument can be summed up in four points. First, modern western culture is in disarray about ethics because we are operating with only the fragments of a long-lost ethical system. Secondly, before the Enlightenment there was a coherent system of morality derived from Aristotle. Thirdly, the Enlightenment project was an attempt to justify morality without recourse to the Aristotelian framework. This it failed to do. Fourthly, the only real choice in ethics is between Aristotle and Nietzsche, or, more accurately, between classical Aristotelianism and modern Western, individualist liberalism. MacIntyre's views will now be discussed under these four headings.

MacIntyre starts *After Virtue* with a very gloomy picture of the moral state of our culture. He believes that all we now possess 'are the fragments of a conceptual scheme, parts which now lack those contexts from which their significance derived'.[2] He believes that this moral confusion can be seen in three areas. The first is the intractability of moral argument. Most people believe that there is no rational way of resolving moral disagreements. People can do no more than state their case and allow other people to state theirs. Moral philosophy is a peripheral discipline preoccupied with questions that only interest a minority. There are no answers, no solutions. This leads to the second area; the moral philosophy of emotivism is indicative of this cultural malaise. It is completely mistaken to imagine that emotivism represents anything more than an account of a certain cultural outlook. Our culture sees moral assertions as the complicated articulation of certain preferences. We live in a subjectivist culture that formerly was not the case. The third area is the rise of certain characters (i.e. social types) which feed upon a post-Enlightenment determinism. We see the rise of the social sciences, which have generated the illusion of the managerial expert. This 'expert' claims to exercise a neutral moral authority much like the natural scientist.[3] MacIntyre goes on to show how inappropriate the managerial expert's claims are, because it is impossible for the social sciences to predict human behaviour exactly. There are just too many elements of human life and activity that are beyond certain prediction.

All this contrasts very markedly with the moral climate before the Enlightenment. The contrast comprises the second point. The dominant moral tradition in the West up until then was Aristotelian. MacIntyre traces the story of this tradition from the heroic epics of Homer to the domestic novels of Jane Austen. The earlier ethical tradition is Aristotelian in that it contains the following features. It starts from man-as-he-is and envisages a telos, that is man-as-he-should-be; and it then employs the 'virtues' as the means for transforming man-as-he-is to man-as-he-should-be. Moreover, it presupposes a context of narrative and practices – 'narrative' is the temporal context in which our lives are made intelligible. In fifth-century Athens, a narrative was provided by the polis. The Aristotelian ethic involves the family, community, and culture with which human beings identify. The 'practices' are defined thus:

any coherent and complex form of socially established cooperative human activity through which goods internal to that form of activity are realized in the course of trying to achieve those standards of excellence which are appropriate to, and partially definitive of, that form of activity, with the result that human powers to achieve excellence, and human conceptions of the ends and goods involved, are systematically extended.[4]

MacIntyre cites as illustrations such activities as football and chess, and, more importantly, the arts, sciences, and politics (in the Aristotelian sense), and the making and sustaining of a family. All are practices with certain internal goods which are inherently worthwhile.

The medieval development of this tradition shifted the telos from a humanly realizable earthly purpose to an other-worldly one requiring divine assistance. The virtues became the means of moving from man-as-we-are-now to man-as-God-intended-us-to-be. But the underlying model remained the same: morality was objective. It was not what an individual happened to desire, but what is, as a matter of fact, best for her. MacIntyre's third point is that this account of ethics was inseparably linked in the mind of post-Enlightenment thinkers with an outmoded Aristotelian science; it is mainly for this reason that the model was rejected.

With Aristotelian science considered outmoded, ethical discussion of a 'telos' for human activity came to seem inappropriate. A model developed which still started from man-as-he-is, and retained the language of the virtues, but which rejected the concept of a telos. This, MacIntyre believes, was always an impossible position to maintain. He feels that this is demonstrated in the failure of Hume, Kant, and Kierkegaard to find an alternative foundation for ethics. Hume suggested the passions; Kant suggested reason; and Kierkegaard suggested criterionless fundamental choice. Each author, in order to sustain his case, has to provide negative arguments against the others. Much is built upon these negative arguments. With common ethical assumptions removed, philosophy became the arena of interminable debate. There was no agreed basis for ethics. Later developments of a language of 'utility' and 'rights' were simply convenient fictions. The Enlightenment project had failed; morality came to be understood as simply the utterance of subjective preferences.

The final point that needs discussion is MacIntyre's claim that the choice amounts to this: either Aristotle or Nietzsche. Nietzsche's genius lies in the fact that he recognized the failure of the Enlightenment project. MacIntyre sums up the position thus:

It was because a moral tradition of which Aristotle's thought was the intellectual core was repudiated during the transitions of the fifteenth to seventeenth centuries that the Enlightenment project of discovering new rational secular foundations for morality had to be undertaken. And it was because that project failed, because the views advanced by its most intellectually powerful protagonists, and more especially by Kant, could not be sustained in the face of rational criticism that Nietzsche and all his existentialist and emotivist successors were able to mount their apparently successful critique of all previous morality. Hence the defensibility of the Nietzschean position turns in the end on the answer to the question: was it right in the first place to reject Aristotle?[5]

Thus, if the Enlightenment was right to reject Aristotle, then Nietzsche must be right. If, however, the Enlightenment was mistaken, then Aristotle must remain an option.

MacIntyre qualifies this simple choice of Nietzsche or Aristotle, and it becomes a more elaborate choice between modern liberal individualism or Aristotelianism. MacIntyre believes that modern liberal society has destroyed the context in which the Aristotelian framework was possible, in that it has eroded the organic (or communitarian) roots of our culture. It is this socially destructive impact of liberal modernity that leaves MacIntyre concluding that a legitimate parallel can be drawn between our current moral state, and the decline of the Roman Empire and the start of the dark ages. MacIntyre writes:

It is always dangerous to draw too precise parallels between one historical period and another; and among the most misleading of such parallels are those which have been drawn between our own age in Europe and North America and the epoch in which the Roman empire declined into the Dark Ages. Nonetheless certain parallels there are. ... What matters at this stage is the construction of local forms of community within which civility and the intellectual and moral life can be sustained through the new dark ages which are already upon us. And if the tradition of the virtues was able to survive the horrors of the last dark ages, we are not entirely without grounds for hope. This time however the barbarians are not waiting beyond the frontiers; they have already been governing us for quite some time. And it is our lack of consciousness of this that constitutes part of our predicament. We are waiting not for a Godot, but for another – doubtless very different – St. Benedict.[6]

Jeffery Stout, in *Ethics After Babel*, disagrees with MacIntyre's analysis. He concedes that MacIntyre's narrative is much better than the Enlightenment's own self-congratulatory story of the journey from superstition to science,[7] but he is less pessimistic about our liberal culture. He offers three criticisms of MacIntyre. First, the latter makes too much of the difficulty of solving disagreements in the public arena. The public arena is bound to concentrate on the differences, not the areas of agreement. And, Stout argues, significant areas of agreement can be found: slavery is considered wrong; women are no longer reckoned as second-class citizens; and liberal political institutions are considered the best form of government. This is not to deny disagreement, but the passions provoked by certain high-profile issues, for example, the abortion debate, can easily obscure the areas of agreement. The second criticism is that another option is available. An alternative between 'smug approval of the status quo and wistful alienation from it'[8] needs to be found. One should not accept MacIntyre's gloomy analysis and utterly impractical suggestions. The areas of agreement in our culture are grounds for hope that need to be developed. And the third criticism is that MacIntyre's narrative needs sweeping revision. This is crucial for my argument. Stout argues that a major factor in the development of liberalism was the polemics and warfare of the Reformation and Counter-Reformation. Theology appeared unable to provide a vocabulary for public discourse without resorting to violence.[9] This intolerance, suggests Stout, is part of the reason why today religious solutions need to be resisted: 'Much contemporary evidence – from Belfast to Beirut, from Teheran to Lynchburg, Virginia – gives ample reason for concern.'[10]

Stout wants to resist religious solutions because he does not trust religion. He wants to affirm liberalism because he wants to affirm tolerance. Much of his argument would crumble if it could be shown that a religious culture can also be a tolerant culture. Such a demonstration is the objective of this book.

We need to start with foundations. As many have shown, including Demant, the foundations of secularism are certain relativist tendencies. Very briefly, the reason why relativism appealed to the secularists of the Enlightenment was that *different religions seemed to make different and incompatible truth-claims. The secularist mind-set considered this both destructive and unjustifiable.* Hume and Kant seem to expose the impossibility of making any certain metaphysical truth-claims. Hume, in *Dialogues Concerning Natural Religion*, has marvellous fun postulating different metaphysical possibilities. Perhaps the order in the world is a result of a large primordial spider, or a committee of Gods, or an Allah, or a Trinity, or just pure chance. For Hume there is no way of knowing for certain which of these hypotheses is true.

This reduces religion from 'the truth' to one of numerous narratives all claiming to be the truth. Given that there is no way of deciding between different cultural narratives, the secularist decided that all positions ought to be tolerated, and none should exercise power over the alternatives. Of course, this tolerance is of a very special kind. Religious faith must not make a social difference because then a person or group might invade the space of others which would be intolerant. So only privatized personal religion is tolerated in the secular society. For the secularist this restriction on religion is self-evidently preferable to wars between intolerant religions.

The secularist position makes the large assumption that Hume is right to say metaphysical issues are unresolvable. It assumes that we cannot decide between Islam, Christianity, Buddhism, or Hinduism. This is the only way the secularist could justify tolerance. In fact, this was always a dangerous argument because, as Nietzsche showed, a commitment to the truth is the only decisive reason for insisting that intolerant forms of racism or facism ought not to be tolerated. However, the virtue of tolerance emerged not because of intolerant anti-realists, but because of religious realists. So the secularist opted to undermine religious intolerance with anti-realist assumptions; she assumed that there is no way of deciding between different cultural narratives. Now there is a major difficulty here. How can one decide between different positions? How can one discover the truth? Isn't it the case that each cultural narrative will have its own criteria of rationality? Even the laws of logic have a cultural history, so even they cannot be used as definitive criteria? This chapter needs to explore the whole question of truth. Anti-realism is the basis of the secularist commitment to tolerance. It is the anti-realist tendency of many advocates of tolerance which frightens the religious adherents. Therefore we need to confront the most basic question of all: how can one discover what is true?

To help us with this issue, we shall start with the debate between Peter Winch and Alasdair MacIntyre. This discussion arose in the context of anthropology and sociology, but it has clear implications for our questions. It will be shown that MacIntyre constructs decisive arguments against Winch, especially as the remaining unanswered questions are resolved in *Whose Justice? Which Rationality?* We then move on to Milbank's work and conclude that he raises legitimate difficulties with MacIntyre's position. However, Milbank's position of theological realism is equally problematic. It is better instead to argue that the critical realist commitment to the ultimate intelligibility of the universe is itself evidence for the Christian tradition. And all those traditions that assume the intelligibility of the universe need a theistic metaphysic. The startling conclusion of this chapter is that it is possible to discover better and worse ways of making sense of the world which provide a stronger foundation for tolerance; however, the whole idea of the truth needs the reality of God.

DISAGREEMENTS BETWEEN CULTURAL NARRATIVES

No one is born entirely alone on a desert island. Even with dramatic technological advances we still need at least one parent or a doctor. This simple fact is responsible for the major epistemological difficulty of modernity. For it follows that our birth setting will determine the family and community in which we grow up. This community will provide the language with which we describe the world. Our culture will provide our rules for rational talk, the conditions for intelligibility. Certain cultural conventions will become for us the 'way things are'. So for example, in a British culture it is understood that people standing in a row next to a post on the side of the street form a 'bus queue'. And if you want a ride on a bus, you join the back of the bus queue. The entire activity is rule-governed. The description of the datum depends on familiarity with the language and culture of Britain. To participate in the activity requires an understanding of the rules of the British culture.

The philosopher Ludwig Wittgenstein was, in his later work, extremely sensitive to the different cultures and 'language games' in the world. In the same way that each game has a different set of rules so has each culture. One cannot be checkmate in a game of basketball for that is to confuse the rules of two different games. So, argued Wittgenstein, it is equally inappropriate to use scientific language in a religious context or for that matter to judge a non-scientific culture by a scientific western rationality.[11]

As this argument is developed by Wittgenstein's disciple Peter Winch, if we are going to compare two different cultures, we will either try to find an objective, external vantage point from which we can decide between the two cultures, or we will end up imposing the standards of our own culture. The attempt to stand outside our own culture is doomed to failure. We are who we are. We were born into a family, and a community, and have lived in a certain way. This is true for everyone. The other option is clearly illegitimate. To impose the standards of one's own culture is a form of imperialism. How do we know that our standards are the right ones? We do not, because we cannot transcend our situation to find out what the world is *really* like or not like.

The implications of this argument are extensive. Consider the following example that is discussed by both MacIntyre and Winch. 'According to Spencer and Gillen some aborigines carry about a stick or a stone which is treated as if it is or embodies the soul of the individual who carries it. If the stick or stone is lost, the individual anoints himself as the dead are anointed.'[12]

Now MacIntyre argues that such a practice is incoherent. One's identity is not linked to a stone; and it makes no sense to anoint oneself as dead unless one is dead. For Winch this is completely illegitimate:

MacIntyre does not say why he regards the concept of carrying one's soul about with one in a stick 'thoroughly incoherent'. He is presumably influenced by the fact that it would be hard to make sense of an action like this if performed by a twentieth-century Englishman or American; and by the fact that the soul is not a material object like a piece of paper and cannot, therefore, be carried about in a stick as a piece of paper might be.[13]

Winch goes on to suggest that the aboriginal practice is not even that strange from the western perspective. 'Consider that a lover in our society may carry about a picture or lock of hair of the beloved ... Suppose that when the lover loses the locket he feels guilty and asks his beloved for her forgiveness: there might be a parallel here to the aboriginal's practice of anointing himself when he "loses his soul". And is there necessarily anything irrational in these practices?'[14]

To Winch, MacIntyre is importing his own cultural standards and imposing a crude scientific rationalism on a different cultural practice. Winch believes that this is totally improper. Why should a different culture be judged by our cultural standards? MacIntyre uses the laws of logic as if the whole world knows that they are valid. Winch explains,

criteria of logic are not a direct gift of God, but arise out of, and are only intelligible in the context of, ways of living or modes of social life as such. For instance, science is one such mode and religion is another; and each has criteria of intelligibility peculiar to itself. So within science or religion actions can be logical or illogical: in science, for example, it would be illogical to refuse to be bound by the results of a properly carried out experiment; in religion it would be illogical to suppose that one could pit one's strength against God's; and so on. But we cannot sensibly say that either the practice of science itself or that of religion is either illogical or logical; both are non-logical.[15]

Winch simply applies what he says of science and religion to the imposition of our own science-influenced cultural values on the aboriginals.

Winch has used a Wittgensteinian analysis to arrive at an anti-realist conclusion, that is, that the human mind cannot transcend its particular frame of reference and know which assertions correspond to reality. Others have arrived at the same conclusion through historicism – a sensitivity to the historical setting of all ideas, so that talk of the absolute truth is seen as impossible to justify.[16] Richard Rorty suggests that to judge another culture or to judge certain strands of our culture from a different tradition is the mistake of Philosophy (with a capital P).[17] It is the philosophy of the metaphysics that Hume and Kant long ago destroyed.

MacIntyre, responding to Winch, emphasizes the areas where he agrees with Winch. Each person is born into a 'rule-governed' setting and, to begin with, activities need to be understood from within that setting. However, he rejects the Winch dichotomy. MacIntyre writes, 'For there are not two alternatives: either embracing the metaphysical fiction of one over-all "norm for intelligibility in general" or fling to total relativism.'[18] MacIntyre wants to take seriously the fact of our historical–cultural setting, but not to surrender the principles of rationality. This quest for a way through the middle of the Winch alternatives has become the dominant theme of Mac-Intyre's work. In immediate response to Winch, MacIntyre has two main problems with the Winch position. He takes up Winch's claims that cultural relativity makes it impossible to ask truth questions, for example, whether the Zande beliefs about witches are true?[19] MacIntyre develops Winch thus:

We can ask from within the Zande system of beliefs if there are witches and will receive the answer 'Yes'. We can ask from within the system of beliefs of modern science if there are witches and will receive the answer 'No'. But we cannot ask which system of beliefs is the superior in respect of rationality and truth; for this would be to invoke criteria which can be understood independently of any particular way of life, and on Winch's view there are no criteria.[20]

Now, MacIntyre goes on, this creates two major problems. First, Winch has made it impossible to explain historical transitions. For example, in seventeenth-century Scotland there was a transition from a culture that believed in witches to one that did not. The determining question was one which Winch thinks impossible, namely, 'Are there witches?' Those living at the time believed that they were moving to a world view that was more accurate than the previous world view. Winch makes this impossible, thereby making any historical narrative in these terms unintelligible.

The second problem is that translation becomes impossible. MacIntyre writes,

Consider the statement made by some Zande theorist or by King James VI and I, 'There are witches', and the statement made by some modern sceptic, 'There are no witches'. Unless one of these statements denies what the other asserts, the negation of the sentence expressing the former could not be a translation of the sentence expressing the latter. Thus if we could not deny from our own standpoint and in our own language what the Azande or King James assert in theirs, we should be unable to translate their expression into our language. Cultural idiosyncrasy would have entailed linguistic idiosyncrasy and cross-cultural comparison would have been rendered logically impossible. But of course translation is not impossible.[21]

This rather startling claim needs further development. For it is not obvious why understanding a different culture cannot be disentangled from making a judgment about that culture. The possibility of translating an idea in one culture into a different culture depends upon a shared framework of reference. Consider the term agape as it was used in the New Testament. Now the difficulties in understanding this term arise precisely because of the cultural distance: a romantic understanding is the predominant and popular understanding of love for us, while in the New Testament this was not the case. So the translator is forced to acknowledge the cultural gap, and in so doing she searches for alternative expressions. Perhaps she suggests that agape described self-giving, openness to others, and a willingness not to count the cost. This alternative description is unlikely to capture *exactly* what agape meant for those writing the New Testament. All that can be claimed for this translation is that it is closer to the meaning intended by the writers of the New Testament. There are two reasons why the translator cannot claim to know exactly what agape meant in a first-century setting. First, such a claim depends on largely inaccessible knowledge, we do not know any first-century Christians to ask whether we have translated agape correctly. Secondly, words and ideas do not have strict definitions. This is why we spend so much time arguing about definitions. So a problem remains: how does our translator have any idea what a different culture meant by a word?

We are forced to assume a fundamental shared humanity. We

assume that all cultures are in the same business of making sense of human life and activity. We are all trying to construct a world view.[22] When it comes to agape, we deduce from the context that the term is trying to describe a certain relationship between God and humanity, and among people. We recognize the experience that St Paul is describing in 1 Corinthians 13 where agape is defined in terms of patience, kindness, and not being irritable or resentful. And we deduce from this and elsewhere a recognizable set of experiences that we express in our language by a certain set of terms that serve as equivalents for agape.

Translation depends on a critical realist claim that all world views attempt to describe a reality which in some ways transcends culture. Solipsism and extreme forms of idealism make translation impossible, but usually we assume the existence of each other, sets of relationships, and an external world. We have to agree on the data that evoke the religious impulse and recognize the experiences that generate different religious world views.

Yet the stubborn anti-realist can quite 'rationally' decide that translation is so difficult as to be virtually impossible; we cannot be sure that an experience in another culture in fact corresponds to the experience described in a certain way in our culture. With this question we are at the outer limits of philosophical judgment. One is either so preoccupied with the distance that one ceases to speak of truth and becomes an anti-realist; or one is sensitive to the distance, but struck by the creative and imaginative human ability to transcend it.

The argument against Winch has consisted of an appeal to the unacceptable consequences of the relativist's position. We were forced to wait until MacIntyre's *Whose Justice? Which Rationality?* for a suggested procedure for deciding between traditions. Here he distinguishes two different but related objections: the relativist challenge and the perspectivist challenge. MacIntyre explains,

The relativist challenge rests upon a denial that rational debate between and rational choice among rival traditions is possible; the perspectivist challenge puts in question the possibility of making truth-claims from within any one tradition. For if there is a multiplicity of rival traditions, each with its own characteristic modes of rational justification internal to it, then that very fact entails that no one tradition can offer those outside it good reasons for excluding the theses of its rival. Yet if this is so, no one tradition is entitled to arrogate to itself an exclusive title; no one tradition can deny legitimacy to its rivals.[23]

Relativism, argues MacIntyre, arises when people insist that rational evaluation of conflicting traditions is only possible when standing outside these traditions; since this is impossible, relativism appears as the only option. MacIntyre commends a different approach. He calls it 'tradition-constituted and tradition-constitutive enquiry'.[24] This approach rejects the expectations of the relativist. It does this in two very important ways: (1) by not expecting to find a neutral standard; and (2) by not expecting to arrive at an all-embracing truth which would be an absolute truth. Underpinning the objections of the relativist is the problem of false expectations. These false expectations have arisen because of the Enlightenment. The Enlightenment project was an unattainable quest for absolute certainty. It is a modern post-Enlightenment problem.

Our current crisis is compared, by MacIntyre, with the development of certain pre-Enlightenment traditions. Within the histories of these traditions, MacIntyre believes the principles of tradition-constituted enquiry are expressed. Although Aquinas did not have a neutral vantage point transcending the various conflicting traditions surrounding him, he still managed to make certain 'rational' judgments. In Aquinas there are two conflicting traditions that are engaged in debate and ultimately synthesized. He harmonizes an Aristotelian structure with an Augustinian psychology. MacIntyre's entire book is a study of the principles of engagement between traditions within a historical and cultural framework. How is this possible?

Initially, traditions are founded within a community. A tradition can be said to begin when the beliefs, institutions, and practices are articulated by certain people and/or in certain texts. In such a community authority will be conferred on these texts and voices. In discussing these texts, procedures for inquiry will be established. A rationality will develop. Problems for the community arise for any of the following reasons: one, when there are different and incompatible interpretations; two, when incoherences and inadequacies are identified; and three, when there is a confrontation with different systems.[25] When these problems arise, the community faces 'an epistemological crisis'.[26] The term 'epistemological crisis' describes a state where the traditional modes of inquiry are generating problems which the tradition lacks the resources to solve. Such a crisis generates the need for an imaginative conceptual innovation,[27] which gives rise to new beliefs that can be compared and contrasted with the older and less adequate beliefs. Such a comparison obviously requires a standard. Here MacIntyre outlines a variation on the correspondence theory of truth.[28] Ultimately, such traditions are trying to explain reality in as comprehensive a way as possible. Truth is ultimately achieved when the beliefs correspond with reality.

A tradition is successfully maintained if it can be shown that any proposed modification in belief and outlook can be demonstrated to stand in a continuity with the rest of the tradition. It is possible that during an epistemological crisis, arising as a result of a conflict with another tradition, the adherents may decide that the new tradition is more appropriate than the earlier one. This is crucial. *MacIntyre believes that it is possible for one tradition when engaging another, to find that the other has better conceptual tools to understand human life and activity. A tradition can founder.* Although there is no neutral rationality to appeal to, the adherents of an existing tradition can come to find a different tradition's rationality more plausible. A judgment has been made between the two traditions. MacIntyre suggests that the developments leading to the science of Newton and Galileo might be of this type.[29]

Naturally, this engagement between traditions is not easy. Communication requires a common language, and language presupposes a rationality. MacIntyre believes that the only way for two traditions, with two different languages, to have dialogue, is for the participants to learn a second first-language. This term captures the necessity of learning the language as we did our first language when children. It is not simply a matter of matching sentences from our first language with our second, but of living and thinking with the concepts within the second language. This MacIntyre argues is both possible and necessary.

Thus MacIntyre's project in *Whose Justice? Which Rationality?* is to find a way to stand within a tradition and yet make judgments between traditions. His position offers an attractive synthesis of historicism and the correspondence theory of truth. John Milbank, in his *Theology and Social Theory*, argues that MacIntyre's position is ultimately untenable. Milbank shares MacIntyre's rejection of an overarching liberal, secular, rationality. However, Milbank goes on, 'MacIntyre, of course, wants to argue against this stoic–liberal–nihilist tendency, which is "secular reason". But my case is rather that it is only a mythos, and therefore cannot be refuted, but only out-narrated, if we persuade people – for reasons of "literary taste" – that Christianity offers a much better story.'[30]

Milbank argues that the problem with MacIntyre is that he is insufficiently historicist. The possibility of living in two traditions does not provide the means of deciding between the traditions, rather both traditions become a part of the person and will coexist in awkward tension.[31] Further, Milbank finds implausible a switch in traditions being legitimated according to the criteria of the older tradition. It makes no sense to imagine a switch in 'rationalities' being determined by the rationality which is becoming obsolete. And finally, Milbank writes, 'It is similarly impossible to adjudicate the claim to "explain more".' Movement in traditions, say from the Aristotelian to the Newtonian, 'have to be interpreted as essentially "rhetorical victories"'.[32]

Milbank, however, is not a straightforward anti-realist. He uses historicism to show that the secular liberal rationality is one of several possible narratives, all of which rest on 'theological assumptions'. In a superb discussion of Nietzsche, he shows that the implications of such a rationality are highly unsatisfactory. Within such a framework, one surrenders to the most powerful. Instead, Milbank suggests the following alternative: it is true that all we have is a range of different traditions, and decisions between traditions cannot be made on some 'tradition-transcendent grounds'. Yet it is possible that one of these traditions is the truth. This is what the Christian narrative claims to be: it is a meta-discourse which can and should embrace all human life and activity. In this respect, he agrees with Demant that the Christian narrative provides a total explanation of all human life.[33] Milbank describes this position as 'a true Christian metanarrative realism'.[34] The confident assertion of the Christian narrative can save us from nihilism and violence. 'Such a Christian logic is not deconstructible by modern secular reason; rather, it is Christianity which exposes the non-necessity of supposing, like the Nietzscheans, that difference, non-totalization and indeterminacy of meaning necessarily imply arbitrariness and violence'.[35] So because Milbank's position is post-modern and historicist, he has protected the Christian narrative from secular objections. But because the narrative is true, he has protected himself against the criticism of nihilism.

In my judgment, Milbank's discussion has pointed to a difficulty in MacIntyre's position. MacIntyre wants to retain the belief that traditions are all in the same business of making sense of reality. For this to work, MacIntyre's 'traditioned-reason' must assume that the standards of coherence and intelligibility cross all traditions. (This is a point we shall return to.) However, Milbank's alternative is equally problematic. There are two difficulties. First, it is odd to affirm the Christian narrative as a meta-discourse and yet with equal tenacity deny any legitimate rational engagement between traditions. For Milbank believes that one is not persuaded by good reasons from one tradition to another; one cannot have dialogue between traditions in a quest for the truth; and one cannot know that one's tradition describes reality in a 'more complete' way than any of the alternatives. All one can do is 'convert' (in a fideistic sense) and enact the narrative in one's life. Milbank makes this explicit in his essay in *Christian Uniqueness Reconsidered*, where he offers the following proposal for Christian relations with other religions:

As regards the general furtherance of the critical understanding of discourses (the minimum that religions can truly share in common) it will be better to replace 'dialogue' with 'mutual suspicion'. As

regards Christian theology and practice, we should simply pursue
further the ecclesial project of securing harmony through difference
and a continuous historical conversation not bound by the Socratic
constraints of dialogue around a neutral common topic. In the course
of such a conversation, we should indeed expect to constantly receive
Christ again, from the unique spiritual responses of other cultures. But
I do not pretend that this proposal means anything other than
continuing the work of conversion.'[36]

Now this is crucial. It is sad that a confident assertion of the
Christian narrative is forced to have this dangerously intolerant
social implication. Our tormented and divided world has more
than enough 'mutual suspicion'. The Milbank outlook feeds the
tribal instinct to which large parts of the Christian narrative are
so strongly opposed.

The second difficulty is that Milbank's historicist assumptions
undermine the possibility of writing an accurate history.
Sometimes he remembers these assumptions. For example,
when criticizing Wayne Meeks, he explains that one cannot get
to a 'pre-textual genesis';[37] but sometimes he forgets. Thus
when he criticizes the liberal Protestant metanarrative as it
initially appeared in Weber, he works through the main
components, concluding: 'Hence Weber was simply wrong to
discover in ancient Judaism the germs of a "protestant"
religion';[38] and later 'there is no reason to suppose any
identifiable Christianity before the emergence of strong ecclesial
themes';[39] and once again, 'it is not true that before the Pope's
assumption of imperial powers, the Church was an essentially
"spiritual" body of individuals'.[40] For Milbank, Weber was
wrong. No reason is given, his ideas are simply not true. This
language implies strongly that the historical judgments of
Weber are less appropriate than the historical judgments of
Milbank. This language can only be used if one accepts that
there is an objective history which can be described in better or
worse ways.

So the position now is as follows: Milbank's theological
realism is too problematic and contains seeds of intolerance.
However, MacIntyre appears unable to justify his traditioned-
rationality. The option I shall now develop is firmly rooted in

the tradition of natural theology. I intend to offer the Thomist cosmological argument as a way of providing a basis for 'traditioned-rationality'.

TRUTH AND THE INTELLIGIBILITY OF THE UNIVERSE

Culturally, we do not really understand what it means to believe in God. God has become an appendage belief. He is in the realm of speculation. There might be a Loch Ness monster; things called ghosts might exist; and there might be this alarmingly large entity called 'God'. Most people assume that God's existence is largely a question about the start of the universe. It is viewed as an 'interesting' question, but peripheral to normal life.

This attitude to religion could not be more mistaken. Religion is a life-transforming world perspective which affects every aspect of life. For the naturalist, the universe is an inanimate entity that through remarkable chance has generated mind and consciousness. All moral values are culture projection. The main theistic claim is the opposite: at the heart of the universe is goodness and love enabling all to be. This is what we mean by God. Theists find themselves in awe and reverence placing ultimate value on this being at the heart of the universe. Worship is not pandering to a giant ego saying 'Oh God, you are jolly big.' Instead, by focusing on God – the ultimate beauty, love, goodness, and joy – believers begin to recognize the appropriate value of everything else. Worship is the realization of the location of ultimate value. Such a disposition forces one to monotheism. This is partly because, given the choice of the 'One' or the 'Many', the One is the simpler explanation. And it is also due to the ultimate nature of worship. It is not simply accidental that the five major world religions tend towards monotheism. Even within Hinduism, Shankara argues that all the different gods and goddesses are expressions of the one – Brahman.[41]

Now this contrast between naturalism and theism has been widely recognized. However, I shall show that a further contrast arises over the nature of truth. For Christians in the Thomist tradition, the naturalist cannot expect the world to exhibit coherence and intelligibility. If the world does exhibit these qualities, then at best they are just 'good fortune' and probably relatively localized. However, the whole idea of truth as a correspondence between descriptions and reality needs a coherent and intelligible reality. So the life-transforming difference in world perspective extends to our very presuppositions about the nature of our experience and whether we can describe our experience. To develop this claim, philosophers started talking about God as a 'Necessary Being'. Now this terminology provokes considerable suspicion. However, it is quite wrong to talk of an opposition between the God of the philosophers and the God of the Bible.[42] The purpose of this philosophical language is to develop two very important strands of the biblical tradition: first, it stresses that God exists in ways which are quite different from the ways in which 'normal' things, like tables, chairs, and people, exist. In other words, it is the ultimate safeguard against anthropomorphism. Second, it explains precisely how the theistic world perspective differs fundamentally from the naturalistic one.

MacIntyre is right to describe the Enlightenment project as an attempt to discover a 'tradition-transcendent rationality'. And MacIntyre is also correct to report that the entire project was a failure. One option considered and rejected by Hume and Kant was the entire tradition of natural theology. The supposed 'proofs for the existence of God' did not succeed because it was always possible to reject the premises. With regard to the design argument, explained Hume, it is always possible to insist that order in nature is not evidence of purpose, but the convenient result of chance. With regard to the cosmological argument, it is possible to hold that the world is just contingent and ultimately inexplicable. And with regard to the ontological argument, one can simply refuse the definition of God as a necessary being existing within all logically possible worlds. In other words, the requirement that the arguments work outside any tradition meant that they were doomed to failure.

The Hume attack completely missed the point of the arguments. They were never intended for the person outside all traditions.[43] Instead they tease out the explanatory power of the Christian tradition.[44] When D. Z. Phillips complains that the God at the end of these arguments is simply an object in the same language game as Loch Ness monsters, he is making the same mistake as Hume.[45] Phillips believes that the whole point of the proofs is to treat God as an object apart from religion – an object within the 'scientific language game'. But the arguments were formed within the Christian tradition. The purpose is to show the explanatory power of the theistic world view. This is not done outside the tradition, but within the tradition. Yet they can be compelling for people outside the tradition, because the proofs illustrate the incomplete nature of their own tradition. However, this is to move on too quickly, let us first return to St Thomas.

The Thomist cosmological argument is frequently misrepresented. It does not claim that as everything has a cause, then the universe must have had a cause, and that cause is God.[46] God is not the great first cause, somewhere back in the mists of time. In fact, when Aquinas discusses the creation of the universe, he implies that rationally his preference is to believe, like his Greek 'masters', that matter is eternal, but on the basis of Genesis 1 he accepts that the universe had a beginning.[47] For Aquinas, in fact, the point of the cosmological argument is not that God was the first cause which led to the development of all else. Rather, it is best seen as an exploration of the concept of intelligibility and explanation. This can be shown as follows:

1. Whenever we experience an event, the natural human instinct is to seek an explanation. For example, most of us want to know the cause of the presence of a fallen tree blocking the road. This is a very basic human instinct.

2. The explanations for most events are contingent. This is to say, the explanations could be otherwise and are dependent upon another layer of explanation. So, returning to our tree, after some enquiry we discover that there was a storm last night that resulted in the tree falling down. This is one explanation among several possible explanations, and it is clearly dependent on the existence of a weather-system.

3. An infinite regress of contingent explanations would still

leave the entire system unexplained. The universe as a whole would make no sense if the explanations were contingent and infinite; any conceivable contingent explanation would become the next stage needing to be explained. So let us suppose, in the case of our tree, that after several layers of explanations, we arrive back at the fundamental laws of physics; the question then is: how do we explain these laws?

At this point, we note that Aquinas excludes two options. He excludes the possibility of an infinite regress of contingent explanations, because that would simply leave the universe as a whole unintelligible. He also excludes the option of simply stopping at a particular point. Bertrand Russell wanted to stop at the universe and decide that 'it is just there, that's all.'[48] But the universe is simply the sum of contingent events that still require explanation.

4. Therefore for the universe to 'make sense', one must have a 'necessary being'. Aquinas says, 'One is forced therefore to suppose something which must be, and owes this to no other thing than itself; indeed it itself is the cause that other things must be.'[49] This is an extremely controversial step. Many philosophers do not think the idea coherent. The 'necessary being' idea is best defined as one existing in all possible worlds and containing within itself the explanation of its own existence. The idea of a necessary being is not vacuous (it does have content), and it has not been shown to be self-contradictory. If the idea of a contingent explanation is coherent, there is no reason why its opposite is not coherent. Further I am persuaded by Keith Ward that it is likely that Aquinas meant a 'logically necessary being'. It is only such a being who can provide the complete explanation for the universe. Finally, we are to identify this being with the God of theism.

This account of the cosmological argument is heavily dependent on Hugo Meynell's *The Intelligible Universe* and Keith Ward's *Rational Theology and the Creativity of God*. Meynell locates the cosmological argument in the following way: 'we can grasp the overall nature of things in very basic outline, and that our successful practice of the sciences depends on the fact that we can do so; and that it is just this basic nature and structure of the world of things, how it cannot but be in order that we may come to know it in the way in which we do, which provides the basis of a cosmological argument for theism'.[50] Ward explains that the argument

is an analysis of the notion of complete explanation, and what is implied in the thought of its possibility. It commits one to the existence of God only if one accepts the intelligibility of the universe. There is no way to force a man to do that; it is an ultimate assumption which will appeal, if it does, by its coherence as a focal point of many related strands of argument to do with the importance of personal being, the objectivity of value, the appropriateness of prayer and the pre-conditions of the pursuit of science.[51]

Ward is correct to emphasize that the argument is not such as to have the capacity to persuade every sane person. To be convinced by it, one needs to assume that an explanation can be found both for the tree across the road and for the entire universe. He is also correct to suggest that one good reason for making this assumption is 'the preconditions of the pursuit of science'. Scientists assume that events have explanations. They accept that the universe 'makes sense'. If one is persuaded by the approach of science, then, Aquinas has shown us, we are committed to the existence of God.

I shall now develop Aquinas and link the argument with the 'critically realist instinct' that traditions can and should make sense of the universe. The argument has the following five stages.[52]

1. MacIntyre's 'traditioned-rationality' depends upon showing the intelligibility of the universe.
2. The intelligibility of the universe requires that the universe is ultimately explicable.
3. An endless set of contingent explanations will leave the universe as ultimately unexplained, for a contingent explanation always requires a further explanation.
4. Therefore for the universe to be intelligible, there must be a necessary being (i.e., a logically necessary being who exists in all possible worlds and is self-explanatory).
5. This is what theists mean by God.

In the first step, I am claiming that the 'critically realist instinct' is that world views attempt to make sense of human experience. 'Making sense' requires that we expect the universe to provide a coherent and stable set of experiences.

In the second step, I claim that if the universe is not ultimately explicable – if there is not an ultimate explanation – then it would be just good fortune that we are able to explain anything at all. Furthermore at any moment the contingency of the universe might destroy the regular patterns that we have so far discerned. In his argument for the third way, Aquinas argues that everything could suddenly cease to be. Categories such as consistency, coherence, and evidence would appear inappropriate in a completely contingent universe.

In the third step, we have the thrust of the Thomist argument. One does not provide an ultimate explanation unless one has an explanation that is not contingent. One cannot just stop at the ultimate laws of physics because these are clearly contingent and therefore themselves require explanation. The ultimate explanation must be necessary.

With the fourth step, we introduce the concept of a necessary being. Despite certain difficulties, I have already defended the coherence of this idea. Finally, we identify this being with the God of traditional theism.

Therefore we arrive at the rather surprising conclusion that 'traditioned-rationality' depends on the 'critical realist' assumption that the world can be explained. If the intention of most world views to explain the world is legitimate, then I have shown that a necessary being is implied. And the idea of a necessary being is part of what we mean by God. Now we are only left with two options. First, a world view which is both realist and theist. Now this, I have shown, is coherent and reasonable. Second, a world view which is explicitly anti-realist. Once you give up on truth and simply articulate your narrative, then you have also given up on intelligible explanations for the world, and therefore God.

One option which has disappeared is naturalism. This is the desire to explain the world without reference to God. Atheism, Marxism, and other naturalistic world views are realist but not theistic. The argument in this chapter exposes the radical incoherence of all naturalistic philosophies. To those who continue to explain the world, but do not believe in God, I can only suggest that they are operating with an *unjustifiable rationality* – quite literally, an irrational rationality. If they have thought through their assumptions, then the best that they can say is that they are seeking 'explanations' that, by some good fortune, *appear* to make sense. This I suspect is all that David Hume would have managed to claim. There is something manifestly problematic about offering explanations when one is uncertain that anything can be explained. It is not surprising that such *unjustifiable rationality* is always vulnerable to relativism and nihilism. Nietzsche saw this with characteristic clarity. For part of his argument was that if God does not exist, then truth simply becomes projection. In the *Twilight of Idols* Nietzsche has a passage entitled 'How the "Real World" at last became a Myth'. In it he works through from Platonism to modernity. For Plato, Nietzsche writes:

1. The real world, attainable to the wise, the pious, the virtuous man – he dwells in it, he is it. (Oldest form of the idea, relatively sensible, simple, convincing. Transcription of the proposition 'I, Plato, am the truth'.)

Nietzsche then works through the medieval Christian, the Kantian, the empiricists, and then:

5. The 'real world' – an idea no longer of any use, not even a duty any longer – an idea grown useless, superfluous, consequently a refuted idea: let us abolish it!
   (Broad daylight; breakfast; return of cheerfulness and bons sens; Plato blushes for shame; all free spirits run riot.)
6. We have abolished the real world: what world is left? the apparent world perhaps? ... But no! with the real world we have also abolished the apparent world!
(Mid-day; moment of the shortest shadow; end of the longest error; zenith of mankind; INCIPIT ZARATHUSTRA.)[53]

Commentators disagree as to exactly what Nietzsche means here. But I suggest that he believes that truth is now nonsense. Projection is all there is. The real world and the apparent world have both disappeared. This, for Nietzsche, would bring true freedom, that is, freedom to invent our own world.

The anti-realist foundation of tolerance for the secularist is still an option. Once God goes, it is the only option left. However, anti-realism is an awkward 'metaphysical basis' for tolerance. The problem is that anti-realism makes it impossible to justify limits of tolerance. We do not want to extend tolerance to forms of fascism and racism. Yet the anti-realist, having surrendered truth, has lost any basis for rational exclusion.

At this point the anti-realist advocate of tolerance will cite the intolerant nature of racism as a grounds for exclusion. But the problem here is that this ground is also the reason given for not permitting a Christian community to have a Christian ethic which might, for example, forbid abortion. The anti-realist advocate of tolerance excludes all moral judgments from the public square. Tolerance becomes an end in itself. On this account, all society consists of is a group of individuals who must coexist in a moral vacuum with minimum interaction.

The thesis of this chapter can be put in two ways: negatively, I am claiming that the only adequate protection against nihilism is belief in God; positively, I am claiming that a *justified rationality* depends on the existence of God. Part of the resistance to this conclusion will come from those who have no grasp of the central significance of the theistic claim. As I have already said, modernity has made God an appendage belief. So it is thought that humanists and Christians can live life agreeing about science and basic moral values, but Christians simply have a need to tag God on to their belief system. But this is a completely wrong way to conceive of religious belief. (I suspect that our modern understanding of the term 'belief' is partly responsible for this mistake.) Both St Thomas and Nietzsche show us that God is a transforming belief, central to how we view everything. Once this fact is grasped, then it is not surprising that belief in God is a necessary condition for rational dialogue.

My conclusion is that truth judgments require a theistic framework. All traditions that attempt truth judgments, but are not theistic are either incomplete (i.e., have not uncovered their epistemological assumptions), or are radically incoherent. This rationality must not be confused with foundationalism, because there is no sense in which this is 'tradition-transcendent'. Instead I have attempted to locate the 'tradition-constituted' rationality of MacIntyre within a cosmological realism, and as part of the theistic tradition. And this rationality includes all the standard tests for intelligibility:

First, coherence is required of our world perspectives. Any self-contradictory world perspective cannot be true.[54] Moreover, coherence implies that the world is consistent. Any world perspective radically inconsistent in its description of human life could be judged as less adequate than those that are more consistent. So a world perspective that claims to be moral yet racist is less adequate than one that is moral and not racist.

Secondly, we shall judge a given world perspective by its explanatory power. The world perspective that explains the data in a better way than its competitors is more likely to be true.

Using the above criteria, we have a basis for rationality, dialogue, and mutual respect. We tolerate those who disagree because they might have a contribution to make in our discovery of the truth. Tolerance for those within the theistic traditions can become a tool in the quest for the truth. In other words, problems in respect of tolerance will be more likely to come from those not committed to a religious world perspective.

In the next chapter I shall develop this argument. We shall discover how a theistic world perspective can provide a foundation for tolerance which is much stronger than the secularist's anti-realist foundation.

CHAPTER 9

Conditions for rational public discourse

In the last chapter we looked at the argument between anti-realism and realism. This was needed because the contemporary commitment to tolerance is largely built on anti-realist assumptions. For the contemporary liberal, tolerance assumes that metaphysical disagreements cannot be resolved; truth in the sense of a correspondence between descriptions and reality is not possible. In evaluating this claim I have shown that this is indeed the case for all those traditions that reject the notion of God. However, the theistic traditions still find it possible to appeal to truth. And it is on theistic assumptions that the language of coherence and evidence can be justified.

We now return to the central question of this book. What world view provides the strongest foundation for tolerance? Let us identify our two extreme options. On the one hand, we have *rational theism*, which is committed to the ultimate rationality of the universe made possible through the creatorial activity of God. On the other hand, we have a *secular anti-realism*, which denies the existence of God and cannot protect itself from the nihilistic implications of much post-modern reasoning. Now I shall show how rational theism, firmly rooted in the Catholic faith, offers both the rational and moral resources for a genuine public discourse. Basically I am bringing out the differences already implied in the last chapter. In working through the argument, I shall take the opportunity to reply to some of the major objections to my position.

RATIONALITY

When it comes to rational dialogue, the theist has the advantage over the secularist in three crucial ways. First, the theist is committed to truth. Secondly, the theist can have meaningful dialogue – a dialogue committed to discovery. And finally, the internal logic of the theistic position leads one to an attitude of 'mutual respect' to competing positions. These three separate points will now be discussed in more detail.

The commitment to truth involves a belief that assertions have a truth-value which will be judged by their capacity to describe the world. At this point I shall not examine the complex arguments for the correspondence theory and against the coherence theory. Suffice it to say that much of this debate is preoccupied with the problem that we do not have any uninterpreted data. All experiences are interpreted. We do not have direct access to Kant's noumenal world; we do not know what things-as-they-are-in-themselves are like. For philosophers like Richard Rorty this makes truth in a correspondence sense absurd. All we have are competing interpretations. To transcend these interpretations in any correspondence sense is impossible.

Although this looks like a strong objection, in actual fact it draws unwarranted implications from the problem. We have already seen in the last chapter, that the bus queue is an observation that requires both language and interpretation. To suggest that this then entails a concept of truth that can only meaningfully be judged by the internal consistency or coherence of a world view, leads to the absurdity that those before the Copernican revolution were making a true statement when they asserted that the world was flat, and those since who assert the opposite are also making a true statement. This cannot be correct.

The alternative to this view of truth does not require that at the Copernican revolution scientists suddenly had access to the way things-are-in-themselves. Rather they discovered the inadequacy of their vocabulary to explain all the data. The position is this: *the world as it really is can disturb the current interpretation of sense-data.* To talk of a correspondence between assertion and reality can easily accommodate the fact that the existing interpretation will always be part of our starting point.

It might still be objected that the idea of 'the truth' implies an unobtainable absolute with intransigent implications. You do not reason with opponents who claim to have 'the truth'. The theist must retort that although there is an 'absolute truth' it would be the height of conceit to claim that we as limited, finite, puny, creatures have this truth. God alone has the absolute truth, for God alone has the perspective and 'vocabulary' in which to describe the complexity of his creation.[1] We shall, at best, have a partial grasp of that absolute truth. Now it is true that some religious people sound as if they have the absolute truth all packaged up. And it is this attitude that can create certain intransigent attitudes. But this attitude is not entailed by a belief that ultimately there is from God's perspective an 'absolute truth'. Indeed most religious traditions are sensitive to the mystery and complexity of God's world. And it is the sin of pride (traditionally the sin of Lucifer) that claims a greater knowledge than any human creature could possibly have. Theists must not claim to have the 'truth' in its entirety, but rather stand ready to be judged by this truth. It is for this truth, and by this truth, that ultimately every theist wants to be judged.

Having defended the claim that an absolute truth is not an absurd or intolerant idea, the theist can go on to the attack. We have seen that the only alternative to this rational theism is secular anti-realism. For the secularist, tending towards nihilism and post-modernism, the crisis within the public square is acute. Public discourse becomes an exercise in assertion, not discussion. Views can only be stated, not judged. The astrological world view, the racist world view, the Christian world view, and the humanist world view cannot be judged by the reality which all are attempting to describe. Neuhaus describes the consequences exactly: '[E]very party will be permitted to contend for their truths so long as they acknowledge that they are their truths, and not the truth. Each will be permitted to propagandize, each will have to propagandize if it is to hold its own, because it is acknowledged that there is no common ground for the alternative to propaganda, which is reasonable persuasion.'[2] Reason has been destroyed; power becomes God.

That quotation illustrates the second advantage the theist has over the secularist. Neuhaus sets against the 'propaganda' of the anti-realist atheist, the 'reasonable persuasion' of the religious person. For the rational theist, dialogue makes perfect sense. We believe that God alone has the absolute truth absolutely. Moreover, such truth as we can comprehend is complicated. Therefore there is a religious imperative for dialogue with different traditions in a quest for higher levels of truth. We need the perspective of others to complement our own. We need the insights of others so that our view of the world can become more accurate.

Dialogue for the secular anti-realist is more of a problem. At best, dialogue will be justified in terms of curiosity about other positions in the market-place. We can be informed, but not enhanced. We can listen, but not share. No synthesis of opposing positions can be discovered. Dialogue with a view to a better understanding of our world is considered impossible. The irrational secularist is offering us a very impoverished view of the world.

The third way the theist can gain over the secularist is in respect to the attitude held to conflicting positions. Irrational secularism is deeply insulting to 'critically realist' world views. The secularist is forced to reduce differences to simply 'different cultural ways of looking at the world'. Real differences over 'matters of fact' make no sense to the irrational secularist. 'Facts' for the irrational secularist do not exist; truth is an absurdity. We cannot gain access to a world beyond our different narratives. Different stories are told that are reducible to different cultural projections. For the secularist, there is no mutual respect. When it comes to the rational theist, this is not so. Even though the Jew and Christian disagree about several major issues, both agree that the disagreement is over matters of truth. Both sides would deny that their view is simply a cultural projection. And both can accept each other's self-understanding that their current view is a claim about the way the world really is.

So in these three ways rational theists can be constructive participants in public dialogue. Rational theists are committed to truth, to dialogue, and to mutual respect. This understanding provides the framework for public discourse; it is to the content of that discourse that we turn next. I shall now argue that the rational theist is in a stronger position than the secularist on the most important disagreement of all – the disagreement over morality.

MORALITY

There is something unavoidably odd about moral assertions. 'I really *ought* to visit my grandmother this evening' is a difficult statement to analyze. The statement seems to imply a conflict between morality and self-interest: we can imagine this person going on to say, 'I would rather go out to the pub, but I really ought . . .' Moral action seems to be in conflict with her personal inclination. Consider, further, that this 'ought' is describing an obligation, a compelling feeling which needs to be satisfied. The language seems to imply an external obligation to act in a certain way. We cannot avoid this obligation anymore than we can wish away the earth's roundness. Or, to take another example, consider a disagreement over abortion. The pro-life advocate argues that abortion is murder, the pro-choice advocate argues that it is wrong for anyone else to make decisions for a woman over her own body. This disagreement is a disagreement over the truth. Each participant is not saying, 'Well, for me, it is wrong to have an abortion, but for you ...' Both use the language of morality to imply that this assertion is wrong or right for the other person. Both are appealing to an external standard that is binding on the other person. Clearly, the language of moral assertions is intended to be 'objective'. Moral assertions appear to refer to an external set of moral truths that are universally true. Terms like 'good', 'right', 'wrong', 'ought', and 'should', sound as if they are external to our mind. Morality is a matter of truth and discovery, not invention.

In sum, the objective character of morality is structured into the very language of moral discourse. Secular anti-realists, however, take issue with this point, arguing that moral assertions are subjective. For his book, *Ethics: Inventing Right and Wrong*, J. L. Mackie chose a telling subtitle, one that expresses exactly the subjectivist claim.[3] Morality is no longer a question of truth and discovery, but of feeling and invention.

Mackie offers two reasons for this position. First, the argument from relativity, which 'has as its premise the well-known variation in moral codes from one society to another and from one period to another, and also the differences in moral beliefs between different groups and classes within a complex community ... Disagreement about moral codes seems to reflect people's adherence to and participation in different ways of life.'[4] So there are certain cultures that permit polygamy; there are others that insist on monogamy. Whether you believe polygamy is permissible will be determined by the culture to which you belong. Different cultures developed different moral systems according to their particular historical experience. You cannot resolve a disagreement over polygamy or any other substantial moral issue, Mackie argues, since morality is more a matter of cultural invention than discovery.

Mackie concedes that the fact of disagreement in morality is not decisive evidence for subjectivity. For scientists disagree constantly over the best way to describe the universe, but clearly the subject matter is objective. He thinks that no parity can be found between a moral disagreement and a scientific disagreement.

However, the moral relativist might want to consider the following situation. We manage to arrange a meeting that includes Aristotle, Newton, and Einstein. We further manage to gather considerable biographical, sociological, and psychological information on each participant. We then settle down to witness the exchange. The argument is heated, with each scientist arguing for his cultural position. Aristotle argues for a universe with set purposes for every plant and animal; Newton is arguing that the universe is best understood as a large machine; and Einstein is arguing that the universe involves a radical relativity especially at great distances and speeds. And as we watch we suddenly notice that a correspondence can be seen between the views of Newton and his psychological and sociological background. Let us imagine that as a child he was obsessed with marbles and machines. We appear to have an explanation for the mechanistic views of Newton. Now along comes our secular anti-realist who argues that all we have here are different projections, and the physicists are not making objective truth-claims.

Now, unlike Mackie, our post-modernist relativist might be happy with this corollary. However, all those sharing the critically realist instinct would be less so. The point is simple. The fact of disagreement and the possibility of psychological explanation does not reduce all truth-claims to merely subjective preferences. Every viewpoint and discovery will have a psychological motivation or aspect, but this fact cannot determine whether the matter involves issues of truth. One can still believe in the objectivity of value and concede that cultural factors do affect our judgment about what we believe that objective moral code consists in. Related to this is another consideration: if morality was simply a matter of personal preference, then argument would be pointless. I like carrots and my wife dislikes carrots. This is a difference in taste; nothing can be gained by a furious argument over carrots. The usual explanation for disagreement is that an issue involves complicated matters of fact. Our three scientists disagree over the ultimate nature of the universe precisely because it is complicated. Likewise a moral objectivist would want to say that disagreement over morality arises because discovering the moral truth is difficult.

J. L. Mackie offers a second argument against objectivity. This is the argument from queerness. Put simply, Mackie points out that the objectivist needs to explain exactly where these moral values are located and how we discover them. With the scientific facts that divide our scientists, their 'facts' are much more obvious than the supposed 'moral facts'. Mackie is requiring that the objectivist offer a framework in which objective moral values would be intelligible. This is perfectly reasonable. And a variety of possible frameworks can be offered. For the Marxist, these objective moral values are located in the dialectic of history. For the theist, these values are located in the character of God. Interestingly, Mackie concedes that,

> To meet these difficulties, the objectivist may have recourse to the purpose of God: the true purpose of human life is fixed by what God intended (or intends) men to do and to be...I concede that if the requisite theological doctrine could be defended, a kind of objective ethical prescriptivity could be thus introduced. Since I think that theism cannot be defended, I do not regard this as any threat to my argument.[5]

This is an important concession. Mackie admits that a theological ethic might be intelligible provided that one has evidence for the existence of God. I am arguing that such evidence is available in precisely the way the theistic claim makes sense of human life and existence. It makes sense of the intelligibility of the universe and the nature of moral discourse.

Having shown the inadequacy of Mackie's arguments against the objectivity of value, I shall now develop three reasons for affirming objective moral values. The first has already been discussed. Close examination of the nature of moral language seems to imply an obligation from beyond us that often conflicts with our self-interest. One of the most inadequate theories to explain moral language is the expressivist theory, according to which moral assertions are just a strange way of articulating one's likes and dislikes. So, for example, 'I think stealing is wrong' really means 'I don't like stealing.' A moment's thought reveals that this cannot be right. For most people the only time one thinks about stealing being wrong is when one is tempted to steal. Even though they would like to steal, they think it is wrong. With the statement, 'I really ought to visit my grandmother', there is the clear implication that I do not really want to visit my grandmother. The expressivist theory is wrong because moral assertions are normally in conflict with our individual preferences. The nature and use of moral assertion provides clear evidence that moral values are objective.

The second reason is the nature of justice. Two cultures disagree over the validity of slavery. Now the subjectivist is stuck. She might be able to express her personal (and cultural) dislike of slavery, but she cannot provide any reason why slavery is wrong for a different culture. If one reduces this to individual crimes, all the assumptions of our legal system start to disintegrate. One defence that is never permitted in our courts is the argument that, given moral relativity, my morality is different from yours and you have no basis on which to judge my action. But of course law-courts must judge and punish a person who commits assault from racist or anti-Semitic motivations, even if (or perhaps especially if) that person regards her anti-Semitism as morally justifiable. Justice presupposes the objectivity of value.

The third piece of evidence for the objectivity of moral values concerns that distinctly modern character – the cynic, defined for our purposes as a person committed to pursuing a completely self-interested life style. The oldest question in the history of ethics is: why not make self-interest the sole criterion for all ethical decisions? Mackie's ethical system is based on egoism. He attempts to argue that it is in our self-interest to have some system of morality. However, he admits that he runs into a difficulty. He explains:

It leaves unanswered the question 'Why should I not at the same time profit from the moral system but evade it? Why should I not encourage others to be moral and take advantage of the fact that they are, but myself avoid fulfilling moral requirements if I can in so far as they go beyond rational egoism and conflict with it?' It is not an adequate answer to this question to point out that one is not likely to be able to get away with such evasions for long. There will be at least some occasions when one can do so with impunity and even without detection. Then why not? To this no complete answer of the kind that is wanted can be given. In the choice of actions moral reasons and prudential ones will not always coincide.[6]

Mackie then moves on to play down the significance of this difficulty. But this will not do.

The cynic represents a major threat to any view of morality. Of course, it is true that self-interest will involve being pleasant to people most of the time. Part of the shift from childhood to adulthood involves this discovery that prudence requires the occasional sacrifice of immediate self-satisfaction for the sake of the group. We learn to share our toys with the other children rather than have constant fights over possession of the toys. However, even here, moral dilemmas arise: for example, it becomes obvious to most people that self-interest and morality do not always coincide. Most decisions requiring moral reflection involve some arbitration between moral principles and personal inclination. Even the decision about visiting grandmother cannot easily be justified on a self-interest criterion. We would have to argue that the satisfaction of family and friends (and of course, grandma) might ultimately make us feel better than an evening at the pub. But I suspect that setting our own long-term satisfaction against the selfish evening in the pub might not be enough to motivate the moral course of action. However, there are other more serious dilemmas that make morality meaningless for the cynic. Consider the cynic who has discovered the means of performing a perfect murder – for example, he has discovered an untraceable drug that causes a heart attack. Consider further that this cynic has a cantankerous, rich, old, yet strong, aunt, and that he is the sole beneficiary in her will. Now in a position where the cynic has nothing to lose and everything to gain, then the rational course of action is to murder the aunt. Fortunately, (especially for aunts) the dilemma in this form is fairly rare, and perfect murders are very difficult to perform. However, equivalent dilemmas are very much part of modern life. It arises in the most acute form when a person has sufficient power to ensure that discovery is unlikely. This can be in a home where a husband is sexually abusing his children, or in a company where the director has access to information that can be used to intimidate his opponents into supporting him. Joseph Stalin is probably the best example of a cynic who protected his position with every means at his disposal. In each case the power the person has ensures that immoral means can be used for selfish purposes.

The character of the cynic is a modern phenomenon. This is not to say that before modernity no one was motivated by self-interest. Such a claim would be absurd. However, it is true that a culture committed to objective moral values can assume that most people know that certain actions are simply wrong, even if these actions are advantageous to their careers. The rise of the cynic ran parallel with an equal concern that in the end the only effective deterrent is discovery. So we now believe that everyone would commit tax fraud if they were certain that they would get away with it. Everyone would take advantage of welfare if they did not fear discovery. In a culture where moral conventions remain strong, and norms are internalized, people can be trusted to some extent. The modern character of the cynic, then, represents a rejection of the true purpose of moral language.

Thus the nature of moral language, our assumptions about justice, and the danger of the cynic provide ample evidence that moral assertions are best understood as objective. However, we now need a framework in which such a claim can be shown to be intelligible. I have already suggested that there are several possible frameworks. In principle (but not in fact) the Marxist position appears to be very strong. In the Marxist system, moral assertions are grounded in the inevitable outcome of history. Why should we always act on the side of revolution and the poor? The Marxist will answer that it is because right and wrong can only be judged against the dialectic of history. As unjust economic relations are bound to generate revolution, then history will judge the rightness of the action. There are many reasons, which are beyond the scope of this book, why the Marxist world view has been discredited both in theory and in practice. Theism, however, is in a much stronger position than alternative world perspectives to provide such a framework.

I shall now attempt a brief sketch of the theistic explanation for morality. The often discussed difficulties with a religious foundation for ethical assertions often presuppose a crudely anthropomorphic God. So let me repeat what exactly the theist is trying to claim. For the naturalist the universe is an inanimate entity that through remarkable chance has generated mind and consciousness. The main theistic claim is the opposite: at the heart of the universe is goodness and love enabling all to be. This is what we mean by God. We find ourselves in awe and reverence placing the ultimate value on this being at the heart of the universe. As I have already said worship is not pandering to a giant ego saying 'Oh God, you are jolly big.' Instead as we focus on God – the ultimate beauty, love, goodness, and joy – we start to appreciate the appropriate value of everything else. Worship is the realization of the location of ultimate value. Such a disposition forces one to monotheism.[7] Further reflection on God establishes the crucial nature of interpersonal relations both with each other and between God and us. The claim that the universe is ultimately personal points to the moral dimension. These moral truths are grounded in the character of God.

At this point, the naturalist raises the spectre of Plato's *Euthyphro* dilemma. This claims that either morality is beyond God and not arbitrary or that morality is determined by God and is arbitrary. If it is the former, then morality is not grounded in God, and if it is the latter then God is not good or loving, because anything God does is good and loving by definition.

Needless quantities of paper have been generated by this problem. The mistake is that the dilemma presupposes a God that is too anthropomorphic. In brief, the problem ignores a further alternative. God's moral attributes belong necessarily in his character; this means that the moral values are firmly rooted in his character. Yet God is not arbitrary, and cannot alter ultimate moral values.[8]

The question now arises: how do we discover these moral values? Certain answers can be eliminated right at the outset. One cannot, for example, simply take any religious scripture and read out the appropriate proof text. Although it was possible for God to provide a certain revelation, it is fairly clear that he did not do so. (This is a point that will be developed in the next chapter.) The quest for these moral values has not been made easy. The Thomist natural-law tradition needs to be developed, but the basic principle is right. Here the central question is: What does God intend for us? In other words, our knowledge of these moral values is discovered by reflection on the creatorial purpose.

However, due to God's desire to respect our freedom, the discovery and implementation of these moral values will require discussion, dialogue, and tolerance. We need to share our mutual insights with each other. At this stage the important point is that theism makes much more sense of moral language than the secularist alternative.

Our argument so far is as follows: the most appropriate foundation for tolerance is not an irrational secularism, but a rational theism. Our culture needs religion, because only religion has the resources for a rich, rational, and moral discourse in the public square.

However, as we saw in Parts II and III, religion needs to concede tolerance as an achievement of modernity. The argument between MacIntyre and Stout in chapter eight illustrated that in the end they were divided over the issue of tolerance. And, as Neuhaus showed, when a theist affirms plurality, she often ends up affirming other elements of modernity as well. But why should theism see itself in opposition to all elements of modernity? We need to affirm all insights into the truth as a part of God's truth. The discovery of tolerance by modernity will lead Christians to discover a deeper and sometimes quite distinctive understanding of their own tradition.

The account of religion I am commending is distinct from the dominant forms of religion prior to the Enlightenment. This is not to say that before the Enlightenment all religion was intolerant and that now all religion in America is tolerant. Such a caricature ignores the complexity and diversity of these cultures. But one can say that the general ethos of medieval Christendom did tend towards intolerance, and the general ethos of the United States does tend towards tolerance. However, it is not just tolerance that divides these two eras. Demant's nostalgia for medieval Christendom is possible only if one ignores the religious wars and the general preoccupation with theoretical contemplation unrelated to ordinary life. Charles Taylor in his seminal study, *The Sources of the Self*, complains that MacIntyre and Bellah both ignore the achievements of modernity: 'The deeper moral vision, the genuine moral sources invoked in the aspiration to disengaged reason or expressive fulfilment tend to be overlooked, and the less impressive motives – pride, self-satisfaction, liberation from demanding standards – brought to the fore. Modernity is often read through its least impressive, most trivializing offshoots. But this distorts.'[9]

Taylor provides a model for the balanced assessment of modernity. First, he accepts that there are areas of tension that threaten breakdown in modern moral culture. Among other things, he is concerned about the modern turn to 'subject-centredness'; a turn that requires self-expression, but lacks any given order by which this expression is controlled. Secondly, he is right to cite the affirmation of the family and work as a distinctively modern insight.[10] Thirdly, he commends the rigorous demanding ethic of modernity. Culturally, we have a heightened sensitivity to suffering.[11] Many of us are opposed to the death penalty and concerned with animal suffering in a way that culturally is quite distinctive. We make exceptional moral demands of ourselves – for example, we expect human rights to be universal.[12] And, finally, Taylor argues that many of these positive changes have their roots in religious dispositions. For example, the affirmation of ordinary life needed the Judeao-Christian creation narratives.

Taylor's account is much more balanced than MacIntyre's, which follows Demant in arguing that without a recovery of a pre-modern tradition, there is no hope for our culture. This is to ignore the achievements of our modern culture. However, one achievement that Taylor fails to emphasize sufficiently is the discovery of tolerance. Tolerance was not a religious discovery. When the church had political power, it tended to be intolerant. Widespread tolerance attitudes were only discovered as the church became a minority in European culture. We needed Locke and Voltaire to persuade the church of the virtue of tolerance. As Neuhaus puts it: 'As the Philistines were to Israel, so Voltaire was to the church.'[13] Secularism was God's way of teaching the church a much needed lesson. If secularism is part of God's revelation, then clearly one cannot dismiss our modern culture in every respect. The theism I am commending feeds upon the Thomist tradition, yet at certain points is at odds with that tradition.

Religious institutions need to embark on a project of constructive engagement with modernity. Images of compromise are inappropriate. All I am arguing is that God has much more to teach us, and his insights can come from a variety of sources. This exercise of engagement should be done with self-confidence. As these last two chapters have shown, religious institutions are needed in our culture.

However, this engagement will not leave our theology untouched. We must find new and different ways of understanding our tradition. In the next chapter I shall offer my suggestions for the Christian tradition. This means that my argument is shifting from general theism to a Christian perspective; others must do the task for the other traditions. What does tolerance imply for the Christian world perspective? What can we learn of God and our faith in the light of our discovery of tolerance? This is a shift in modes. Our cultural analysis is forcing us back to our theology. We need a Christian theology that can accommodate plurality.

CHAPTER 10

Plurality and theology

In this part the bulk of the argument has been in our second mode of enquiry – the cultural. This chapter will concentrate on the problem of tolerance in the first mode – the theological mode.

In chapter eight we looked at John Milbank's confident assertion of the Christian metanarrative. In his engagement with modernity, Milbank insisted that dialogue among different world perspectives and judgment between them are both impossible. According to Milbank, we are only able to articulate our vision of human society and hope that others are taken up with the narrative. I argued that Milbank's position has dangerously intolerant implications. If we can learn nothing from these different world perspectives, if other world perspectives imply an 'ontology of violence', then perhaps these other world perspectives should be quietly (and non-violently) excluded from the public square. The difficulty here is: what sort of theology can enable a constructive Christian contribution in a pluralist society?

I have argued in the last two chapters that theological assertions make realist claims about the nature of the world, and that theism is a more coherent description of life than any alternative world perspective. Belief in God is part of an attempt, in various traditions, to explain and make sense of human life and experience. A world perspective has two explanatory functions. The first concerns the positive features of human life and experience; so, I have argued that theism makes sense of the objectivity of value and the intelligibility of the universe. These are positive features of the world in that they are phenomena which can be cited as evidence for the world perspective. The second concerns the negative features of human life and experience; for the Christian world perspective this would include the fact of evil and, more importantly for the public square, the existence of different religions. What exactly would be classified as a negative or positive feature would vary from world perspective to world perspective, but the important point is the fact that each world perspective must, if it is going to be successful, provide some sort of explanation for those features that appear to count against itself. One of the most important explanations a world perspective must provide is the existence of world perspectives that disagree. In other words, each world perspective must supply an explanation of disagreement.

I shall now argue that the explanation of disagreement offered by orthodox Christianity is the reason why the Christian tradition has such strong tendencies towards intolerance. Much of my argument has drawn on the Thomist tradition, but, as regards the explanation of disagreement, the tradition needs radical modification. We shall start this discussion with a summary of the Thomist explanation for both positive and negative features of human experience.[1]

Thomism had immense explanatory power and was in many respects very popular and successful. St Thomas' whole system of natural theology was intended (and I think succeeded) to demonstrate irrefutably that one cannot understand the world without believing in God. However, there are some people who do not believe in the Christian God. This was a problem for St Thomas. The *Summa contra Gentiles* was written as a source book for missionaries involved in converting Muslims and Jews. In his account of unbelief St Thomas shows how his system can explain the existence of other religions. He is careful to distinguish between different types of unbelief, or, to use his language, different types of infidelities. He writes:

we should conclude that considered in relationship to the virtue of faith, there are several infidelities determinate in number and kind. For its sinfulness consists in the resisting of the faith, and this may come about in two ways: either the faith is fought against before it has been accepted, such is the unbelief of pagans or heathens; or that is done after the Christian faith has been accepted, whether in figure, and this is the unbelief of the Jews, or in the revelation of the very truth, and this is the unbelief of heretics. And so, broadly speaking these three may be reckoned as kinds of unbelief.[2]

The Thomist model operating here is at first sight very sophisticated. It is a universal account: it explains the Jews who rejected the figure, that is the 'shadow' Christianity which he believed was in the Old Testament, and foreshadowed the true revelation of Christ; it explains other religions who choose to fight against the revelation; and it explains the heretic who rejects the revelation of the truth despite having grown up with it. St Thomas believes that the root of resistance to the faith is human sinfulness. He accepts the logic of his position, so, although Jews and heathens should not be compelled to believe, because belief is always voluntary, 'the faithful, if they are able, should compel them not to hinder the faith by their blasphemies or evil persuasions or even open persecution. It is for this reason that Christ's faithful often wage war on infidels... [As for heretics and apostates] these are to be submitted to physical compulsion that they should hold to what they once received and fulfil what they promised.'[3]

This is only half of St Thomas' explanation: it is the human perspective, which sounds plausible enough. But the other explanation of disagreement is still very much within his world perspective. It is the doctrine of predestination. In short, the reason why some people disagree is because they are not chosen. So Aquinas writes, 'Some people God rejects. We have seen already that predestination is a part of providence, and that its working allows failures in the things in its charge. Since by divine providence human beings are ordained to eternal life, it also belongs to divine providence to allow some to fall short of this goal.'[4] So the ultimate answer to the problem of people disagreeing is simply this: they were not chosen. Now such a response is open to all sorts of objections. One might want to question the consistency of the Thomist world perspective and ask such questions as: how is predestination compatible with human freedom? And St Thomas was sensitive to these objections; his world perspective is not crude or obviously mistaken. He was aware of the existence of other religions, and does try to explain this fact.

The Thomist explanation for disagreement is ultimately a closed account of them. It is closed because the reasons people disagree are given as human sinfulness and God's divine predestination – a type of explanation present in many forms of Christianity and Islam. I take a closed explanation to be one where a single factor or group of factors within a world perspective are taken as the explanation for all disagreement. Now of course they vary in terms of sophistication, and, as has already been noted, the Thomist account is one of the most developed closed accounts of disagreements.

It might be objected that it is wrong to identify St Thomas' account of unbelief with an account of disagreement. After all, Plato and Aristotle were both pagans, but Aquinas considered it important to engage rationally with their work. There are two important remarks I must make in response to this objection. First, Plato (certainly) and Aristotle (slowly) had the special status of Christian pagans. St Thomas was already familiar with the range of Fathers who had interpreted Plato as a man who had foreseen the final revelation of God in Christ. They were not covered by his blanket explanation for pagans. Secondly, it is true that, despite these internal explanations of different traditions, certain influences over a long period from a different world perspective can be accommodated. Neither, moreover, was Aristotle put under the same heading as the Muslims. MacIntyre misrepresents the situation when he presents St Thomas primarily as an example of a man rationally engaging with two conflicting traditions.[5] The major problem for Aquinas was the existence of completely different religious traditions (namely, Judaism and Islam); it was from that perspective that he managed to synthesize the Augustinian and Aristotelian traditions. After all, the Augustinian and medieval Aristotelian traditions are both clearly Christian. This was a remarkable achievement; but, with this internal explanation for these different religions, St Thomas finds it difficult to accommodate Judaism and Islam. Although he does want to correct certain

Islamic interpretations of Aristotle, his only explanation for the existence of Judaism and Islam is to refer on the one hand to human sin, and on the other to predestination. This explanation makes it impossible for these traditions to be harmonized with Christianity.

Other world perspectives that provide closed explanations can be found in the more doctrinaire forms of politics: for example, where disagreements are interpreted solely in terms of protecting class interests. This crude, closed type of explanation is the explanation of the fanatic. From the Islamic fundamentalist to the revolutionary Marxist, the same closed account can be seen. Dialogue between two religious groupings with such a closed explanation for disagreements is virtually impossible. It is not that neither will listen to the other, but that each is interpreting the disagreement according to his own world perspective which has already provided the explanation of why people disagree with it. The irony here is that the explanation that they will be giving for each other probably will be very similar; both believe that the other is resisting the truth because of the other's sinfulness.

Many of my examples have been taken from very 'reactionary' forms of religion, and, although such religion provides an excellent example of closed accounts of disagreement, it is wrong to assume that the same tendency cannot be seen in more 'liberal' forms of religion and politics. Some evidence has arisen that many institutions in the American academy require a political orthodoxy that makes it very difficult for the conservatives (both politically and theologically) to contribute to the debate. 'Political correctness' is underpinned by an internal explanation for disagreement that dismisses all those who disagree with liberal, relativist assumptions as racist, sexist bigots. All closed explanations of disagreement lead to intolerance within that world perspective. This is true of both the intolerant fundamentalists and the liberals.

The orthodox religious accounts of disagreement are very unlikely to be true. First, they ignore the complexities of traditions, their own and that of others, in terms of their

historical and cultural development. Christianity captured
Europe, and Islam captured parts of the Middle East for
complicated historical reasons, largely beyond the control of
individuals. This makes any claim that one of these religions is
being wilfully sinful very implausible. Secondly, these closed
accounts ignore the similarities in terms of argument both for
belief and for each other. It is not simply ironic that two
religions agree in attributing the other's disagreement to
sinfulness; rather it reflects on the inadequacy of the description.
Any claim to sinfulness depends on identifying deliberate
intention to avoid the truth. The fact that both believe they
have the truth makes the explanation in terms of sinfulness
implausible. Thirdly, this closed account collapses when a
believer in one faith meets believers from a different religious
tradition. The sincerity, integrity, and goodness seen in believers
from a wide variety of traditions makes the closed account very
unlikely. If goodness comes from God, then goodness in a
different religious tradition must come from God.

Rationally, then, closed accounts are improbable. Historically, this discovery is the product of our post-Enlightenment
liberal tradition. It is partly due to our sensitivity to the ease
with which evidence can be deduced for different traditions,
and partly to the destruction of the closed accounts which opens
up the possibility of tolerance, in the hope of dialogue leading to
the truth. When the Enlightenment project for absolute
certainty failed, these closed accounts were seen as highly
improbable. *We now accept that absolute certainty about the nature of
the world is clearly unobtainable.* This has created the possibility of
an 'open account' for disagreement. An 'open account'
concedes the possibility that there may be truth in other world
perspectives that disagree. It is open because it recognizes the
tentative nature of human knowledge, and because it recom-
mends tolerance as a necessary means of ascertaining the truth
about the world. It is liberal, because it captures a thread most
liberals have had in common – that the world is open to a
variety of interpretations, and that God intended it to be so.
(This form of liberalism does not deny the possibility of discovery
of the truth, it just emphasizes the difficulties of knowing exactly

when one has discovered the truth. This places it in a world apart from a liberal, relativist, secularism with all its nihilistic dangers.) Open account of disagreements captures the complexity of the world, assesses the evidence with care, and makes enormous demands in terms of intellectual consistency.

These two different types of explanation – closed and open – for disagreement enable us to understand the problems with dialogue and the nature of commitment. The possibility of dialogue depends on an open account of disagreement. Two people with closed accounts of disagreement will produce the most intractable dispute. Such an exchange has already been described. Two people with open accounts of disagreements have the most potential for progress, because both parties assume that there must be *an element of truth in the other's world perspective*. Two people with differing accounts of disagreement will often leave one person interpreting the interest as evidence that conversion is possible; and the other, puzzled as to why there is so little understanding of her own position.

The nature of commitment is often justified by a closed account for disagreement. This internal explanation provides the necessary device that entitles one to be committed. Commitment to a tradition is partly shown by the attitude one has to different traditions that disagree. MacIntyre is right to define traditions within communities. And, when one appreciates that traditions arise from a historical context within a community, one also understands the nature of these internal explanations for different traditions. *They are devices that enable a community to retain its identity against other communities*. They are the means by which commitment is justified. In declaring the truth of one's own tradition and believing that other people in different traditions are simply being sinful, one is showing one's commitment. True faith requires the capacity to believe despite the opposition; this for most people is only possible when one has a fairly simple internal explanation for those who are opposing. Clearly, it is possible to think of different models of commitment, and some traditions are much more open than others. However, for the major theistic traditions in the West, these simple explanations for disagreement justify for most believers their commitment.

We can now understand why tolerance is such a problem for the major theistic traditions. Also we can see the theological task we have set ourselves. However, before developing this task, one further clarification is needed. It is possible that a closed explanation for a disagreement can be true. Indeed most people will have a world perspective made up of both closed and open elements. In deciding whether one accounts for another world perspective in an open or closed manner one should ask this simple question; is there any possibility that there could be an element of truth in this conflicting world perspective, or is it just completely wrong? So I have an open account when it comes to other religions, but have a closed account when it comes to an overtly racist or sexist world perspective. This is because I explain the racist as a person who holds an irrational prejudice against a group of people; this is a closed explanation for the racist. However, for reasons already stated, it is now very difficult for any Christian to use the traditional closed account to dismiss adherents in the other major religious traditions.

This closed explanation for disagreement provides the main impetus towards intolerance. After all, you do not 'tolerate' the sinful and evil. However, there have been other strands within the Christian traditions that appear more open to pluralism and tolerance. I shall start by examining three such arguments firmly embedded in the orthodox Christian tradition. I shall show that before the Enlightenment these arguments were not decisive, but that they must now be considered so. The point slowly emerges that the denial of these closed accounts for disagreement has a far-reaching effect.

1. *Jesus required his followers to 'love one another'. If you love one another you will tolerate one another.*
This looks fairly encouraging, after all, you do not kill those you are commanded to love. Unfortunately, historically we have ample evidence of Christians who felt able to love the heretic to death. One problem is that these positive sentiments in the New

Testament coexist with less loving sentiments. For example, consider how much anti-Semitism has been built on Jesus' irate attack on the Pharisees as described in Matthew 23: 'Woe to you, scribes and Pharisees, hypocrites.' Or the instruction in 2 John: 'Do not receive into the house or welcome anyone who comes to you and does not bring this teaching; for to welcome is to participate in the evil deeds of such a person' (2 John: 10). Historically, the church used these intolerant strands to provide the spectacles through which the loving sentiments were interpreted. The possibilities have been: love everybody except the heretic or sinner; love the sinner but do everything we can to confine (or stop) the sin; or in love for the sinner make it impossible for the sinner to carry on sinning. The last option might require killing, but, of course, better that than permitting the continuing blasphemy.

2. *It is always a sin to act against your own conscience.*
For St Thomas it is always a sin to act against your conscience. Now conscience for St Thomas is the individual's moral reasoning. Once one has decided what one thinks is right, one must then do it. It is always a sin to act against your conscience, even if in so doing you act rightly. One is guilty of sin because one did not believe that one was doing the good. This priority of conscience has certain positive implications for tolerance. Atheists or Muslims who disagree with the Christian account of reality ought to do this if their consciences tell them that their belief-systems are true. If they converted to Christianity without really believing it, they would be guilty of sin. Unfortunately, this strand in St Thomas is easily obscured. On the one hand, we are trusting people's report as to the state of their consciences. We have all heard people who imply that they thought an action was right, but really knew it was wrong. St Thomas believed that the Jew and Muslim were being wilfully sinful, so he did not permit the conscience argument to extend to them. And, on the other hand, even if a believer respects the conscience of those of other faiths, she might not want others contaminated. For the sake of children and friends, she might argue that a

vigorous form of censorship was necessary. Historically, these two considerations overcame St Thomas' argument for the toleration of conscience.

3. *Out of respect to God's sovereign saving activity and human freedom, people ought to be tolerated.*

This argument is implied in the New Testament and developed by some of the Reformers. The argument took two forms: God alone saves and therefore those people not fortunate enough to have the gift of faith should be prayed for until they are redeemed. Two, the gift of human freedom must be allowed to run its course, even if it is in rebellion against God.

These considerations were, unfortunately, often outweighed by the worry that the sinner, especially the sinner vocal in the public square, might prove very destructive. One could permit the quiet sinner, but the vocal one is just too risky. Remember that, from the perspective of eternal damnation, there is much at stake. It was believed that to tolerate one sinner, out of respect for her freedom, was very dangerous. Consider the following calculation: permit one free sinner and the result is twenty damned souls or censor the sinner and reduce the pernicious influence. Most Christians have opted for the latter. The unquestioned belief that hell would be the eternal destination of the unsaved soul partly explains why tolerance was very unpopular.

Due to the total disregard of these tolerant strands in the Christian tradition, the world needed the Enlightenment. David Hume, in his witty attack against belief, forced the church to discover the virtue of tolerance. Hume illustrated that the certainties, on which theism was based, were not that certain. In his *Dialogues Concerning Natural Religion* Hume showed that metaphysics is very difficult to justify. How can the theist exclude the hypothesis that perhaps God is not very powerful? Or that God was only responsible for a small section of the universe? It is by extension that one ends up with: Is the one true God corresponding with Allah, or Yahveh, or Krishna, or a Holy Trinity? Now David Hume was, in my judgment, needlessly skeptical. But he did expose a problem. Clearly, God has not made his revelation so utterly incontrovertible and incontestable. There are numerous conceptual possibilities (i.e., reasonable, metaphysical, logical possibilities). If God exists, then God has made his revelation deliberately tenebrous.

Now MacIntyre is right: Hume was making, quite literally, unreasonable epistemological conditions for a knowledge-claim. Hume found himself forced into skepticism by his method. He failed to appreciate that reasoning should not start from nowhere and be constructed for a 'traditioned-transcendent' individual. However, it is also true that Hume shattered any epistemological certainty for any single tradition. The temptation before Hume was to believe that one's tradition was simply self-evidently true – a complete description of the entire universe. Working with this assumption, the closed accounts of disagreement were much more plausible. However, Hume shows us that a particular culturally conditioned tradition to have the absolute truth is highly improbable: such a claim would require a 'tradition-transcendent' vantage point, which perhaps he was wrong to seek, but which he also proved could not exist. (It was also theologically inappropriate for, as I have already argued, God alone has the capability to know the absolute truth.) The cultural givenness of human activity makes the acquisition of knowledge a difficult task. This is not to surrender to cultural relativism, but to admit to a challenge which, for the theist, God has built into the universe.

I shall now outline three modern arguments for tolerance founded on Humean assumptions. We assume that God does not intend any tradition to have the absolute truth.

4. *Human sinfulness has affected religion.*
Keith Ward takes this line in his *Images of Eternity*. Ward writes:

It would be so easy to divide the world into the good and the bad: to say that all professing Muslims are saved and all unbelievers are damned. Believers do sometimes say that sort of thing: but it shows a remarkable lack of reflection on the compassion of God. For a start, there are thousands of different religious traditions, and many subdivisions even of the five main traditions I have considered here. In a world of sin and illusion, religion itself must partake of that illusory and sinful nature.[6]

Here Ward is bringing together a cluster of arguments. He appeals to the compassion of God, the diversity of traditions, and the fact of human sin. The steps from human sin to tolerance run as follows: humans are sinful, which implies that everything partakes in human sinfulness. Therefore we must be constantly humble and sensitive to the possibility of error. Therefore we ought to be tolerant. The idea that the Christian religion has been affected by sin is a modern one. It would have sounded improper to most Christians of past ages to say that God's revelation has been partially thwarted by human sin. However, Ward accepts that God has not produced an absolute incontrovertible revelation. This is to accept the insight of Hume, and assign the lack of incontrovertibility to the existence of sin.

5. *Until the eschaton, we cannot have complete certainty.*
This is Neuhaus' preferred argument. We saw that this sense of living in the 'now' for the 'not yet' is, Neuhaus believes, the meaning of the two-world doctrine. It acknowledges a dualism that sets itself against monism – the monism of the liberation theologians who believe that a certain political system is the kingdom of God; the monism of the pre-Vatican II Rome that believed that Christendom could be a Christian society; and the monism of those wanting a Christian America by taking biblical principles and imposing them on the rest of society. The two-kingdoms doctrine excludes all monisms because it concedes right at the outset that anything in this world will always at best be an approximation of the kingdom that will be fully realized only at the eschaton. Neuhaus writes:

Genuine democratic pluralism depends upon dualism. It depends on an acknowledgement that nobody has the correct fit between the ultimacies of God's self-revelation in Christ and the penultimacies of the ordering of our political life ... This means that public life, the ordering of the polis of the city of man, will always be for us an unsatisfactory business ... Politics is not only the art of the possible, as is commonly said; it is also the art of finding out what may be possible. It explores how the life of the polis, of the city of man, might be better ordered, more justly ordered. Indeed there is high adventure in it, with all the challenges required to fully occupy human capacities for courage and daring and imagination. And yet, after saying all that, politics is not satisfactory and never will be. It is second best. Everything is second best compared to the city from which we are born and to which our journey tends, the City of God.[7]

This is a strong argument. God alone knows the ideal human political framework and one day it will be realized. However, until then, the church must contribute to the public dialogue in appropriate humility, ready and willing to learn from others. Yet where Neuhaus would differ from Martin Luther is in the range of groups with which Neuhaus is willing to learn. Luther would not entertain dialogue with Jews.[8] Neuhaus requires more than just the two-kingdoms to justify this sort of pluralism. Luther's emphasis on the limited nature of our earthly pilgrimage would provide a basis of dialogue between the Christian sects, but why extend it to those opposed to the revelation of God in Christ?

6. *God desires freedom and dialogue hence the deliberately ambiguous nature of the world.*
Hick calls this the 'epistemic distance' between God and humanity.[9] God could have easily overridden our freedom by being blindingly obvious at every turn; so to protect our freedom we require a special set of circumstance which enables us to grow into maturity.

On this theory the very ambiguity of the world is intended as a challenge. God is calling us to live together, to understand, and to learn to love. It is part of our creatureliness that certainties are hard to come by. When we become too certain, we imagine that we are as God. This sin of hubris consists in the pretension that our partial insights are complete truths that need no connection or clarification from insights elsewhere. Such pretension is sheer arrogance, since only God can know with certainty the complete truth. Believers are called to offer our insights with a measure of humility, and with a genuine interest in the insights of others. On this view, dialogue is not an optional extra for theism, but a religious imperative.

A THEOLOGY OF GENUINE DEMOCRATIC PLURALISM

MacIntyre describes the Enlightenment project as a mistake – I want to describe it as a discovery. It is an insight – albeit rather ironical – into the truth of the human situation. For a Christian it can be described as a revelation. Hume showed us that our partial understanding of the universe does not entitle us to claim omniscience. Further it does not imply that God has not given insights about the universe to other cultures and traditions. Now the extent to which this post-Enlightenment insight transforms the nature of Christian faith is a crux of contemporary theological debate. I have argued that the affirmation of plurality depends on a recognition of our epistemological uncertainty. However, a Christian could still accept this and yet be relatively conservative. Humility is a very traditional virtue. Although God's revelation is not confined to Christianity, it remains possible that Jesus provides the definitive revelation. One can still talk about the authority of the Bible and the scandal of Christian particularity. It is wrong to insist that the affirmation of plurality depends upon accepting Hick's pluralist hypothesis;[10] a fairly conservative theology can be both tolerant and open.

Having said all that, there are certain problem areas for the more extreme conservative accounts. Much Christian intolerance has arisen from the conviction that to be saved from hell depends on the acceptance of Jesus as Lord.

The major calculation made by our Christian predecessors when reflecting on public affairs was the weighing of freedom for the heretic against damnation for the group influenced by the heretic. Given the certainty of hell, this appears extremely reasonable. However, most contemporary Christians are much less sure about the existence of hell. Our predecessors were mistaken in giving such significance to the small number of passages in the Bible that speak of eternal damnation. It was always a fairly awkward move from the Bible to Dante. In the Hebrew Bible, hell is not mentioned. The Jews had a shadowy underworld known as 'sheol', and some time after the exile started talking about the 'resurrection of the dead'. And in the New Testament, it is mainly Matthew, John, and the book of Revelation who are preoccupied with this theme. Matthew writes about 'Gehenna' which is derived from a rubbish tip outside Jerusalem; and John works with an opposition between the church and the world which along with the book of Revelation is more extreme than any other part of the Bible. It is a small foundation for such a large edifice. It was always misguided to place such extreme emphasis on this doctrine. This is not to say that the language does not capture any truth whatsoever. There might be some truth in the idea that God will not override the selfishness of a person who refuses to respond to love. But this is quite different from the idea that the devout Muslim or Jew is damned simply for not being a Christian. This form of the doctrine is a severe problem.

So there are good theological reasons why the church does not take the eternal destiny of unbelievers as the major consideration in public policy. Those who continue to emphasize the doctrine in their politics find themselves forced to intolerant positions. In the United Kingdom, schools have a legal obligation to bring pupils together for a time of worship. Those with a strong doctrine of hell would want Christian evangelists to have access, but deny the same right to the Muslims. It is difficult for certain communities to affirm genuine democratic pluralism when they believe that the other groups are misleading people to damnation. Interestingly, many Christians pay lip-service to the doctrine, but do not let it affect their relations with other communities. This is tantamount to surrendering the doctrine. It would be healthier if this was done overtly.

So then, aside from doctrines such as hell, which are in need of revision, a conservative theology *can* sustain plurality. There remains a plausibility problem. To keep alive literal talk about the imminent return of Jesus, or the inerrancy of scripture, maintains a world perspective that has been rendered implausible by our contemporary historical and biblical discoveries.

It is not my task in this book to explain why these traditional theological options are problematic. But I do want to illustrate ways in which more liberal theological options can provide interesting arguments for plurality.

Three such arguments are especially important. They all share the post-Enlightenment assumption that God has not given Christians complete certainty. The first argument stresses the universal elements of the Christian faith rather than the particularist claims. This can take a trinitarian form: God is the creator of the whole world, therefore he is active in the whole world; Jesus illuminates all human beings everywhere (John 1: 4, 9) and died for all; and the Holy Spirit is active throughout the world bringing knowledge of righteousness (John 16: 8).[11] These universal claims make it impossible to confine God's activity to ancient Israel, Jesus, and then the church. It is impossible to believe that the Triune God would ignore Africa, Asia, and the Americas for all this time and concentrate only on the middle East and Europe.[12]

A second argument emerges from our changed understanding of the Bible. No longer is the Bible a monolithic entity, dictated from God to humanity. Instead it has become an account of the human struggle to make sense of the divine. It has very little overtly about plurality and tolerance. Tolerance was not considered a virtue in the first century. As Houlden explains:

Nobody in first-century Judaism had a theory about the positive value of the existence of a plurality of voices among them, or saw the different practices of the Pharisees and the men of Qumran as fascinating complementary contributions to the richness of Jewish experience. Nor did the authorities feel that as long as you only squabbled about the Sabbath you were bound to be harmless. On the contrary, any issue might turn into a threat to social stability and thus to established power; and once that move had taken place, authority could afford only a violent response.[13]

Houlden finds the affirmation of plurality in an area which modern New Testament scholarship has opened up to us. We are fortunate to have three synoptic gospels which paint such different portraits of Jesus. Houlden explains that our good fortune is probably due to the distinguished authorship attributed to them, the limited circulation and lack of machinery to eliminate elements which might be disapproved of, and finally the inability of later writers to discern major theological differences between the gospels. Then Houlden writes: 'That Matthew and Luke wrote, at least in part, out of positive disapproval of Mark and other predecessors is overwhelmingly likely, and, in the case of Luke, explicit. Yet the diversity of testimony to Jesus survived, as we can now see inadvertently and by a misconception, for us to contemplate as exemplifying the theological pluriformity of first-century Christianity.'[14] What we have here is a 'biblical' argument for plurality. Preserved, however inadvertently, within the pages of the canon are major theological disagreements about the most fundamental questions of all. Who was Jesus? What was his message?[15] We can now see that to be truly biblical one should be truly open. One should engage with fundamental disagreements both inside and outside the community in a spirit of mutual respect and affirmation. This is clearly the spirit found in Matthew and Luke, for they both used and took issue with Mark.

The third argument is an appeal to the nature of love. Too often accounts of love have stressed the personal and individualistic. When it comes to plurality, love has a corporate nature; we need to see the link between individuals and cultural identity. Language, religion, rituals, and feelings cannot be disentangled. The Christian message stresses the link between love, identification, and pain: this is in part what the incarnation shows. George Carey makes a similar link between toleration and pain:

Genuine religious toleration is achieved when people hold their religion as so important, so absolute that to part from it is to die, and at the same time realize from their absolute centre of being that *another* person's values and beliefs are just as important and as real. That is the moment of genuine tolerance, because there is a cost *involved* in the act of tolerating another person's way of living and believing. The pain involved is not only in preserving inviolate one's own convictions but enduring the reality of the other person's, and, while deeply disagreeing, respecting them – with a consequent sharing of *their* pain as well as their own.[16]

Carey is right to stress the link between identity, culture, and beliefs. And true love is the recognition that what Christians feel about their faith is also true for those of other religions. Christians need to cultivate a strong sense of empathy and identification with different cultures.

So the discovery of tolerance grounded in the deliberately ambiguous creative activity of God is best located in a theology that can be defined legitimately as 'post-liberal'. It is liberal in the sense that it accepts that there is no unchanging central core to Christianity. All of our images develop as new information and knowledge is revealed. And it is 'post'-liberal in the sense that it is completely opposed to the relativist, subjectivist strand of much contemporary liberalism.

The American democratic experiment can take much of the credit for showing the world that it is possible to be committed to both truth and plurality. Tolerance is an American virtue affirmed in the First Amendment and celebrated in its cities. However, the church must not rest content with tolerance. Tolerance is good in that it is infinitely preferable to intolerance. But in certain forms tolerance can be very shallow. We need to move beyond tolerance, to active engagement and concern in the life of others, to dialogue, to collaborative truth-seeking and an enrichment of life through the insights of others. This is constructive plurality in the fullest sense, the kind that the Christian church must make central to its public proclamations in the world.

For the secularist in America to exclude religion from the public square is wrong for two reasons. First, the basis for rational dialogue in secularism is extremely weak. And second, religion in America is not a threat to plurality. Most of the religious traditions in America affirm plurality and are ready and willing both to offer and to receive religious insights for the ordering of public life. American culture needs the religious contribution.

Plurality and post-modernism

In attempting to explore the relationship between Christian ethics and plurality, we have examined many complex issues, from method in ethics to the theology of plurality. The problem was the fact of plurality and difference. We live in a world that is enormously diverse: different cultures reflecting different languages, different rituals, and different metaphysical accounts. For those committed to a world perspective that claims to explain the nature of ultimate reality, all this diversity has posed a problem. If one tradition has the truth, why don't others recognize it? And how do we stop others leading people into error?

The argument of this book is that there is now a new way of looking at this diversity. Instead of viewing plurality as a threat to be overcome, it should be viewed as a challenge requiring engagement. While the European experience continues to stress the need for a unitary culture, the American experience has opened up a new approach. America was the haven for minorities. Diversity and difference were part of the American experience right from the start. For Americans, plurality is a fact to be welcomed.

In many ways this is a post-modern book. The term is contentious: for much post-modernism has anti-realist connotations of relativism and subjectivism. However, in a more general sense, post-modernism is a movement that claims we are on the verge of a new way of looking at the world: one that moves beyond the uniformity of secular modernity to the diversity of a post-modern society.

For pre-moderns, the ideal was a unitary culture. This meant a Christian culture, speaking the same universal language, sharing the same values, living in harmony, with a clear and shared 'idea'. The culture was formed around the highest common denominator – a metaphysical ideal – that suggested a hierarchy from God, to king, to the people. Each was given an appropriate part to play.

For modernists also, the ideal was a unitary culture. This meant a culture built on science, secularism, and liberal rationality. Religion was an outmoded superstition that needed to be controlled. It was permitted provided that it remained private and personal. But ultimately the great secular hope was that religion would slowly wither and fade away. Here the values had to be non-religious, and united around the lowest common denominators of economic life and production.

For modernity, the debate on plurality was confined to the limits of integration. The tolerant strand argued that people could adapt and integrate into a culture; the less tolerant strand argued that this was only possible very gradually and over a long period of time. Both parties in this debate presupposed that a unitary culture was the ideal. Too much diversity in a nation cannot be accommodated. Difference was threatening; assimilation was the only way forward.

The most powerful argument of the secular modernists was tolerance. It was believed that secularism was the only framework in which freedom of expression could be protected. Two Muslim scholars, Sardar and Davies, capture both the sentiments and problems of modernism:

One of the most pernicious myths of modern times is that freedom of expression can only be guaranteed by a secular worldview. The corollary is that all traditional cultures enslave the individual in their social and cultural environments; it is modernization that has brought mankind liberation from social bondage and genuine freedom. To be modern is to be a free individual, to be unattached to the compulsion of anything sacred, to be indifferent to traditional and social customs, to be free to express oneself when and as one likes, to ridicule and abuse as one wishes. This freedom, however, is only an illusion. It is a freedom that ensures the silence of other points of view, for their expression is to invite ridicule or that uncomprehending raise of the eyebrow that asks, 'Can there really be people who think like that in this day and age?' It is not that there is no freedom to differ, just that those who demur from secularism have attained merely the freedom to be unheard and to become invisible. It is a freedom that has bred apologia, where those who differ must grovel for a quizzical hearing on the terms set down for them, terms that deny the validity and meaning of what they have to express. It is a freedom that enslaves others to ensure the freedom of a select few.[1]

In the battle between these two creeds many Christians felt that the only legitimate opposition to a secular 'idea' was a Christian 'idea'. As we saw with the Christendom Group, this was the nature of the British debate over plurality.

For post-moderns, the ideal requires the affirmation of difference. This envisages nations made up of different communities, speaking different languages, having different histories, bringing different experiences to the common life. And the political vision proposed does not require that everyone surrender their culture, past, and language, but asks that while everyone affirm their own culture, they also permit others to do the same.

There is a political proposal underpinning this book. The post-modern proposal requires a policy of political enrichment, which involves both separateness and engagement.

THE POLITICAL PROPOSAL

Instead of a unitary culture where one language, one religion, one history, and one set of images dominate, we need a diverse culture where different languages, many religions, several narratives and images coexist in stimulating tension. Let us welcome the diversity of foods, the different religious options, and the variety of perspectives. Instead of the schools and media promulgating one 'idea', let different communities articulate different 'ideas'. In short what we need is a policy of *cultural enrichment*.

Cultural enrichment requires three different processes. First, we must develop the separateness of each community. We should empower communities to create the space for their tradition to be affirmed. Once one sees that faith is grounded in communities that have a history and language, then tolerance requires support for these communities. Such communities need the space to protect their history and language.

The second process within cultural enrichment is that of community engagement, implying dialogue, disagreement, and a mutual exploration of truth. We have to learn to live in many communities. We cannot remain monolingual, but will have to become bilingual or even trilingual. Each person will live in several communities, moving between them and feeding on the differences in language, history, habits, and religion.

The third process is that of faith communities discovering their voice within the public square. Public policy requires the moral dimension. Much of this book has stressed the dangers of the moral contribution being excluded from public debate. The proposed decentralized power to these different communities does not entail a complete *carte blanche* being given. For example, no community would be permitted to hold or keep slaves. A consensus in western Europe and America has agreed that slavery is a fundamental indignity to the image of God within each person. People are not to be treated as commodities owned and used at will. Slavery would not have been abolished without such moral insights. And those who argue that such moral considerations extend to the unborn child need to be taken seriously.

This is not the place for an extended discussion of the abortion issue. Suffice it to say, the campaign against abortion is not incompatible with the general affirmation of a tolerant and pluralistic society. What this debate needs is a thoughtful examination of the moral issues. The logic of the secularist excludes moral considerations from the agenda. The matter is often reduced to a question of formulations to enable coexistence between competing 'opinions' on abortion. In Roe v. Wade the issue is simply one of power between the states and the centre. Moral questions are not directly relevant.

The abortion debate needs a moral vocabulary that the religious traditions can provide. As Hunter in his excellent *Culture Wars* shows, a significant spectrum of positions is taken within religious communities. The debates within and between religious communities ought to provide powerful witness to the way in which moral questions can be raised and resolved. Sadly, this is often not the case. All too often churches reduce debates to the political manœuvring of the proposers and opposers of motions.

Yet there are encouraging signs. Hunter reports on, what he calls, 'the new ecumenism'. This 'new ecumenism' is 'the cooperative mobilization, in which distinct and separate religious and moral traditions share resources and work together toward common objectives'.[2] As Hunter shows, Roman Catholic and Protestant groups link up with Jewish and Muslim groups to form alliances on certain moral issues. From these cross-community alliances a new moral consensus might emerge: a consensus that confronts the moral issues embedded in the debates surrounding such issues as abortion, race, and the environment.

THE THEOLOGICAL FOUNDATION

Theologically, cultural enrichment is grounded in the God who welcomes diversity. It is a God who created the planet with immense diversity; it is a God who demands respect for persons especially if they disagree with you. The fact is God has deliberately created the world in such a way that the truth is not obvious. God has given each one of us a perspective that makes it very difficult to see the truth. All our perspectives are limited, partial, and incomplete. God has done this because he welcomes the fact that we are forced to supplement our perspective with the perspectives of others.

The theology that underpins this book affirms plurality because God intended it. God requires that as an expression of love we learn the lesson of humility and the need for dialogue.

CONCLUSION

The substance of the study has concentrated on two claims, one philosophical and the other historical.

The philosophical claim attempts to illustrate that the

contemporary threats to plurality do not come from religion, but from secularism. The secularist, who has given up the quest for truth and therefore moral debate and rational dialogue, is the greater danger to tolerance. A religious foundation for tolerance is grounded in the reality of God that ensures the intelligibility of the universe. This foundation is the only effective antidote to secular reason, which cannot avoid the dangers of nihilism. Truth-claims depend upon the conviction that the universe is intelligible, and that in turn depends upon belief in God.

The subsidiary historical claim is that the United States has made a cultural discovery. It has found good religious reasons why we ought to affirm plurality. The British debate about plurality is still firmly rooted within the confines of pre-modernity and modernity. However, the nation of immigrants was forced, right from the start, to engage with plurality. And slowly a culture emerged that was both religious and tolerant. This led some to suggest that America had created a new religion – civil religion, whereas in fact Christians, Jews, and Muslims were discovering the importance of plurality. Despite all the problems in America, much of its success can be attributed to this remarkable cultural discovery.[3] In this sense Americans are post-modern.

This discovery, as with all important discoveries, has come the hard way. It is easy to find examples of American intolerance. Yet, despite the tensions provoked by such diverse religious and racial groups, Americans should take pride in the general ethos of their culture.

So to sum up: we started with the secularist challenge. Religion must be confined to the personal and private because it is intolerant; it cannot cope with plurality. We explored the British response that wanted to reject this secular unitary culture and replace it with a Christian unitary culture. This is a debate tied to the confines of modernity and pre-modernity. In the States a different outlook emerged. Here religious communities have sound religious reasons for affirming plurality. The foundation of this religious tolerance is much stronger than the secular foundations. It offers a new vision for nations. Instead of forcing minority cultures to fit in around the majority culture, we create the space for cultural enrichment: for cultures separate, yet linked; self-confident, yet in dialogue.

No longer need the churches feel defensive on the issue of tolerance. Christians can join the debate in the public square confident that our contribution is desperately needed. We have gone from plurality as a problem, to plurality as a providentially intended part of God's creatorial design. We have gone from plurality as a threat, to plurality as God's method for teaching us about the appropriate way to live.

Notes

INTRODUCTION: THE SECULARIST CHALLENGE

1 It is worth noting that this picture of unrelenting decline in church attendance in Britain has recently been challenged by Robin Gill in *Moral Communities* (Exeter: University of Exeter Press 1992), pp.44–8.
2 The current English usage of 'civility' is politeness. I am using civility in the older sense to mean behaving in ways appropriate for a citizen. In the classical sense a civilization needed its citizens to participate in the running of the social structures. The argument of this book is that the sense of mutual respect and participation can be best protected by an engagement with religious and moral dispositions.

I PLURALITY AND SECULARISM

1 For John Hick, see *The Interpretation of Religion* (Basingstoke: Macmillan 1989).
2 Within the Christian theology of other religions, exclusivism is the view that conscious knowledge of God's saving activity in Christ is essential for salvation. Inclusivism believes that all salvation is through Christ, although not confined to those who consciously accept.
3 For an excellent discussion of the meaning of toleration see Bernard Crick, *Political Theory and Practice* (London: Penguin 1972), chpt. 3.
4 Marcuse in Wolff, Marcuse, and Moore, *A Critique of Pure Tolerance* (Boston: Beacon Press 1965), p. 84. To be fair to Marcuse, tolerance is sometimes used to mean 'permission', and such permission is exercised when one turns 'a blind eye' or fails to recognize injustice. However, this meaning of tolerance needs to be sharply differentiated from the meaning I am advocating. It is not appropriate to link the achievement of tolerance between two

groups strongly opposed towards each other, with this inadvertent permission.

5 I shall not discuss Spinoza further, even though he defends toleration fifteen years before Locke's first *Letter Concerning Toleration*. His argument had less impact and rests on rather peculiar interpretations of natural law and natural right.

6 See John Plamenatz's excellent discussion in *Man and Society* (Harlow: Longman 1963), 1, pp. 70–6.

7 To start with Augustine was fairly tolerant, but then he changed his policy. He provides a good illustration of how pragmatic defences of tolerance are inherently weak. For an excellent discussion see John Rohr, 'Religious Toleration in St. Augustine', in *Journal of Church and State* 9 (1967), 51–70.

8 See Charlesworth, *Church, State, and Conscience*, (St. Lucia 1973), chpt. 1.

9 Although the Reformers themselves were generally intolerant, they did provoke the issue of tolerance. And, as I shall discuss further in chapter nine, the early Luther did argue that compelling one to believe was impossible, because you cannot compel a human heart.

10 A. J. Ayer, 'Sources of Intolerance', in Mendus and Edwards (eds.), *On Toleration* (Oxford: Clarendon Press 1987), p. 83.

11 For a good discussion of Locke's arguments on toleration see Maurice Cranston, 'John Locke and the Case for Toleration' in Mendus and Edwards, *On Toleration*. For a good general introduction to Locke see Maurice Cranston, *John Locke: a Biography* (Oxford: Oxford University Press 1985).

12 Cranston in *John Locke: a Biography* argues that Locke's primary purpose in the *Two Treatises* is to answer Filmer's polemic, *Patriarcha*.

13 Everyone agrees that the idea of 'tacit consent' is problematic. For an excellent discussion see Charles Beitz, 'Tacit Consent and Property Rights', in *Political Theory*, 8 (1980), 487–502.

14 It should be noted that, for Locke, it is only the propertied individuals who matter. The rest are subsumed under their property-owning employers or masters. Locke's real concern is with the seventeenth-century issue of establishing the rights of the propertied not to have their wealth interfered with (e.g. by taxation) without their consent (e.g. by the arbitary exercise of royal favour).

15 In Britain homosexuality became the issue in the Hart/Devlin debate which is superbly discussed in B. Mitchell, *Law, Morality,*

and Religion in a Secular Society (Oxford: Oxford University Press 1970).

16 For David Hume see the marvellous way that Philo speculates on metaphysical possibilities in *Dialogues Concerning Natural Religion* (London: Hafner Press 1948). For a good and balanced report on the kinship between scepticism and toleration in the seventeenth century see Richard Tuck, 'Scepticism and toleration in the seventeenth century' in Mendus (ed.), *Justifying Toleration* (Cambridge: Cambridge University Press 1988), chpt. 1.

17 C. L. Ten, *Mill on Liberty* (Oxford: Oxford University Press 1980), p. 124.

18 J. S. Mill, *On Liberty* (Harmondsworth: Penguin 1974), p. 81.

19 C. L. Ten, *Mill on Liberty*, p.126. Italics mine.

20 See Michael Creuzet, *Toleration and Liberalism* (Chulmleigh: Augustine 1979).

21 See for example Richard Morgan, 'Religious and Social Tolerance', in *Churchman*, 99 (1985), 234f.

2 PLURALITY, CULTURE, AND METHOD

1 See Karl Barth, *Church Dogmatics* (Edinburgh: T. and T. Clark 1936–77), II/2 and III/4 for Barth's most sustained discussion of ethical questions. It is my impression that Barth was in practice much more involved in political and social questions than one would expect from his theology.

2 I do not intend to discuss the middle axioms proposal. Too often this appeared to ignore the cultural dimension, and simply treat ethics as the problem of theological principles and application. For middle axioms see R. Preston, *Explorations in Theology 9* (London: SCM Press 1981), chpt. 3.

3 For Denys Munby see *Christianity and Economic Problems* (London: Staples Press 1969). For Ronald Preston see his evaluation of V. A. Demant in R. Preston, *Religion and the Persistence of Capitalism* (London: SCM Press 1979).

4 Richard Niebuhr, *Christ and Culture* (New York: Harper and Row 1951), p. 32.

5 Richard John Neuhaus, *The Catholic Moment* (San Francisco: Harper and Row 1987).

6 See Stanley Hauerwas, *A Community of Character* (Notre Dame: University of Notre Dame Press 1981) especially chpt. 5.

7 With due apologies to all Canadians, all references to America will refer to the United States. For Richard John Neuhaus see, *The Naked Public Square* (Michigan: Eerdmans 1984).

8 For Alasdair MacIntyre see *After Virtue* (London: Duckworth

1988). MacIntyre probably would not describe himself as a Christian ethicist, but plenty of ethicists who are christians are using his work.

9 As Berke shows if one judges Reinhold Niebuhr's practical, political judgments by recent history, especially the 1989 revolution in Eastern Europe, then many of his judgments are vindicated. See Matthew Berke, 'The Disputed Legacy of Reinhold Niebuhr', in *First Things* (November 1992) 37–42.

10 For a good recent study on Reinhold Niebuhr see K. Durkin, *Reinhold Niebuhr* (London: Geoffrey Chapman 1989).

11 See J. Fletcher, *Situation Ethics* (London: SCM Press 1966).

12 R. Niebuhr, *The Children of Light and the Children of Darkness* (London: Nisbet and Co. 1945), p. 88.

13 R. Niebuhr, *The Children of Light and the Children of Darkness*, p.93

14 Ibid., p. 94.

15 Ibid.

16 Ibid., p. 95.

17 For a good discussion see R. J. Neuhaus, 'Why Wait for the Kingdom? The Theonomist Temptation', in *First Things*, (May 1990) 13–21.

3 PLURALITY AND THE CHRISTENDOM GROUP

1 See C.Gore introduced *The Return of Christendom*, By a group of Churchmen. (London: 1922).

2 Alan Porter (ed.) *Coal; A Challenge to the Nation's Conscience* (London: Hogath Press 1927). V. A. Demant, *The Miners Distress and the Coal Problem* (London: SCM Press 1929); and J. V. Delahaye (ed.), *Politics: A Discussion of Realities* (London: C. W. Dent 1924).

3 See R. Kojecky, *T. S. Eliot's Social Criticism* (London: Faber and Faber 1971), p. 171f. The minutes included the bracket.

4 Letter is reprinted in T. S. Eliot, *The Idea of a Christian Society*, 2nd edition (London: Faber and Faber 1982), pp. 97–8. Alex Vidler also a member of the Moot group wrote *God's Judgement on Europe* (London: Longmans 1940) at about the same time. This book follows very closely V. A. Demant's argument in *The Religious Prospect* (London: Muller 1939).

5 See Adrian Hastings who makes this point extremely well in *A History of English Christianity 1920–1985* (London: Collins 1986). For the history of the Tractarians and Christian Socialists see O. Chadwick, *The Victorian Church* (London: Adam and Charles Black 1970), ii, chpt. 5, sections 4 and 8.

6 See E. Mascall, *He who is: a Study in Traditional Theism* (London: Darton, Longman and Todd 1966).

7 The unpublished sermons are held by his son Jocelyn Demant at Headington, Oxford.

8 Maritain's study, *True Humanism* (London: Century Press 1939) provoked considerable interest in the United Kingdom; and for Dawson see Beyond Politics (London: Sheed and Ward 1939).

9 V. A. Demant, *God, Man, and Society* (London: SCM Press 1933), p. 42.

10 This is found scattered throughout Demant's writings. Probably the most systematic statement is his Malvern lecture which he published in *Theology of Society* (London: Faber and Faber 1947), p. 75f.

11 T. S. Eliot, *The Idea of a Christian Society*, p. 41

12 Ibid., p. 80.

13 For Dawson see, *Religion and the Rise of Western Culture* (London: Sheed and Ward 1950); for Maritain see, *True Humanism*.

14 Demant had considerable difficulty with the appropriate terminology. 'Dogmas' are normally conscious and explicit. Elsewhere he suggested 'aims' and 'assumptions', but, as the bulk of this argument is taken from *The Religious Prospect* (London: Muller 1939), I have retained this terminology.

15 V. A. Demant, *The Religious Prospect*, p. 29.

16 Ibid., p. 57.

17 V. A. Demant, *God, Man, and Society*, p. 162.

18 Ibid., p. 162.

19 Demant's interpretation of Kant is contentious. In one sense Kant's entire system was an attempt to refute David Hume and justify objective truth. All Demant means here is that ultimate truth resides in the noumenal world which is inaccessible.

20 Ibid., p. 163.

21 V. A. Demant, *The Religious Prospect*, p. 57.

22 All three quoted by Demant. Ibid., p. 38.

23 Ibid., p. 13.

4 THE TOTALITY OF THE CHRISTIAN NARRATIVE: CAPITALISM AND ECOLOGY

1 V. A. Demant, *Religion and the Decline of Capitalism* (London: Faber and Faber 1952), p. 20.

2 Ibid., p. 23.

3 Ibid., p. 48.

4 Ibid., p. 22.

5 See R. H. Preston, *Church and Society in the Late Twentieth-Century: the Economic and Political Task* (London: SCM Press 1983), p. 40–5, for a very clear account of the nature and origin of the market economy.

6 V. A. Demant, *Religion and the Decline of Capitalism*, p. 22.

7 Ibid., p. 31.

8 Ibid., p. 34.

9 Ibid., p. 48.

10 Ibid., p. 147.

11 Ibid., p. 89.

12 Ibid., p. 95.

13 Ibid., p. 102.

14 Ibid., p. 102.

15 Ibid., p. 173.

16 The article was commissioned by Professor Gordon Dunstan for a proposed, but never published, *Dictionary of Business Ethics*. Dunstan wrote to Demant on 24 April 1980. Copies are held by Professor Dunstan and Jocelyn Demant at Headington.

17 T. S. Eliot, *The Idea of a Christian Society* 2nd edition (London: Faber and Faber 1982), p. 80.

18 For guild socialism see, M. B. Reckitt and C. E. Bechhofer, *The Meaning of National Guilds* (London: Cecil Palmer 1920). The best-known theologian supporter was Jacques Maritain.

19 A. J. Penty in 'Has Machinery Causal Importance?' in *Christendom* (October 1925), 272f.

20 T. S. Eliot, *The Idea of a Christian Society*, p. 62.

21 V. A. Demant, *Christian Sex Ethics* (London: Hodder and Stoughton 1963), p. 116.

22 See for example T. S. Eliot, 'Education in a Christian Society' in the *Supplement to the Christian News-Letter*, 13 March 1940, reprinted in *The Idea of a Christian Society*. p. 140f.

5 PLURALITY AND CONTEMPORARY BRITISH CHRISTIAN ETHICS

1 For Preston's main discussion of Demant see *Religion and the Persistence of Capitalism* (London: SCM Press 1979), pp. 13–16. Preston and Munby are in complete agreement on the economic weaknesses of Demant *et al.* Munby's criticisms of Demant are found in *Christianity and Economic Problems* (London: Staples Press 1969), p. 283f.

2 R. Preston, 'The Malvern Conference', in *The Modern Churchman* (1942), 16. The Malvern Conference, convened by William

Temple in 1941, provided the Christendom Group with a major platform to propagate their analysis of society.

3 Ibid., p. 19.

4 See Preston's discussion in *Church and Society in the late Twentieth Century: the Economic and Political Task* (London: SCM Press 1983), p. 34f.

5 R. Preston, *Religion and the Persistence of Capitalism*, p. 14.

6 Ibid., p. 15.

7 For example, see E. J. Mishan, *The Costs of Economic Growth* (London: Staples Press 1967), p. 127f.

8 D. L. Munby, *The Idea of a Secular Society* (London: Oxford University Press 1963), p. 14.

9 Ibid., p. 17.

10 Ibid., p. 21.

11 Ibid., p. 27.

12 Ibid., p. 30.

13 It is important to note that Munby was a strong advocate of welfare provision by the state. So by minimum I mean the extent of ethical imposition by the state. Munby is an economic interventionist, but a social liberal. He supported the National Health Service, but opposed the restrictions of trade on a Sunday. It is interesting that during this century western states have taken more intervention on themselves (welfare, education, transport etc.), but ceased to impose a metaphysic as religion. Precisely the reverse of the tendency of the Middle Ages right up to the nineteenth century.

14 The problem with this liberal confidence in objective reason has been exposed by Alasdair MacIntyre in *After Virtue* 2nd edition (London: Duckworth 1985). I discuss this work and these issues further in chapter 8.

15 For a good biography of Powell, see Andrew Roth, *Enoch Powell: Tory Tribune* (London: Macdonald 1971). For an excellent study of the impact of Powell on the British political scene see Douglas Schoen, *Enoch Powell and the Powellites* (London: Macmillan 1977). He suggests that Powell's position on political questions might have had a decisive effect on two general elections.

16 For the text of the speech see T. E. Utley, *Enoch Powell: the Man and his Thinking* (London: William Kimber 1968), pp. 178–90.

17 For an excellent defence of this view see Roger Scruton, *The Meaning of Conservatism* (London: Penguin 1980).

18 Communitarian is the term preferred in the United States. This emphasis on community in opposition to liberal individualism has been taken up by many not wanting to identify with the Conservativism of Enoch Powell.

19 See J. E. Powell, *Still to Decide* (Kingswood: Elliot Right Way Books 1972), p. 170f.

20 Ibid., p. 172.

21 Edmund Burke is probably the more explicit ideological ancestor of Powell. However, Hooker provides the more overtly religious account of society, so I shall concentrate on Hooker.

22 J. E. Powell, *Still to Decide*, p. 190.

23 Ibid., p. 202f.

24 Ibid., p. 204.

25 Some of these television and radio debates with Powell are found in Enoch Powell, *No Easy Answers* (London: Sheldon Press 1973). See especially the debates with Trevor Huddleston and Douglas Brown. Thirteen debates have been held in the Church of England Synod from the 6th November 1969 to 11th November 1981. The bulk of the debates focused on three Acts of Parliament. They were the 1970 Race Relations Act, the 1971 Commonwealth Immigrants Act, and the 1981 British Nationality Act.

26 T. Huddleston as found in E. Powell, *No Easy Answers*, p. 106.

27 Ibid., p. 101.

28 Speech by Enoch Powell in April 1968 reprinted in T. E. Utley, *Enoch Powell*, p. 188.

29 Andrew Roth, *Enoch Powell* p. 341.

30 Ibid., p. 341.

31 The best sustained treatment of events up until September 1989 is D. Pipes, *The Rushdie Affair* (New York: Birch Lane Press 1990). Much of the account that follows has been taken from D. Pipes.

32 The precise motives of the ayatollah are the subject of much dispute. I am persuaded by Daniel Pipes that he did not respond earlier because he did not know about the book. Furthermore, it was not political factors that provoked the *fatwa*, but his religious convictions that apostasy and blasphemy must be punished. For D. Pipes see *The Rushdie Affair*, pp. 87–104.

33 See L. Appignanesi and S. Maitland (eds.), *The Rushdie File* (London: Fourth Estate Ltd. 1989), p. 100. See also p. 27.

34 For an excellent and very fair analysis of this article, see R. Webster *A Brief History of Blasphemy: Liberalism, Censorship and 'The Satanic Verses'* (Southwold: The Orwell Press 1990), pp. 85–103.

35 The difficulties with this conversion are outlined by M. Ahsan and A. Kidwai (eds.) in *Sacrilege versus Civility. Muslim Perspectives on 'The Satanic Verses' Affair* (Leicester: The Islamic Foundations 1991), pp. 45–52.

36 D. Pipes, *The Rushdie Affair* p. 54.

37 Despite Rushdie's denial in the *International Herald Tribune*, 18–19 February 1989, cited in Z. Sardar and M. W. Davies,

Distorted Imagination: Lessons from the Rushdie Affair (London: Grey Seal Books 1990), p. 187.

38 The argument revolves around the reliability of the classical Muslim historian al-Tabari (d. 923). He is the source of the story. Sardar and Davies in *Distorted Imagination* provide the case against, while some western scholars, operating on the principle that it is such an unlikely story that no one would invent it unless there was a basis in fact, believe that it is likely to be authentic.

39 Rushdie does mitigate this impression in places, not least by the device of a dream. But the hypothesis is suggested, which to devout Muslims is bound to cause upset.

40 Ali A. Maxrui, *The Satanic Verses or a Satanic Novel? The Moral Dilemmas of the Rushdie Affair* (New York: Greenpoint Committee of Muslim Scholars and Leaders of North America 1989), p. 13.

41 'Limits of Tolerance', in The *Daily Telegraph*, 6 February 1990.

42 Letter from Bishop L. Newbigin in *The Independent*, 21 February 1989. Reprinted in Ahsan and Kidwai, *Sacrilege versus Civility*.

43 It was banned, for example, from Cornwall. For Richard Webster's discussion see *A Brief History of Blasphemy*, chap. 1. Ahsan and Kidwai also cite the controversy over *American Psycho* by B. E. Ellis which has offended feminists in the States. Ahsan and Kidwai, *Sacrilege versus Civility*, p. 40.

44 Fay Weldon as cited in Sardar and Davies, *Distorted Imagination*, p. 228.

45 The Star, 21 February 1989, cited in M. Ruthven, *A Satanic Affair. Salman Rushdie and the Rage of Islam* (London: Chatto and Windus 1990), p. 120.

46 Z. Sardar and M. W. Davies, *Distorted Imagination*, p. 88.

47 *The Independent on Sunday*, 11 February 1990, as cited by G. D'Costa, 'Secular Discourse and the Clash of Faiths: "The Satanic Verses" in British Society', in *New Blackfriars* (October 1990), 425f.

48 D. Pipes, *The Rushdie Affair* p. 220f.

49 St Thomas, *Summa Theologica*, 2a.2ae, Question 11, article 3, translated by Thomas Gilby xxxii, (London: Blackfriars 1975), p. 89.

50 Al Azhar, the oldest Muslim institution in the world, took this line. For a good discussion of these issues see Sardar and Davies, *Distorted Imagination*, chap. 7.

51 *The Independent*, 22 February 1989. In 1990 he appeared to change his mind.

52 G. D'Costa, 'Secular Discourse and the Clash of Faiths: "The Satanic Verses" in British Society', in *New Blackfriars* (October 1990), 430.

53 Julie Flint, *The Observer*, 11 February 1990, as cited by Richard Webster, *A Brief History of Blasphemy*, p. 107.
54 Sardar and Davies, *Distorted Imagination*, p. 242.
55 Ibid., p. 273.
56 The best contributions came from Gavin D'Costa, Lesslie Newbigin, and Michael Dummett.
57 See, for example, the essays in S. Lee, *Law, Blasphemy and the Multi-Faith Society: Report of a Seminar* (London: Commission for Racial Equality, 1990).

6 PLURALITY AND THE AMERICAN EXPERIENCE

1 There is a major problem here which requires ongoing reflection. The native American experience can easily feel excluded from the main 'white European' narrative. For a good discussion of this see David Chidester, *Patterns of Power. Religion and Politics in American Culture* (New Jersey: Prentice Hall 1988), chpt. 4.
2 John Winthrop, 'A Modell of Christian Charity' from the *Winthrop Papers*, (Boston: The Massachusetts Historical Society 1931), II 40–3.
3 John Rolfe, 'A Relation of the State of Virginia 1616', cited in David Chidester, *Patterns of Power*, p. 18.
4 David Chidester, *Patterns of Power*, p. 20.
5 See Ruth Block, 'Religion and Ideological Change in the American Revolution' in Mark Noll (ed.), *Religion and American Politics. From the Colonial Period to the 1980s* (New York: Oxford University Press 1990), p. 48. She illustrates how important this covenantal terminology was at the time of the revolution.
6 Historians disagree over the validity of the label 'deism' to describe the faith of the founders. Please note there was considerable variety amongst the founders. Although in general the belief in a designer providing a basis for morals is a theme of the deists, the belief in providence is not. I shall retain the term as it does capture the different emphasis from the more Puritan strands of American religion.
7 John Murrin, 'Religion and Politics in America from the First Settlements to the Civil War', in Mark Noll (ed.), *Religion and American Politics*, p. 31.
8 Most European forms of deism did not believe in providence. For a good discussion see Peter Byrne, *Natural Religion and the Nature of Religion* (London: Routledge 1989).
9 For a good account of Washington's beliefs see R. Pierard and R. Linder, *Civil Religion and the Presidency* (Grand Rapids: Academie Books 1988), chpt. 3.

10 John F. Wilson, 'Religion, Government and Power in the New American Nation', in M. Noll (ed.) *Religion and American Politics*, p. 84.

11 Supreme Court, Everson v. Board of Education (1947).

12 This point is nicely illustrated by H. Stout in Mark Noll (ed.) *Religion and American Politics*, p. 62f.

13 This is usefully described in David Chidester, *Patterns of Power*, p. 142. See also F. Colombo, *God in America. Religion and Politics in the United States* (New York: Columbia University Press 1984), pp. 17–27.

14 James Reichley, 'Religion in American Public Life', in Mark Noll (ed.), *Religion and American Politics*, p. 203.

15 Ibid., p. 203.

16 Ibid., p. 204. The most moving description of this is found in E. D. Genovese, *Roll, Jordan, Roll: The World The Slaves Made* (New York: Pantheon Books 1974). For a good critique of Genovese see King's article in A. Weinstein, F. O. Gatell, and D. Sarasotin (eds.) *African Negro Slavery. A Modern Reader* (New York: Oxford University Press 1979).

17 See Reichley in Mark Noll (ed.), *Religion and American Politics,*. p. 212.

18 For example, some Christians linked the black with descendants of Ham, condemned by God to be servants of servants. (Genesis 9: 18–27).

19 Robert Bellah, *The Broken Covenant: American Civil Religion in Time of Trial* (New York: Crossroads 1975), p. 52.

20 Pierard and Linder, *Civil Religion and the Presidency*, p. 112.

21 This is especially true since Everson (1947).

22 R. Bellah in Richey and Jones (eds.) *American Civil Religion* (New York: Harper and Row 1974), p. 256.

23 See Herberg in Richey and Jones (eds.) *American Civil Religion*, p. 76f.

24 For a very readable survey of presidents and civil religion see Pierard and Linder, *Civil Religion and the Presidency*.

25 W. Lloyd Warner in Richey and Jones (eds.), *American Civil Religion*, p. 96.

26 Ibid., p.14.

27 For example, one of the most interesting is M. W. Hughey, *Civil Religion and Moral Order Theoretical and Historical Dimensions* (Westport: Greenwood Press 1983). He argues that Bellah is making inappropriate Durkheimian assumptions.

28 G. A. Kelly, *Politics and Religious Consciousness in America* (New Brunswock: Transaction Books 1984), p. 242.

29 See Moltmann in Rouner (ed.), *Civil Religion and Political Theology* (Notre Dame: University of Notre Dame Press 1986), p. 41.

30 Noll, *One Nation Under God? Christian Faith and Political Action in America* (San Francisco: Harper and Row 1988), Appendix A.

31 Neuhaus in Rouner (ed.), *Civil Religion and Political Theology*, p. 101.

32 Bellah in Richey and Jones (eds.), *American Civil Religion*, p. 257.

33 Wilson in E. A. Smith (ed.), *The Religion of the Republic* (Philadelphia: 1971).

34 Neuhaus in Rouner (ed.) *Civil Religion and Political Theology*, p. 102f.

35 Richey and Jones, *American Civil Religion*, p. 14f.

36 Sidney Mead, *The Nation with the Soul of a Church* (Macon: Mercer University Press 1975), p. 22.

37 Herberg in Richey and Jones, *American Civil Religion*, p. 86.

38 R. N. Bellah, 'Civil Religion in America' in *Daedalus* (Winter 1967), 16.

39 R. N. Bellah, 'American civil religion in the 1970s', in Richey and Jones (ed.) *American Civil Religion*, p. 271f.

40 R. N. Bellah, *The Broken Covenant* p. viii.

41 Ibid., p. 116.

42 Ibid., p. 142f.

43 Ibid., p. 143

44 Ibid., p. 159.

45 Ibid., p. 136.

46 Sociologists have, on the whole, been very critical of the methods employed in this study. Greeley suggests that one could use the same methods to arrive at diametrically opposed conclusions. It is beyond the scope of this study to comment on this disagreement. Generally, I assume that Bellah has identified elements of American life that are at least partially true. For Andrew Greeley see 'Habits of the Head', in *Society* (May/June 1992) 74–81.

47 R. N. Bellah, R. Madsen, W. M. Sullivan, A. Swidler, and S. M. Tipton, *Habits of the Heart* (Los Angeles: University of California Press 1985), p. 275.

48 Ibid., p. 271

49 Ibid., p. 284.

50 Ibid., p. 281.

51 Ibid., p. 286.

52 See C. Dawson, *Beyond Politics* (London: Sheed and Ward 1939), p. 24f, and V. A. Demant, *Theology of Society* (London: Faber and Faber 1947), p. 194.

53 R. Bellah et al. *Habits of the Heart*, p. 287. (My italics).

54 R. N. Bellah, 'Competing visions of the Role of Religion in American Society', in R. N. Bellah and F. E. Greenspahn, *Uncivil Religion: Interreligious Hostility in America* (New York: Crossroad 1987), p. 230.

55 R. N. Bellah, 'The Role of the Church in a Changing Society' in *Currents in Theology and Mission* (June 1990), 183.

56 Ibid., p. 189.

57 Andrew Greeley, 'Habits of the Head', 78.

58 For comparison with Europe see R. N. Bellah, R. Madsen, W. M. Sullivan, A. Swidler, and S. M. Tipton, *The Good Society* (New York: Alfred Knopf 1991), p. 88f. The main proposals are found in the conclusion.

59 Andrew Greeley, 'Habits of the Head' 77.

7 PLURALITY AND PUBLIC PHILOSOPHY

1 See R. J. Neuhaus, *America Against Itself: Moral Vision and Public Order* (Notre Dame: University of Notre Dame Press 1992), p. 81.

2 R. J. Neuhaus, 'Religion and Public Life: The Continuing Conversation', in *Christian Century* (11 July 1990).

3 See R. J. Neuhaus, 'Abortion: the Dangerous Assumptions' in *Commonweal* (1967). For his most recent discussion of abortion see *America Against Itself*, chpts. 6 and 7.

4 R. J. Neuhaus, 'Religion and Public Life', 670.

5 P. Berger and R. J. Neuhaus, *Movement and Revolution* (New York: Anchor 1970). See the Wager at the end. p. 239f.

6 Ibid., p. 152f.

7 Ibid., p. 141.

8 R. J. Neuhaus, *In Defense of People: Ecology and the Seduction of Radicalism* (New York: Macmillan 1971), p. 31f.

9 Ibid., pp. 162–201. Here Neuhaus discusses the work of Ehrlich.

10 Ibid., p. 199.

11 Ibid., p. 242. See also p. 230f.

12 Ibid., p. 170.

13 R. J. Neuhaus, *Time Toward Home: The American Experiment as Revelation* (New York: The Seabury Press 1975), Introduction. p. vii.

14 Ibid., p. 201.

15 Ibid., p. 19.

16 Ibid., p. 54.

17 Richard John Neuhaus clarified this issue in conversation with me. It is interesting to note that in many respects it is very similar to the view of other nations found in Maimonides.

18 M. Noll, *One Nation Under God? Christian Faith and Political Action in America* (San Francisco: Harper and Row 1988), p. 189f.
19 R. J. Neuhaus, *Time Toward Home*, p. 113.
20 Ibid., p. 76.
21 Ibid., p. 104.
22 See P. L. Berger and R. J. Neuhaus, *Against the World For the World: The Hartford Appeal and the Future of American Religion* (New York: The Seabury Press 1976).
23 The lack of the cultural mode is the problem with this book. It is partly due to the requirements for the book to serve as discussion material in the Lutheran Church.
24 R. J. Neuhaus, *Christian Faith and Public Policy* (Minneapolis: Augsburg Publishing House 1977), p. 13.
25 Ibid., p. 22.
26 I have already criticized this procedure in my chapter on method.
27 R. J. Neuhaus, *Christian Faith*, p. 37.
28 J. Nuechterlein, 'Christians and Politics' in *The Cresset*, (April 1978) 9.
29 Ibid., p. 10.
30 R. J. Neuhaus, *The Naked Public Square*, p. 150.
31 Ibid., pp. 151–2.
32 Ibid., p. 86.
33 Ibid., p. 116.
34 Ibid., p. 128.
35 R. J. Neuhaus, 'What Fundamentalists Want' in R. J. Neuhaus and M. Cromartie (eds.), *Evangelicals and Fundamentalists Confront the World* (Washington: Ethics and Public Policy Center 1987), p. 11.
36 Ibid., p. 18.
37 R. J. Neuhaus, *The Catholic Moment* (San Francisco: Harper and Row 1987), p. 24.
38 See R. J. Neuhaus, 'The Pope Affirms the New Capitalism', in the *Wall Street Journal*, 1 May 1991. This is also the theme of his latest book *Doing Well and Doing Good: The Challenge to the Christian Capitalist* (New York: Doubleday 1992).
39 P. Berger and R. J. Neuhaus, *To Empower People: The Role of Mediating Structures in Public Policy* (Washington: Institute for Public Policy Research 1977), p. 2.
40 Ibid., p. 6.
41 R. J. Neuhaus, *America Against Itself*, p. 185.
42 Ibid., pp. 185–6.

8 GOD AND TRUTH

1 Although the Reformers themselves were not very democratic, it is generally agreed that the idea of democracy was helped by the 'priesthood of all believers' doctrine. Power to interpret the Bible no longer resides with the pope or bishops but with lay people.
2 A. MacIntyre, *After Virtue*, 2nd edition (London: Duckworth 1985) p. 2.
3 Ibid., p. 107.
4 Ibid., p. 107.
5 Ibid., p. 117.
6 Ibid., p. 263.
7 J. Stout, *Ethics after Babel* (Boston: Beacon Press 1988), p. 209.
8 Ibid., p. 232.
9 Ibid., p. 209.
10 Ibid., p. 223.
11 Wittgenstein did not in actual fact talk much about religion. However, his followers have drawn this conclusion from his work. Along with Peter Winch see D. Z. Phillips, *Faith after Foundationalism* (London: Routledge 1988).
12 See MacIntyre in B. Wilson (ed.), *Rationality* (Oxford: Basil Blackwell 1970), p. 68.
13 Winch in B. Wilson. Ibid., p. 109.
14 Ibid., p. 109.
15 P. Winch, *The Idea of a Social Science* (London: Routledge and Kegan 1958), pp. 100–1.
16 See for example Dennis Nineham, *The Use and Abuse of the Bible* (London: Macmillian 1976).
17 For a good introduction to Rorty's work, see K. Kolenda, *Philosophy Democratised* (Florida: University of South Florida Press 1990).
18 A. MacIntyre in B. Wilson, *Rationality* p. 66.
19 Ibid., p. 79f.
20 Ibid., p. 129.
21 Ibid., p. 129.
22 J. Stout in *Ethics After Babel*, makes much of this point about translation needing a common frame of reference. See pp. 61–7.
23 A. MacIntyre, *Whose Justice? Which Rationality?* (London: Duckworth 1988), p. 352.
24 Ibid., p. 389.
25 Ibid., p. 355.
26 Ibid., p. 361.
27 Ibid., p. 362.

28 Ibid., p. 356.
29 Ibid., p. 365.
30 J. Milbank, *Theology and Social Theory* (Oxford: Basil Blackwell 1990), p. 330.
31 Ibid., p. 341f. At this point Milbank makes certain interesting observations on the nature of translation.
32 Ibid., pp. 346–7.
33 Milbank explicitly acknowledges his debt to Demant in 'A Socialist Economic Order', in *Theology* (September 1988) 413f.
34 J. Milbank, *Theology and Social Theory*, p. 389.
35 Ibid., p. 5.
36 J. Milbank in G. D'Costa (ed.) *Christian Uniqueness Reconsidered* (Maryknoll: Orbis Books 1990), p. 190.
37 J. Milbank, *Theology and Social Theory*, p. 114.
38 Ibid., p. 94.
39 Ibid., p. 94.
40 Ibid., p. 95.
41 See Keith Ward in *Images of Eternity* (London: Darton, Longman and Todd 1987) for an excellent treatment of orthodox thinkers in the five major world religions and the striking similarity in the concepts of God.
42 In this respect M. Buckley in *At the Origins of Modern Atheism* (New Haven: Yale University Press 1987) is wrong. It is not so much the God of the Philosophers, but the God of Deism which lies behind the rejection of belief in our culture. It is a God who is peripheral to human existence, instead of the God at the heart of a transforming world perspective.
43 This might seem a surprising claim, however, I am certain it is true. St Anselm formulated his Ontological Argument in the context of worship; and St Thomas was commending the elegance of the Christian narrative as a total explanation.
44 This view of the proofs is widespread amongst philosophers, for example, Richard Swinburne, *The Existence of God* (Oxford: Clarendon Press 1979).
45 See D. Z. Phillips, *Faith After Foundationalism*.
46 This is the parody of the argument offered by Bertrand Russell in the debate against Copplestone.
47 See St Thomas, *Summa Theologica*, 1a, Question 46, article 3, translated by T. McDermott, VIII (London: Blackfriars 1964), p. 79.
48 B. Russell, *Why I am not a Christian* (London: Unwin books 1967), p. 140.
49 St Thomas Aquinas, *Summa Theologica*, 1a, Question 2, article 3, translated by T. McDermott, 11 (London: Blackfriars 1964).

50 H. Meynell, *The Intelligible Universe* (London: Macmillan 1982), pp. 84–5.
51 K. Ward, *Rational Theology and the Creativity of God* (Oxford: Basil Blackwell 1982), p. 12.
52 Meynell's summary of the Cosmological argument is very similar to the argument I am offering here. The slight differences are, first, I follow MacIntyre in accepting that knowledge is tradition-constituted; and, second, Meynell's concept of God I find unnecessarily anthropomorphic. For Meynell see *The Intelligible Universe*, p. 118.
53 F. Nietzsche, *Twilight of Idols*, Translated by R. J. Hollingdale (Baltimore: Penguin 1968), pp. 40–1.
54 So, for example, a world perspective that insisted on talking about 'square-circles' would be incoherent. For, as these terms are currently understood, squares are shapes with sides and angles, circles have no sides and no angles, therefore one cannot have a shape with both sides and angles, and yet no sides and no angles.

9 CONDITIONS FOR RATIONAL PUBLIC DISCOURSE

1 This was a theme of B. L. Hebblethwaite's paper 'God and Truth' at the Society for the Study of Theology Conference in Oxford 1989.
2 R. J. Neuhaus, 'Can Atheists Be Good Citizens?', in *First Things* (August 1991).
3 The terminology in this debate is apt to be confusing. At this stage in my argument, the term objective is equivilant to moral realism. Subjectivism is a denial of objective moral truths. My argument will start by concentrating on the different attitudes to morality. The precise status of these objective moral values will become apparent later on.
4 J. L. Mackie, *Ethics* (London: Penguin 1977), p. 36.
5 Ibid., p. 48.
6 Ibid., p. 190.
7 This argument for monotheism was made in the last chapter. See p. 147.
8 Stephen Clark's treatment of the *Euthyphro* dilemma in *Mysteries of Religion* (Oxford: Basil Blackwell 1986) is extremely useful.
9 C. Taylor, *Sources of the Self* (Cambridge: Harvard University Press 1989), p. 511. In a footnote, Taylor makes it explicit that he is thinking of MacIntyre and Bellah here.
10 Ibid., p. 226f.
11 Ibid., p. 394.

12 Ibid., p. 516.
13 Richard John Neuhaus has used this expression several times in conversation with me. I have yet to find it in print.

10 PLURALITY AND THEOLOGY

1 The argument that follows is a revised version of material that first appeared in the following articles: 'World Perspectives and Arguments: Disagreements about Disagreements', in *Heythrop Journal*, 30 (1) (1989), 1–12, and 'Faith and Reason: Reflections on MacIntyre's 'tradition-constituted enquiry''', in *Religious Studies*, 27 (1991), 259–67.
2 St Thomas Aquinas, *Summa Theologica*, 2a. 2ae, Question 10, article 5, translated by Thomas Gilby XXXII, (London: Blackfriars 1975), p. 53.
3 Ibid., p. 63.
4 St Thomas Aquinas, *Summa Theologica*, 1a, Question 23, Article 3, translated by Thomas Gilby V (London: Blackfriars 1967)
5 See A. MacIntyre's treatment of St Thomas in *Whose Justice? Which Rationality?* (London: Duckworth 1988), chpt. 11.
6 K. Ward, *Images of Eternity* (London: Darton, Longman and Todd 1987), p. 176.
7 R. J. Neuhaus, 'The Ambiguities of "Christian America"', in *Concordia Journal* (July 1991), 291–2. This line seems to appeal to those of an orthodox or evangelical disposition, see, for example, Richard Morgan, 'Religious and Social Tolerance', in *Churchman*, 99 (3) (1985), 238.
8 See R. J. Neuhaus and L. Klenicki, *Believing Today: Jew and Christian in Conversation* (Grand Rapids: Eerdmanns 1989).
9 J. Hick, *Evil and the God of Love* (London: Collins 1968), p. 322.
10 Hick's pluralist hypothesis is described briefly in chapter 1 (see pages 9–10). For the most sustained statement of his position see *The Interpretation of Religion* (Basingstoke: Macmillan 1989).
11 Michael Nazir-Ali develops this argument, see 'Dialogue in an Age of Conflict', in Dan Cohn-Sherbok (ed.), *Many Mansions: Interfaith and Religious Intolerance*, (London: Bellew 1992), pp. 73–4.
12 This argument is common among inclusivists. While I am unhappy with the label, I am happy to endorse this argument. For my views on the pluralist, inclusivist, exclusivist paradigm see, 'Creating Options: Shattering the "Pluralist, Inclusivist, and Exclusivist" pardigm' in *New Blackfriars* (January 1993).
13 J. L. Houlden, *Bible and Belief*, (London: SPCK 1991), p. 153.
14 Ibid., p. 161.

15 Houlden brings out the differences between Matthew and Mark in his delightful book, *Backward into Light* (London: SCM Press 1987).

16 George Carey, 'Toleration', in Dan Cohn-Sherbok (ed.), *Many Mansions*, p. 9.

11 PLURALITY AND POST-MODERNISM

1 Z. Sardar and M. W. Davies, *Distorted Imagination: Lessons from the Rushdie Affair* (London: Grey Seal Books 1990), p. 238.

2 J. D. Hunter, *Culture Wars* (Basic Books 1991), p. 97.

3 It is interesting to note that T. S. Eliot was genuinely surprised that America succeeded. Eliot could not see how a diverse (and he thought completely secular) culture could survive. See *The Idea of a Christian Society*, 2nd edition (London: Faber and Faber 1982), p. 69f. Yet we now see how the problems of Ireland and Israel depend upon an imitation of America and this post-modern discovery. In a future study I hope to show how the modern state of Israel is making progress in this respect.

Bibliography

Ahsan, M. M. and Kidwai, A. R. (eds.), *Sacrilege versus Civility. Muslim Perspectives on 'The Satanic Verses' Affair* (Leicester: The Islamic Foundation 1991).

Akhar, S., *Be Careful with Muhammad. The Salman Rushdie Affair* (London: Bellew Publishing 1989).

Appignanesi, L., and Maitland, S., (eds.) *The Rushdie File* (London: Fourth Estate Ltd 1989).

Aquinas, Thomas., *Summa Theologica*, 1a, 2–11, translated by T. McDermott, II(London: Blackfrairs 1964).

Summa Theologica, 1a, 19–26, translated by Thomas Gilby, v(London: Blackfriars 1967).

Summa Theologica, 1a, 44–49, translated by Thomas Gilby, VIII (London: Blackfriars 1967).

Summa Theologica, 2a 2ae, 8–16, translated by Thomas Gilby, XXXII (London: Blackfriars 1975).

Barth, K. *Church Dogmatics*, II and IV (Edinburgh: T. and T. Clark 1936–77).

Beitz, C. 'Tacit Consent and Property Rights', in *Political Theory*, 8 (4) (November 1980), 487–502.

Bellah, R. N. 'Finding the Church: Post-Traditional Discipleship', in J. M. Wall and D. Heim (eds.), *How My Mind Has Changed* (Grand Rapids: Eerdmans 1991).

'The role of the Church in a Changing Society', in *Currents in Theology and Mission* (June 1990), 183–91.

The Broken Covenant: American Civil Religion in Time of Trial (New York: Crossroads 1975).

'Civil Religion in America', in *Daedalus*, 96 (Winter 1967), 1–21.

Bellah, R. N. and Greenspahn F. E. *Uncivil Religion: Interreligious Hostility in America* (New York: Crossroad 1987).

Bellah, R. N., Madsen, R., Sullivan, W. M., Swidler, A., and Tipton, S. M., *The Good Society* (New York: Alfred Knopf 1991).

215

Habits of the Heart (Los Angeles: University of California Press 1985).

Berger, P. and Neuhaus, R. J. (eds.), *Against the World For the World: The Hartford Appeal and the Future of American Religion* (New York: The Seabury Press 1976).

Berger, P. and Neuhaus, R. J. *Movement and Revolution* (New York: Anchor 1970).

To Empower People: The Role of Mediating Structures in Public Policy (Washington: Institute for Public Policy Research 1977).

Berke, M. 'The Disputed Legacy of Reinhold Niebuhr', in *First Things* (November 1992) 37–42.

Buckley, M. *At the Origins of Modern Atheism* (New Haven: Yale University Press 1987).

Byrne, P. *Natural Religion and the Nature of Religion* (London: Routledge 1989).

Chadwick, O. *The Victorian Church*, II (London: Adam and Charles Black 1970).

Charlesworth, *Church, State, and Conscience* (St. Lucia 1973).

Chidester, D. *Patterns of Power. Religion and Politics in American Culture* (New Jersey: Prentice Hall 1988).

Clark, S. *Mysteries of Religion* (Oxford: Basil Blackwell 1986).

Cohn-Sherbok, D. (ed.), *Many Mansions: Interfaith and Religious Intolerance* (London: Bellew 1992).

Colombo, F. *God in America. Religion and Politics in the United States* (New York: Columbia University Press 1984).

Cranston, M. *John Locke: a Biography* (Oxford: Oxford University Press 1985).

Creuzet, M. *Toleration and Liberalism* (Chulmleigh: Augustine 1979).

Crick, B. *Political Theory and Practice* (London: Penguin 1972).

D'Costa, G. 'Secular Discourse and the Clash of Faiths: "The Satanic Verses" in British Society', in *New Blackfriars* (October 1990).

(ed.), *Christian Uniqueness Reconsidered: The Myth of a Pluralistic Theology of Religion* (Maryknoll: Orbis Books 1990).

Dawson, C. *Beyond Politics* (London: Sheed and Ward 1939).

Religion and the Rise of Western Culture (London: Sheed and Ward 1950).

Delahaye, J. V. (ed.), *Politics: A Discussion of Realities* (London: C. W. Dent 1924).

Demant, V. A. *The Penumbra of Ethics* (Unpublished Gifford Lectures).

Christian Sex Ethics (London: Hodder and Stoughton 1963).

Religion and the Decline of Capitalism (London: Faber and Faber 1952).

Theology of Society (London: Faber and Faber 1947).

The Religious Prospect (London: Muller 1939).

Christian Polity (London: Faber and Faber 1936).

God, Man and Society (London: SCM Press 1933).

The Miners Distress and the Coal Problem (London: SCM Press 1929).

Durkin, K. *Reinhold Niebuhr* (London: Geoffrey Chapman 1989).

Eliot. T. S. *The Idea of a Christian Society*, 2nd edition (London: Faber and Faber 1982).

Fackre, G. *The Religious Right and Christian Faith* (Grand Rapids: Eerdmans 1982).

Fletcher, J. *Situation Ethics* (London: SCM Press 1966).

Genovese, E. D. *Roll, Jordan, Roll: The World The Slaves Made* (New York: Pantheon Books 1974).

Gill, R. *Moral Communities* (Exeter: University of Exeter Press 1992).

Gore, C. Introduced *The Return of Christendom*, By a group of Churchmen. (London: 1922).

Greeley, A. 'Habits of the Head', in *Society* (May/June 1992), 74–81.

Hart, R. *The Political Pulpit* (West Lafayette: The Purdue University Press 1977).

Hastings, A. *A History of English Christianity 1920–1985* (London: Collins 1986).

Hauerwas, S. *A Community of Character* (Notre Dame: University of Notre Dame Press 1981).

Hebblethwaite, B. L. 'God and Truth', unpublished SST Conference paper delivered in October 1989.

Hick, J. *The Interpretation of Religion* (Basingstoke: Macmillan 1989).

Evil and the God of Love (London: Collins 1968).

Houlden, J. L. *Bible and Belief* (London: SPCK 1991).

Backward into Light (London: SCM 1987).

Hughey, M. W. *Civil Religion and Moral Order Theoretical and Historical Dimensions* (Westport: Greenwood Press 1983).

Hume, D. *Dialogues Concerning Natural Religion* (London: Hafner Press 1948).

Hunter, J. D. *Culture Wars* (Basic Books 1991).

Kelly, G. A. *Politics and Religious Consciousness in America* (New Brunswick: Transaction Books 1984).

Kojecky, R. *T. S. Eliot's Social Criticism* (London: Faber and Faber 1971).

Kolenda, K. *Philosophy Democratised* (Florida: University of South Florida Press 1990).

Lee, S. *Law, Blasphemy and the Multi-Faith Society: Report of a Seminar* (London: Commission for Racial Equality, 1990).

Locke, J. *Letter Concerning Toleration* (New York: Promethius Books 1991).

Two Treatises of Government (London: Dent and Sons 1924).

MacIntyre, A. *After Virtue*, 2nd edition (London: Duckworth 1985)
   Whose Justice? Which Rationality? (London: Duckworth 1988).

Mackie, J. L. *Ethics* (London: Penguin 1977).

Maritain, J. *True Humanism* (London: Century Press 1939).

Markham, I. S. 'Creating Options: Shattering the "Pluralist, Inclusivist, and Exclusivist" paradigm', in *New Blackfriars*, 74 (1993), 33–41.
   'Faith and Reason: Reflections on MacIntyre's "tradition-constituted enquiry"', in *Religious Studies*, 27 (1991), 259–67.
   'World Perspectives and Arguments: Disagreements about Disagreements', in *Heythrop Journal*, 30 (1) (1989), 1–12.

Marty, M. E. *A Nation of Behavers* (Chicago: The University of Chicago Press 1976).

Mascall, E. *He who is: a Study in Traditional Theism* (London: Darton, Longman and Todd 1966).

Maxrui, A. A. *The Satanic Verses or a Satanic Novel? The Moral Dilemmas of the Rushdie Affair* (New York: Greenpoint Committee of Muslim Scholars and Leaders of North America 1989).

McElroy, R. W. *The Search for an American Public Theology – The Contribution of John Courtney Murray* (New York: Paulist Press 1984).

Mead, S. E. *The Nation with the Soul of a Church* (Macon: Mercer University Press 1975).

Mendus, S. (ed.), *Justifying Toleration* (Cambridge: Cambridge University Press. 1988).

Mendus, S. and Edwards, D. (eds.), *On Toleration*, (Oxford: Clarendon Press 1987).

Meynell, H. *The Intelligible Universe* (London: Macmillan 1982).

Milbank, J. *Theology and Social Theory* (Oxford: Basil Blackwell 1990).
   'A Socialist Economic Order', in *Theology* (September 1988).

Mill, J. S. *On Liberty* (Harmondsworth: Penguin 1974).

Mishan, E. J. *The Costs of Economic Growth* (London: Staples Press 1967).

Mitchell, B. *Law, Morality, and Religion in a secular society* (Oxford: Oxford University Press 1970).

Morgan, R. 'Religious and Social Tolerance', in *Churchman*, 1985, 99 (3), 230–40.

Munby, D. *Christianity and Economic Problems* (London: Staples Press 1969).
   God and the Rich Society (London: Oxford University Press 1961).
   The Idea of a Secular Society (London: Oxford University Press 1963).

Neuhaus, R. J. *Doing Well and Doing Good: The challenge to the Christian Capitalist* (New York: Doubleday 1992).

America Against Itself: Moral Vision and Public Order (Notre Dame: University of Notre Dame Press 1992).

'Can Atheists Be Good Citizens?', in *First Things* (August 1991).

'The Ambiguities of "Christian America"', in *Concordia Journal* (July 1991).

'The Pope Affirms the New Capitalism', in the *Wall Street Journal* (1 May 1991).

'Religion and Public Life: The Continuing Conversation', in *Christian Century* – 'How my mind has changed' series (11 July 1990), 669–73.

'Why Wait for the Kingdom? The Theonomist Temptation', in *First Things* (May 1990), 13–21.

The Catholic Moment (San Francisco: Harper and Row 1987).

The Naked Public Square (Michigan: Eerdmans 1984).

Christian Faith and Public Policy (Minneapolis: Augsburg Publishing House 1977).

Time Toward Home: The American Experiment as Revelation (New York: The Seabury Press 1975).

In Defense of People: Ecology and the Seduction of Radicalism (New York: Macmillian 1971).

Neuhaus, R. J. and Cromartie, M. (eds.), *Piety and Politics: Evangelicals and Fundamentalists Confront the World* (Washington: Ethics and Public Policy Center 1987).

Neuhaus, R. J. and Klenicki, L. *Believing Today: Jew and Christian in Conversation* (Grand Rapids: Eerdmanns 1989).

Niebuhr, Reinhold. *The Children of Light and the Children of Darkness* (London: Nisbet and Co. 1945).

Niebuhr, Richard. *Christ and Culture* (New York: Harper and Row 1951).

Nietzsche, F. *Twilight of Idols and the Anti-Christ*, translated by R. J. Hollingdale (Baltimore: Penguin 1968).

Nineham, D. *The Use and the Abuse of the Bible* (London: Macmillian 1976).

Noll, M. A. (ed.), *Religion and American Politics. From the Colonial Period to the 1980s* (New York: Oxford University Press 1990).

One Nation Under God? Christian Faith and Political Action in America (San Francisco: Harper and Row 1988).

Nuechterlein, J. 'Christians and Politics', in *The Cresset*, 41 (6) (April 1978).

Penty, A. J. 'Has Machinery Causal Importance?', in *Christendom* (October 1925).

Phillips, D. Z. *Faith after Foundationalism* (London: Routledge 1988).

Pierard, R. V. and Linder R. D. *Civil Religion and the Presidency* (Grand Rapids: Academie Books 1988).

Pipes, D., *The Rushdie Affair* (New York: Birch Lane Press 1990).

Plamenatz, J. *Man and Society*, 1 (Harlow, Longman 1963).

Porter, A. (ed.), *Coal: A Challenge to the Nation's Conscience* (London: Hogath Press 1927).

Powell, E. *Still to Decide* (Kingswood: Elliot Right Way Books 1972). *No Easy Answers* (London: Sheldon Press 1973).

Preston, R. H. 'The Malvern Conference', in *The Modern Churchman* (April 1942).

'The Theology of the Malvern Conference', in *Christianity and Society*, 7 (3) (1942).

Explorations in Theology 9 (London: SCM Press 1981).

Religion and the Persistence of Capitalism (London: SCM Press 1979).

Church and Society in the Late Twentieth Century: The Economic and Political Task (London: SCM Press 1983).

The Future of Christian Ethics (London: SCM Press 1987).

Reckitt, M. B. and C. E. Bechhofer, *The Meaning of National Guilds* (London: Cecil Palmer 1920).

Richey, R. E. and Jones, D. G. (eds.), *American Civil Religion* (New York: Harper and Row 1974).

Rohr, J. 'Religious Toleration in St. Augustine', in *Journal of Church and State*, 9 (1967), 51–70.

Roth, A., *Enoch Powell: Tory Tribune* (London: Macdonald 1971).

Rouner, L. S. (ed.), *Civil Religion and Political Theology* (Notre Dame, University of Notre Dame Press 1986).

Rushdie, S., *The Satanic Verses* (London: Viking 1988).

Russell, B. *Why I am not a Christian* (London: Unwin books 1967).

Ruthven, M. *A Satanic Affair. Salman Rushdie and the Rage of Islam* (London: Chatto and Windus 1990).

Sardar, Z., and Davies, M. W. *Distorted Imagination; Lessons from the Rushdie Affair* (London: Grey Seal Books 1990).

Schoen, D. *Enoch Powell and the Powellites* (London: Macmillian 1977).

Scruton, R. *The Meaning of Conservatism* (London: Penguin 1980).

Smith, E. A. (ed.), *The Religion of the Republic* (Philadelphia: 1971).

Stackhouse, M. *Public Theology and Political Economy* (Grand Rapids: Eerdmans 1987).

'An Ecumenist's Plea for a Public Theology', in *This World*, 8 (Spring/Summer 1984) 47–79.

Stout, J. *Ethics after Babel* (Boston: Beacon Press 1988).

Swinburne, R. *The Existence of God* (Oxford: Clarendon Press 1979).

Taylor, C. *Sources of the Self* (Cambridge: Harvard University Press 1989).

Ten, C. L. *Mill on Liberty* (Oxford: Oxford University Press 1980).

Utley, T. E. *Enoch Powell: The Man and his Thinking* (London: William Kimber 1968).

Vidler, A. *God's Judgement on Europe* (London: Longmans 1940).

Ward, K. *Images of Eternity* (London: Darton, Longman and Todd 1987).

  Rational Theology and the Creativity of God. (Oxford: Basil Blackwell 1982).

Webster, R. *A Brief History of Blasphemy. Liberalism, Censorship and ' The Satanic Verses'* (Southwold: The Orwell Press 1990).

Weinstein, A. and Gatell, F. O. and Sarasotin, D. (eds.), *American Negro Slavery. A Modern Reader* (New York: Oxford University Press 1979).

Wilson, B. (ed.), *Rationality* (Oxford: Basil Blackwell 1970).

Wilson, J. F. *Public Religion in American Culture* (Philadelphia: Temple University Press 1979).

Winch, P. *The Idea of a Social Science* (London: Routledge and Kegan 1958).

Winthrop, J. *Winthrop Papers* (Boston: The Massachusetts Historical Society 1931).

Wolff, R. P., Moore, Jr., B., and Marcuse, H. *A Critique of Pure Tolerance* (Boston: Beacon Press 1965).

Index